ROY

ROY

The Official Autobiography of
Roy of the Rovers

Roy Race
with Giles Smith

arrow books

13 5 7 9 10 8 6 4 2

Arrow Books
20 Vauxhall Bridge Road
London SW1V 2SA

Arrow Books is part of the Penguin Random House group of companies whose
addresses can be found at global.penguinrandomhouse.com.

Penguin
Random House
UK

Copyright © Roy of the Rovers, Egmont UK Ltd 2014
Copyright © TPC&G Ltd 2014

Roy Race has asserted his right to be identified as the author of this
Work in accordance with the Copyright, Designs and Patents Act 1988.

First published by Century in 2014
First published in paperback by Arrow Books in 2015

www.randomhouse.co.uk

A CIP catalogue record for this book is
available from the British Library.

ISBN 9780099598664

Printed and bound by CPI Group (UK) Ltd, Croydon, CR0 4YY

MIX
Paper from
responsible sources
FSC® C018179

Penguin Random House is committed to a sustainable future for our
business, our readers and our planet. This book is made from Forest
Stewardship Council® certified paper.

For the Basran Eight: Noel Baxter, Trevor Cassidy, Vic Guthrie, Carl Hunt, Neville Jones, Kenny Logan, Steve Naylor and Jimmy Slade.
Gone, but not forgotten.

And for Penny, always.

Introduction

Incredible. That's the only word I can use.

Ten league titles, eleven FA Cup wins, three European Cups and 481 goals across a thirty-eight-year playing career at the highest level.

Incredible. But it's the story of my life.

Throw in management, marriage, three children, a surprisingly high number of kidnappings, an assassination attempt that put me in a coma and not one but two narrowly escaped earthquakes . . .

Incredible.

What's the phrase? 'Roy of the Rovers stuff'. Well, I guess this stuff really is 'Roy of the Rovers stuff'. It's my autobiography.

Of course, it hasn't all been glory and last-gasp winners. There has been tragedy too – some actual last-gasping. So much tragedy, in fact, that I now realise I didn't get round to mentioning in the following pages the deaths, in 1964, of my team-mates at Melchester Rovers, Dave Williams and Bob Roberts, who were killed at a charity speedway event. I would like to apologise to their families and hope that a prominent mention here at the front of the book is some recompense. It was a terrible loss, and somehow so poignantly unnecessary. Bob had never even been on a motorbike before. Talk about being out of your comfort zone.

Lasting scars, then. And not least from the Basran car-bomb massacre of 1986 and the tragic loss of eight further great team-mates, colleagues, peers, friends. This book is dedicated to them. And to my wife, my one and only Penny.

I'm aware, of course, that a lot of the events of my life were well documented at the time in the press. However, as everybody knows, you can't always believe what you read in the papers, and, in any case, what got into print wasn't even the half of it. Hence this book.

A few words of thanks, if I may, before we get under way. It was Ben Dunn at Random House who, over a series of lunches at Antonio's Trattoria in Melchester, a couple of which he kindly offered to pay for, persuaded me that the time was finally right to put pen to paper. The logic of his argument ('if you don't, some other bugger will') was crisp and persuasive. Another piece of Ben's considered advice ('try to leave out the bits that people don't bother to read') also stayed with me.

Once the project was in motion, I had cause, as I have at every point of my life, to be bottomlessly grateful to my oldest friend and former team-mate, the legendary William 'Blackie' Gray. When my own recollections grew misty – as inevitably they would, from time to time – it was great to know that I could always ring Blackie and, if it was one of his good days, the nurses would go and get him and put him on the end of the phone and, in conversations that sometimes ended up lasting for two or three hours, my old pal would help me fill in one or two of the gaps. Cheers, Blackie.

Last of all, I would like to thank Bob Dickens of the *Melchester*

Evening Chronicle for helping me put my story in order. Bob and I have been stumbling into one other for a long time, and it's entirely fair to say that, even though we tried, no journalist could be found who was closer to the ins and outs of life at Melchester Rovers during my career.

Unquestionably, Bob's work as a beat reporter put him at the centre of a few lively debates in the club car park down the years. Both of us still laugh about the time Duncan 'Big Dunc' McKay, Rovers' uncompromisingly fiery centre half, got upset by something Bob had written in an article about Big Dunc's wife and a male striptease ensemble called Pecs-Tacular. Dunc dragged Bob out of his car and into the kit room, pinned him to the tumble dryer and threatened to pull his tongue out with the laundry tongs on the grounds that 'ninety-five percent of what you write is bare-faced frigging lies, Dickens, and the other five percent is plain wrong.'

It was great to have Bob on board for this book.

Roy Race, Upper Cobdon, nr Melchester, 2014

1

Early Doors

The date is 21 October 1938; 8.43 a.m. German forces under the command of Adolf Hitler have recently annexed the Sudetenland and the tension is rising all across Europe. Indeed, it probably wouldn't be going too far to say that storm clouds are gathering.

None of that, though, is of any concern at this particular moment to Mrs Marjory Race, who is, as our story opens, well into injury time in the protracted but never less than absorbing, end-to-end contest which will eventually result in her squeezing into the world a 13lb 11oz bundle of life: her only child, Roy.

Mum, for her part, would always tell people that she knew I was going to be a footballer from the amount of kicking I did, not just on the way out of her uterus during that brutal and ultimately exhausting forty-three-hour labour, but in the weeks afterwards, lying contentedly on my back in my cradle.

'Kick, kick, kick,' she used to say. 'He simply never stopped!'

It's an interesting story, but I was able to put that particular piece of motherly wisdom to the test many years later, when my own children came along. My son, Roy Jr, was a big kicker in his Babygro – and, of course, he did go on to enjoy a fruitful career in the professional game. But so, equally, was his twin sister Melinda, and she went on to run a car respraying workshop in Brighton with her partner Carol, so it's probably not safe to infer too much from those early physical manifestations.

Back to the beginning, though. Home for Mr and Mrs Race and their new baby was a terraced house in Sutton Street, about ten minutes east of Melchester town centre on the number 49 tram – and, as I would later discover, about the same by bike if you had the wind behind you and the energy to make it up Shirley Hill without getting off and pushing.

Ours was a humble working-class house in a humble working-class area. Downstairs was a front parlour kept 'for best' – which mostly seemed to mean Christmas – and beyond that was what we called 'the back sitting room', which in turn led into the small, square kitchen. Upstairs were two bedrooms and a small 'box room' or storage space. Mod cons? Not really. The lavatory was in a lean-to, out in the back yard. When it was bath night, Mum would take the tin tub down from its hook on the back door, fill it with water warmed in a pan, and we would perform our ablutions right there on the kitchen floor in front of the cooker, and frequently, also, under the watchful eye of Old Mr Hotchkiss, who would often be standing at the top-floor window of the house that backed onto ours and to whom I would always offer a cheery wave of the soap. The set-up sounds primitive now, by today's luxurious standards, but at the time it seemed completely normal and perfectly adequate.

Obviously, for nearly six of my first seven years on the planet, an unprecedentedly violent global conflict was raging, but my memories of that are, to be perfectly honest with you, sketchy. Impact-wise, Melchester seemed to get off fairly lightly. The town certainly wasn't subject to the systematic bombing raids that afflicted so many British cities. The closest we came to devastation from the air was when a German plane, apparently on its way back from a raid on Seaford, dumped the remainder of its load on some of the warehouses down by the Mel Estuary. It's chilling to think that, had that plane's route put it on a course just a quarter of a mile to the east, Mel Park, the home of the Rovers, would have taken a direct hit, possibly changing the entire course of history. As it was, the bombs simply took out a candle factory and a deserted Victorian book depository which, according to rumour, was used for illegal bare-knuckle boxing bouts. No big loss.

Food was rationed, of course, but, again, I barely noticed. What Mum could do with a simple scrubbed carrot and a packet of lard defied belief. She was also, as mothers were in those days, a genius at making a scrag end of lamb furnish meals for up to a fortnight, ensuring that we never went to bed hungry in Sutton Street. All in all, our parents must have taken care to shield us from the worst of things in that difficult time. In any case, we were probably too busy thinking about the subject which almost instinctively became our prime concern: football.

The street was our playground – which is to say, our football pitch, because all we kids wanted to do in those days was kick a ball around. William 'Blackie' Gray from opposite – my oldest, firmest friend and later, of course, my faithful Rovers team-mate – would call round, or I would call for Blackie, and then we would go and knock up Stephen Collard or Howard Billings and very soon we would have enough for a match or, at the very least, a game of three-and-in. Fortunately from our point of view, not too many people had cars in those days and there was very little traffic up and down the road, give or take the odd grocery van and the occasional coal cart, so we had the space to play in, with the kerbs as our touchlines and (of course) jumpers for goalposts.

And play we did, for hour after hour, until it was almost dark, except for the soft glow from the gas streetlights, and until our suppers were long cold and our mothers were calling for the fourth or fifth time from the front doors to bring us in.

No doubt football kept us out of mischief and, as such, our parents must have been grateful for our interest in it – give or take the inevitable cost of a few accidentally broken windows along the way. The most damage we caused in that respect was when Harry 'Bonkers' McCrory, one slightly rainy evening in about 1949, attempted what was, for his age, and given the conditions, an extremely ambitious diving header, and slightly mistimed it. The ball ended up going through the window of number 11, and Bonkers ended up going through the window of number 13. No subs in those days, either, remember. But such incidents were relatively rare, and everyone soon saw the funny side – even Bonkers, three weeks later, when he was eventually discharged from the children's ward.

There was another unfortunate incident one afternoon, not long after this. An eleven-a-side street-match was in full flow. As memory has it, we were 1–0 down at the time and pressing for an equaliser when I heard a familiar voice shout, 'Roy! To me!' I looked up and spotted Blackie, who had made a blindside run up the right flank and was now drifting in, completely unmarked, towards the corner of the penalty area. Using the outside of my left foot, I picked him out with a looping, diagonal ball over the defence, inviting the volley. Alas, as the ball dropped, Blackie got his shape all wrong, sliced it wildly and then watched in frozen horror as the ball flew about twenty yards up the street and smacked against the shiny brown backside of the horse belonging to the window cleaner, who must have been working around the back of someone's house and had left his cart parked up by the kerb.

Startled by the impact, the horse reared up on its hind legs, let out an eerie, high-pitched whinny and then bolted up the street, the cart careering behind it and shedding buckets and cloths as it went. None of us had ever seen a horse move that fast – and the poor dumb beast was showing no sign of slowing down when it turned left at the top of the road and disappeared in the direction of the town centre.

Blackie was in a right old state. 'Christ, Roy; what am I going to do?'

I thought about it for a moment. And then I told him that one thing he could do was try to get his head more over the ball, which would enable him to keep it down. I also pointed out that he might have assessed the developing situation better. 'You had time, in that case, to take a touch,' I said, 'which would have helped you bring the ball under control, and also might have given you the chance to open up a better angle on goal.'

Blackie was always hungry to learn, and he nodded eagerly.

Football ran in our blood – but perhaps especially in mine. The game was embedded in the Race family history. My grandad, Billy Race, had captained Melchester Rovers in its formative years at the turn of the twentieth century, piloting the club out of the Southern League and enjoying, among other things, the career-capping honour of an FA Cup victory in 1907. Some of my earliest and happiest childhood memories are of the Sunday afternoons when Mum and Dad would take me to my grandparents' house for tea. Grandad's medals were on display in a glass-fronted cabinet on a dark polished sideboard which bulked large in the tiny, immaculately tidy sitting room, and they twinkled like objects of enormous wonder to me – impossibly shiny treasures brought back from some rare and exotic land. The air would be rich with the smell of Gran's freshly baked upside down cake, the fire would be crackling in the grate, and I would sit, enchanted, at Grandad's slippered feet and listen to his tales of football glory – the goals scored in the dying seconds, the last-ditch tackles made, the trophies lifted. I would never tire of hearing those stories. OK, I tired of them a bit, later on, when he started telling the same one, five or six times in succession, and when he would sometimes come into the room with no trousers on, looking confused. But not until then.

My dad would have loved to have followed Grandad to the top of the professional game – and my understanding is that only an unfortunate and permanent groin strain prevented him from doing so. Where and how that groin strain was sustained, and what the full extent of it was, I simply don't know. I assume it was the same injury that prevented him serving in the war. But it was never talked about.

Actually, Dad didn't talk about much altogether. He was a quiet man – indeed, almost completely silent from one week to the next. However, he had clearly inherited his dad's love for football. And football was capable of wringing from this otherwise silent and undemonstrative man expressions of passion that nothing else inspired. He never missed a Rovers home game, pulling on his coat and striped scarf and leaving the house at 2.35 on the dot, and the result could affect his mood for hours, and even days afterwards. If the Rovers had won, that evening there would be an unmistakable lightness about the way he sat in his armchair, listening to the radio and largely ignoring us.

When Rovers lost, though . . . now, that was when you had to watch out! Somehow our cat, Silky, who must have had some kind of telepathic connection with Mel Park, would know the result in advance and be off out the back door like a streak, even as Dad's key was in the front door. A fond family legend tells of the winter's evening when, in the wake of a shock FA Cup third round defeat at home to unfancied Shermall United, Dad, having already rolled the cooker onto its side in the kitchen, went into the yard and pulled the cistern off the wall in the outside lavatory. Furthermore, only the combined efforts, over the ensuing three quarters of an hour, of my mum and Mr Sexton from next door, who came round in a hurry, prevented Dad from using the cistern to beat down the low brick wall that separated the two properties. Even as a young and oblivious child during incidents such as these, innocently lying on the rug with a wooden toy train or similar in my hand, I must have noted and absorbed at some level the colourful tapestry of emotions that the game of football could inspire.

Dad, of course, was the first to see some potential in me as a footballer. Indeed, my early development as a player owed everything to him. He was the one who set me on the path to my destiny in football, and he was the one who made sure, in no uncertain terms, that I stayed on that path. On Sunday mornings, really from almost as soon as I could walk, he would take me over to what we called 'the fields' but which was really just a large expanse of flattened, largely grassless and as yet undeveloped land on the city's outskirts. (It's now an out-of-town shopping facility, featuring a PC Realm and a branch of Pets 4 U.)

Once we were there, just the two of us, he would run me through his specially devised training regimen. What was interesting, and even pioneering, about Dad's sessions was that we would spend at least the first two and a half hours working entirely without the ball. The emphasis in those early stages was mainly on stamina and fitness. He would set down a couple of rusty paint tins and make me sprint between them, breaking the silence only to say things like

'Again' and 'Faster'. Then I had to do press-ups and toe-touches and star jumps – and then various combinations of all three. And then I would do running on the spot with pieces of concrete attached to my thighs with a couple of leather straps that Dad had resourcefully adapted at home from an old suitcase. He had also, equally imaginatively, made his own medicine ball using an old velvet cushion cover and a second-hand set of encyclopaedias, and I would lie on the ground while he dropped this package on my stomach over and over again to encourage abdominal toning. Only when these exercises were completed to Dad's satisfaction would he introduce the ball, whereupon he would run me through another extensive set of drills designed to improve dribbling, passing, shooting and tackling. The session would always wind down with a four-mile run.

Hard work? Yes, but rewarding. And then we would walk home together in contented silence, both of us, I'm sure, eagerly anticipating the lamb-stock and carrot soup with all the trimmings that Mum would have been preparing in our absence and which would be ready on the table as we came through the door.

This is what I have found myself trying to explain to youngsters over and over again down the years. You can have all the God-given talent in the world, but it won't get you anywhere if you don't also have the willingness to do the work, and to put in the hours as a four-year-old, with the concrete lumps tied to your thighs.

Later, of course, as I became involved in school teams and moved on into youth football, the need for Dad to be involved in my training in a hands-on way inevitably receded. But all along, and right up until 1967, when he eloped to Spain with the Sextons' eldest daughter, Bethany, he remained my prime source of encouragement – always there with a word as I left the house on the morning of a game. 'Don't bother coming home if you don't win,' he would say. 'I won't, Dad,' I would laugh, heading off up the street with my kitbag as the door slammed behind me.

Needless to say, it was Dad who took me to see the Rovers for the first time – perhaps the most immensely formative experience of my young life. I had been on at him to let me go to a match for some while, but he had always refused. 'You're too little,' he would say, on the occasions when I could get him to explain. 'You won't see anything.' Did my mum, who knew about my desperation to see the Rovers in the flesh, eventually have a quiet word with him? Or did Dad have a plan all along? Was he just determined to time it right? All I know for sure is that after lunch one Saturday (14 February 1947, when I was eight), Dad abruptly stood up and said, 'Get your coat. We're going to the match.'

We took the tram across town and then walked through the streets towards the stadium, caught up in a gradually thickening flow of humanity, channelling towards the ground as if irresistibly drawn that way like a tide. And as we walked I drank it all in, in a state of semi-disbelief: the mingled smells of cigarette smoke, fried food and police horse; the cries of the souvenir hawkers in the front gardens and the rosette sellers on the pavements: 'Get your favours!' 'Programme!'

And suddenly the flow of humanity had become a slow, concerted press, and the imposing outer walls of Melchester Stadium were rearing like mountains above us and my dad was shoving me ahead of him through the stiff, clanking ironwork of the turnstile. Then we were among an energised throng, pushing our way along a dim, echoey corridor and up a flight of whitewashed concrete steps, my hand clinging to the belt on Dad's overcoat, my mind fighting the fear of being swept away from him and separated forever. And suddenly we were out in the open air again, though all I knew of it was a patch of wintry sky above me because all around me were coats and macs and grown-up legs. And now we seemed to be

edging sideways through people, along a broadish concrete step,
until we could apparently get no further and stopped at what must
have been Dad's chosen place in the ground, with me still entirely
hemmed in by legs and coats, and realising with a sinking heart that
Dad had been right all along – that I *wouldn't* see anything, that I
was too small . . . but then, in that very moment of bitter regret,
feeling Dad's hands go under my arms and lift me up – surely the
first time he had done this since he had swung me above him as a
baby – and plant me on the metal beam of a crush barrier, from
where, with a suddenness that stole my breath, I could see, spread
out before me, the whole colourful, jostling panorama of Mel Park
in all its match-day glory.

The records show that there were 74,690 people wedged into
the ground that day – a perfectly standard attendance for a Rovers
league match at that time. We were, as I now saw, high up and to the
right, behind the goal at the Melchester Road End, but I had only
just begun to get my bearings and absorb the view when there was
a noise like thunder – a thunder which seemed to shake the ground
beneath us. I must have looked frightened and turned instinctively
back towards my dad. But Dad in turn leaned in to me, pointing
with a thick finger to the halfway line where the Rovers were running out in their red and yellow hoops as the ground exploded in
welcome.

As the teams lined up, the man standing next to my dad gave me
a serious look.

'First time, son?'

I nodded stiffly.

'Well,' he said, 'if we win, you can come again.'

And then he laughed loudly, cuffed me on the shoulder and
handed me a toffee. And with that his attention returned to the
pitch and he bellowed, louder than I had ever heard anyone bellow,

'Come on you Rov-aaars!'

I didn't even unwrap that toffee. It remained clenched in my palm and ignored until half-time, by which time it had melted so much that it could only be extracted from its paper with surgically precise use of the fingernails. Meanwhile, I had been entirely absorbed, unable to think of anything beyond the spectacle unfolding in front of me. I had never been where there were so many people at the same time, and all concentrated on the same thing, feeling the same swirl of emotions as the ball travelled from one end of the pitch to the other. Moreover, I found myself, to my unyielding amazement, in the presence of the actual, real-life Rovers: Roger Girling, Bob 'Streaky' Bacon, Frank Denselow, Philip Hensher – mythical figures who, until now, had only existed for me in the form of cherished cigarette cards and smudged photographs, carefully clipped from newspapers and glued in scrapbooks . . . And now here they were, moving before my eyes, human beings, and yet somehow so much more than that, in a world within a world where everything was brighter, louder, more intense. I was dazzled, open-mouthed, lost in it.

Rovers led from the thirty-second minute with a headed goal from George Dawson but carelessly conceded an equaliser from a set piece just two minutes from the end and dropped a point. Dad, of course, was incandescent with fury and got into a fight outside the ground with a police horse. Me? I barely even thought about the result or its consequences. I would think about those things the following day as I pored over the report in Mum's Sunday paper, the report itself taking on the status of a mystical totem in my eyes: printed evidence of an event that I had witnessed in person!

But in the immediate aftermath, I floated home in a daze, my head filled with a torrent of sounds and images – that bright green rectangle of grass with its crisp white lines, the roaring crowd, George Dawson flexing his neck and shaking his arms as he stood over the ball in the centre circle, waiting for the referee to whistle and start the game.

It had lit the fire. I knew, without any shadow of a doubt, where I wanted my future to take me.

2

Schoolboy Level

I passed my eleven plus and, to the enormous gratification of my mum, and probably of my dad too, earned a place at Melchester Grammar – thus becoming the first member of the Race family ever to pass through those distinguished academic portals and into the well-appointed, red-bricked buildings beyond.

I will never forget setting out from home on my first morning, a bundle of nerves and anticipation, in the uniform that my mum had broken into the holiday savings to buy: the purple and yellow striped cap, the purple and yellow striped tie and the purple and yellow striped blazer. That was quite an unusual outfit – and, no question, made us a bit of a target on the way to and from school for some of the Hill Road Secondary boys and their empty pop bottles. Still, it wouldn't be the last time I pulled on an unfashionably bright strip and went out in public! What's more, sprinting down the alley behind Heather Lane in a flop-sweat once or twice a week, or scattering from the bus stop as the chunks of glass began to rain down and seeking sanctuary inside the door of Jack's the chemist's, seemed a small price to pay for the pride that I instinctively felt as a Grammar School boy. I was probably even prouder than my parents, if the truth be known.

As a scholar, though . . . well, I guess you would have to say that school books weren't where my heart was. Sure, I worked hard during lessons and got decent enough grades, by and large. The report from my form teacher, Mr Longland, at the end of my first year, said: 'He seems to have a steadying influence on his fellow pupils' – which, if true, was good to hear. But, as diligent as I was in the classroom, I think it was pretty obvious to everyone who taught me that I was really just waiting for the bell to ring so that I could stow my pencils and ruler in my pencil case, put my books tidily in my desk, return any remaining apparatus to its appropriate cupboard or shelf and rush out into the playground to kick a ball around.

Football, football, football: those were my three priorities in those days! In that order! Unless we had a biology test the next day, in which case I would go home, have my tea and mug up as best I could.

I was certainly never in trouble – except on one occasion that I recall. A couple of the lads – I think it was Stinker Boyce and Robbie Shorter; it was usually them! – had balanced a waste-paper bin full of scrunched-up paper just above the classroom door, ready to startle our hapless physics master, Mr Kerslake, who was known widely as Nobby Kerslake, although, in fairness to him, those allegations were never proven and the case never came to court.

Anyway, the classroom was buzzing in anticipation of this lark when I stood up and pointed out to everyone that the bin itself, which was metal in construction and had a crude and slightly sharp seam at the rim, would inevitably follow the admittedly harmless paper down, generating quite a lot of speed from the height of at least seven feet, and could potentially cause a nasty injury, which wouldn't be amusing for anybody involved.

'Roy's got a point,' said Fatty Yeats. With the rest of the lads murmuring in agreement, I climbed on a chair to remove the bin . . . only for the classroom door to open and reveal me at precisely the moment I was reaching up to fetch the bin down from its ledge.

Caught red-handed in the act of setting a potentially dangerous trap! Or so it seemed to the immediately irate Mr Kerslake.

My punishment – issued instantly by a puce Nobby – was to spend that lesson (a double) standing in the corridor and then, that night, to write out, 750 times, the sentence 'I must not engage in childish pranks.' Unfair? Well, yes, clearly, in the circumstances. And you've got to remember that this was still some time before the advent of CCTV, which, questions of civil liberty aside, has obviously sorted out a lot of these kinds of problems for the newer generation. Nevertheless, I resigned myself quietly to my fate – and certainly didn't attempt to incriminate the true culprits. I'm fairly sure I earned a little extra respect from Stinker and Robbie for that – and, certainly, the flow of crudely crayonned drawings of male and female genitalia, which had been finding their way with tiresome frequency into my satchel, and whose source I had never been able to identify, slowed considerably after the waste-paper bin episode. Indeed, I'm confident all of us in that classroom, in various ways, learned a lesson that day.

I like to think I was a popular pupil who rubbed along perfectly well with nearly all his peers, and had time and a word of encouragement for everyone – even Angus Honeyman, who wore glasses and had limited bowel control and was most often to be found weeping in the store cupboard.

There was, however, one fellow student with whom I struggled for a long time to make a connection – and that was Bert Beston.

Bert's dad owned a big builders' supplies company, enabling them to live in a large detached house over on Cobnut Hill, in the posh part of Melchester, and Bert would often be delivered to school in a silver Bentley, inspiring a certain amount of awe among some of the lads – and possibly even a touch of envy. Well, I could understand that reaction, although my feeling has always been that if people have worked hard in their lives and made a bit of money, they should be free to enjoy it, and, so long as it isn't harming anyone else, good luck to them. Was Mr Beston's Bentley causing any harm? OK, sometimes it could pass you a bit close as it swept off the school drive, with its deep-throated engine roaring and its tyres spitting out loose stones. But otherwise, no.

Still, some people make a decision not to like you and won't change their minds, no matter what you do, and I guess Bert was one of those people. He seemed determined to take against me, whether I was helping Mr Longland found the wildlife appreciation society, giving it my all as Cassius in the summer-term production of *Julius Caesar* or getting involved in setting up an after-school homework club for kids in the area with limited literacy skills. It didn't matter what I did, frankly: I couldn't please Bert Beston.

And I certainly couldn't please him as his team-mate and captain in the football team. Bert fancied himself as a bit of a player, and with some justification. He certainly had the flicks and the tricks, although he perhaps lacked the innate positional sense and, still more importantly, the application that would enable him to take the game to a higher level. He was also quite fat, and tended to stand upfield, demanding the ball, rather than tracking back and working to retrieve it, and although, in those days, such tendencies didn't entirely rule out a career in the professional game, they made it that little bit harder for a player to get noticed.

Nevertheless, especially in our U15 season, Bert set up a couple of relatively important goals from the inside left position and made one or two useful contributions at set pieces, especially corners, where he was a handy extra body in the box. You would think he might have drawn satisfaction from that, and from being part of a winning unit, yet, for some reason, for Bert, it never seemed to be enough. I got the impression that he hankered after my number nine shirt, and quite fancied the captaincy to go with it – and, of course, he was used to getting what he wanted, and not used to being thwarted. His view, I suppose, was that I stole the glory that could have been his. I could never understand that attitude, nor how anyone could prioritise their own feelings of fulfilment over the fulfilment of the team as a whole. I remember pointing all this out to Blackie on the way home from school one day, after a 7–4 victory over Holbrooke County High in which I had scored four, set up three and had two more disallowed on the back of marginal offside decisions.

'There's no "I" in "team", Blackie,' I said.

'Isn't there, Roy?' said Blackie, who could be quite slow sometimes, but would normally pick up on things eventually.

'To be fair,' I went on, 'there's a "me" in there. And also a "mat". Plus "tea", obviously. "Eat", too. But you take the point I'm making.'

'Whatever you say, Roy,' said Blackie.

It was soon after this that odd things started happening that I couldn't explain. There was the occasion, for instance, when I went to get changed before a match and discovered that my left boot wasn't in my kitbag. What had become of it? I was certain that I had packed both boots: I was absolutely fastidious about getting my kit together on the night before matches, cleaning the boots, giving them a layer of dubbin and buffing them to a high sheen, then carefully laying out each item of clothing on the bed, checking and rechecking before folding everything, equally carefully, into the bag. There was no way I could have left a boot behind. That boot definitely wasn't there now, though.

Adapting to the circumstances as best I could, I played the match barefoot and was able to score the winner in an eagerly contested five-goal classic. Mind you, my toes ached for days after. And who would have thought it could take toe nails so long to grow back?

Despite the plaudits ringing in my ears, along with the generous offers of plasters, I had mixed feelings afterwards as I got changed. A lost boot! I left for home with a sinking heart at the prospect of breaking the news to my parents. Dad, in particular, was unlikely to see the funny side. It wasn't as though they could afford to rush out and buy me a new pair.

But even as these miserable thoughts were descending upon me, my eyes alighted on a familiar black shape, mysteriously wedged into a litter bin outside the changing rooms. The missing piece of footwear!

But who put it there, and why? My thoughts turned instinctively to Beston, who was about 100 yards up ahead of me, running towards his dad's car. But he wouldn't have . . . would he? I let it drop.

There was also the time, just moments into a game with Kingswood Secondary, when my skin was suddenly on fire with irritation. It seemed to start slowly, in the small of my back, and then spread rapidly until my whole body was raging beneath my shirt, shorts and socks. The more I scratched and plucked and wriggled, the worse it got.

Could it be that someone had doused my kit with itching powder? But who would want to do a thing like that?

Two words, again, sprang to mind: 'Bert' and 'Beston'. My suspicions hardly diminished when, in the grip of this ticklish agony, I tried to make eye contact with Beston across the pitch and found him strangely preoccupied with retying his bootlaces.

Fortunately the location of Kingswood's pitch meant I was able to leave the field, dash down the hill and plunge into the adjacent tributary of the River Mel, soaking the powder out of my kit. I then dashed back up the hill and rejoined play, just in time to get onto the end of a wickedly searching cross from Blackie and lash the ball home for the opening goal in what turned out to be a 5–1 victory.

There were one or two other incidents around this time – one of them extremely unsavoury and involving a nappy, and all of them seemingly designed to throw me off my game. However, though I had my strong suspicions, I was never able to identify the saboteur definitively and I didn't want to accuse Beston without hard evidence. To do so would have been to risk infuriating him and unsettling the spirit within the team in a crucial phase of the season.

In any case, the incidents of attempted kit-sabotage gradually slowed to a trickle and then dried up entirely. In the meantime, Beston and I had grown to be more and more friendly – talking to each other, sharing tips, working together well on the pitch – to the point where I came to feel ashamed of myself for having suspected him of harbouring a grudge. Whoever had played those undermining pranks on me, I decided, it wasn't Beston.

I finally felt able to abandon my suspicions of Beston completely when Melchester Grammar were drawn to play a regional cup game on a Saturday morning away at Collerton Park Senior School, a side we had never come up against before.

Leaving school on the Friday afternoon, with Blackie and Beston, I suddenly realised I had forgotten to copy down the directions to the pitch, which had been posted by Gobber Hughes, the school football coach, on the noticeboard alongside the team sheet.

'It's OK, Roy,' Beston said. 'I know the way. In fact, I even know a couple of shortcuts.'

And with that, he tore a page from his rough book and sketched out a map, showing an extremely clear and easy-to-follow route from my doorstop on Sutton Street to Collerton's pitch.

'See you tomorrow, boys,' he said, and skipped over to his dad's waiting Bentley.

'You know what, Blackie?' I said. 'I've had Beston down for a bit of a wrong 'un. In fact, when you take the trouble to know him, he's a perfectly decent lad.'

'Indisputably so, Roy,' said Blackie.

The following morning, I called for Blackie bright and early and, with our kitbags slung over our shoulders, we set out together on the hour's walk across Melchester to Collerton. It was Saturday, the sun was beginning to peer through the smog and there was the prospect of a football match ahead of us: we couldn't have been happier. We talked as we walked and the journey sped by, bringing us to a trim recreation ground in the far western suburbs bang on the appointed hour of nine a.m., just as Beston had predicted.

'We're the first here, Blackie,' I said. 'We've even beaten the groundsman,' I observed, noticing the padlocked doors on the changing rooms and the goalposts which hadn't yet been hung with their nets.

We dumped our bags on the grass and stood around, waiting. Ten minutes passed. Nobody appeared. Another ten minutes. Still nobody. I was growing more than anxious.

'We're meant to be kicking off in five minutes. Where is everyone?'

At that moment a black dog bounded onto the field, followed at a distance by its owner. I asked him if this was where Collerton school played their matches.

'Not here, son,' said the dog walker. 'This is Collerton Hill. You'll be needing the pitches over at Collerton Brook on the other side of the city.'

That devious Beston had only gone and given us directions to the wrong ground!

Hastily absorbing directions from the dog walker, Blackie and I snatched up our bags and began to run, down a succession of seemingly endless suburban roads, left then right, then right then left, both of us silent the whole way, sick with panic. By the time we reached the pitches at Collerton Brook, the game had been underway for twenty-five minutes.

Gobber Hughes watched us running towards the touchline with his arms folded. His fury was tangible.

'What time do you call this, Race?'

'I'm sorry, sir. We had some . . . difficulties finding the ground.'

'Did you, indeed? Well, we've had some difficulties too in your absence. Our nine men are getting run ragged out there. We're already three–nil down.'

'We'll do our best to make it up to you and to the team, sir.'

'You better had, Race. The honour of the school is depending on you, not to mention our continuing participation in this year's Regional Schools Cup, for which everyone connected with the school, and not least the headmaster, has been nurturing unprecedentedly high hopes.'

I was able to pull a goal back before half-time before adding a second in the opening exchanges after the interval. Blackie then nodded home an equaliser and, with only a minute remaining, I picked up the ball just inside the opposition's half, went on a jinking run which took me past four haplessly back-pedalling Collerton defenders and crashed home the decider from the edge of the penalty area.

Even Gobber Hughes looked emotional as the final whistle blew. I was chaired off by my grinning team-mates, all except for Beston, I noted, who left the pitch on his own with a dark scowl on his face, absorbed by his thoughts.

We went on to win the Regional Schools Cup that year, beating Havering Grove Academy 2–1 in the final. But we did so without Bert Beston. His father was headhunted to run a big leather goods and imported tiger-skin operation in America, and Bert was taken out of Melchester Grammar and sent to a boarding school, which probably suited him better, all things considered.

For many years after leaving school, I often found myself wondering what became of Beston. Looked at a certain way, his questionable attitude to teamwork, his slippery nature, plus his inherent sense of superiority and entitlement, could be thought to amount to a combination of characteristics in a person that might not come to much good in future life. But, again, you can judge too soon: in the course of researching this book, I found out that he became a senior police officer.

What was to become of me, though? My future path was about to become very much clearer as the direct result of a chance encounter in a park with a mustachioed man in a raincoat.

3

Spotted

I guess every life has its pivotal moments: those points where a number of elements coincide and something happens which sends your journey in a certain direction. And of course it always feels odd to think back and reflect on how different things might have been if those elements hadn't come together at that exact point, or had come together in another way, which would have led you in another direction entirely.

I guess what I'm talking about (without wishing to get too deep about it!) is fate, or, if you like, chains of consequence – how you arrived, on a certain day, at a certain crossroads, at the same time as someone else, and ended up being led up a certain road for certain purposes; and yet how different everything might have been had you arrived, for some reason, five minutes later, and met someone else and gone down another road for quite different purposes, or even taken the bus on the day in question.

For instance (to pluck an example at random): what if a

sharp-witted, unusually self-possessed young woman with long black hair and really prominent organisational skills hadn't, one particular day in June 1975, come to work at Melchester Stadium as secretary to team manager Ben Galloway? What if that young girl had instead taken up the offer which, as she later told me, lying in my arms on our honeymoon in Crete, had been on the table for her at the time – namely, to work as the personal assistant to a Norwegian mountaineer and independent documentary film-maker called Rock Thorgessen? Could that somehow mean – impossible thought! – that life would never have paired me with Penny Laine, my dear, late, lamented wife, the mother of my children, my sole love?

Or would life have gone on and simply ordered itself differently? Would Ben Galloway, in that instance, with Penny's polite but firm letter of rejection on his desk, have offered the secretarial job to someone else – possibly Jennifer Eckles, who was working in the commercial department at the time, and almost certainly applied when the post became vacant, and who had lovely, tumbling chestnut hair and a shy laugh and softly downturned eyes? And would Jennifer and I then have courted each other, tenderly, sweetly, with sometimes unbearable yearning, and would I have ended up happily married to Jennifer, possibly somewhere hot?

The mind reels, especially with hindsight. You only need to remove one little piece from the jigsaw – one little coincidence of time and place – and fling it across the room, and the whole picture of your life rearranges in front of your eyes. It's amazing when you think about it.

So, along the same lines: what if Alf Leeds, with his pale, belted raincoat, his thinning, slicked-down black hair and his shiny moustache, hadn't been on Wandlebury Common on that sharply sunlit morning in September 1954?

What if he hadn't been standing on the touchline at the exact moment when, with the scores tied at 1–1 between Melchester Grammar and Clacton Hill High, and with only seconds remaining, I latched on to a long throw-out from Albie Ingleton in our goal, set off on a diagonal run to the edge of the opposition's penalty area, feinted left but went right, losing the last defender, and curled the ball into the top corner for a last-gasp winner?

What if something or someone had detained Alf in the adjacent woods that day? Or what if the agonising kidney stones that were sadly to plague the trusty club servant in later life had crystallised in his ureter that much sooner and kept him busy at home on the floor of his bathroom on the Saturday in question? Or what if a thousand other perfectly plausible things had occurred, preventing me on that fateful morning from getting talent-spotted and offered a trial with Melchester Rovers on the spot? Would I have gone on to have the amazing career and the humbling amounts of success in the professional game that I eventually had? Or was that my moment, my one chance to seize the greatness that would otherwise have eluded me?

Actually, now I come to think about it, I probably would have been all right. Even in the Fifties, the Rovers' scouting network was a fairly sophisticated and broad-ranging operation, employing a number of agents, and not just Alf, all of them briefed to patrol the local scene and report back in detail on their findings in regular Monday morning meetings with senior personnel at the club, making as sure as they possibly could that no likely talent slipped through the net.

Consider too that, in the period we're talking about, I was getting plenty of exposure on public pitches around Melchester. It's something I always stress to youngsters starting out in the game: practice is important, obviously, but there's no substitute for actual match experience, so seek out as much of it as you possibly can. I certainly did, and I know it paid dividends later on.

Accordingly, this is how my weekends panned out, at this stage of my life, around my sixteenth birthday. On Saturday mornings, I was playing school football for Melchester Grammar. Then I would get changed quickly in order to turn out in a lunchtime kick-off for Melchester Royals, a local youth club outfit who played over at Howards Marshes. And after that I would change quickly again and head up to Aldersham on my bike to appear in the afternoon for an U18 unit there, Aldersham Harriers.

Then, on Sunday, I would represent the Melbrook Boys Club in the Melchester & District U21 Combined League, prior to changing and going directly over to Cromwell Park, on the south side of the city, to play for Cromwelleynians in Inter-Counties Division One, before changing again and finishing the day in the blue and white hoops of Belton United, who played at U19 level and had quite a decent little side at the time. Combine all that with appearances, as and when called upon, for the Railway Tavern pub team, and as a ringer for a couple of works sides that my dad put me forward for, and I guess the chances are that I would have been spotted eventually, Alf Leeds or no Alf Leeds.

All that football at the weekend meant a lot of washing for poor old Mum, of course! Sometimes every window in the house would be misted up and you couldn't move in our tiny kitchen for the drying shirts draped on every surface, and frequently there would be socks all the way up the stairs, not to mention a pile of soiled shorts awaiting Mum's plunger in the hall. Making sure I had all the correct kit when I set out at the start of the day was quite a military operation too. That said, I'm proud to tell you that I only got it wrong once – on a busy Sunday in October 1954, when I arrived at Aldersham Rec, plonked down my bag, reached through the four

sodden sets of clothing from the day's earlier matches and realised to my horror that I hadn't packed my all-black Beacham Boys
Wanderers kit.

What on earth was I going to do?

My spirits hardly improved when I went round the rest of the
team and found out that nobody had any spare items they were
ready to lend me – not so much as a solitary sock.

'Ah, well. Looks like we'll just have to get by without you this
week, Roy,' said club captain Alan Small, his equable tone belying,
I felt, the despondency that he clearly would have been feeling
about going into the game under-strength.

I wasn't going to let the team down so easily, though, and I
continued to scour the surroundings for alternative clothing. There
was nothing suitable on the floor in the showers, nor in the rudimentary, battered lavatory block out the back. But outside the
building, on my way to conduct a search of the car park, I spied
something. As fortune would have it, the changing rooms at the Rec
were in the process of being rebuilt at this time, and, up on the
scaffolding at gutter level, probably left there by a builder in a hurry
to get off home on the Friday evening, was a bucket.

And in that bucket, as I discovered when I shinned up onto the
scaffolding to take a peek, was some roofing tar – now cold but not
yet completely set.

Roofing tar being, of course . . . black.

Yes!

I did the obvious thing and, standing on the scaffolding, stripped
down to my underpants before smearing a hearty dollop of the tar
over my chest and arms and down my legs to the tops of my knees.
I then gave a further coating to my calves and shins before tying on
my boots. Hey presto! You would hardly have known anything was
awry, apart from the slightly sickly smell and the stickiness.

And, sure enough, thus 'attired', I duly went on to bag a hat-trick in an impressive 5–0 romp, to the obvious delight of the lads.

Excellent insulating material, tar, by the way! Cycling home, I don't think I'd ever been so warm. Removing the stuff that night, out in the weakly moonlit back yard at home, proved a bit of a challenge, though, I must say. Indeed, for a couple of hours there I thought I was going to have to live with tar-caked nipples for the rest of my life! However, Mum never gave up, and indeed, with Mr Sexton from next door gamely shining the torch on the relevant areas, we eventually discovered that the offending matter lifted off relatively easily if she applied enough meths and a broad-gauge chisel.

As I recall, my nipples were still quite tender and pronounced all those weeks later, on that Saturday morning when Alf Leeds pulled me aside as I left the Wandlebury Common pitch in the company of my jubilant school-mates, already peeling off my shirt in my haste to get changed for the next match in my tight schedule.

His raincoated figure seemed to glide up silently out of nowhere, and suddenly, in an abrupt waft of stale tobacco and cough sweets, there he was, blocking my way. 'You're too good to be playing at this level, son,' said Leeds, looking me sternly in the eye, and only occasionally allowing his curious gaze to drift down to my engorged chest area. 'How do you fancy coming along to Melchester Stadium on Monday morning at eleven a.m. for a trial with the Rovers?'

'You're offering me a trial with the Rovers?' I gasped.

It wasn't, perhaps, the most penetrating question I could have asked at that point. But Alf was clearly a man who was used to seeing surprised expressions on young lads' faces.

'You heard me right, son. I'm offering you a trial. Report to the ground at eleven and tell them Alf Leeds sent you.'

How to communicate the tumultuous mixture of joy, anticipation and sheer astonishment that flooded over me at that moment?

Gobsmacked doesn't begin to describe it. Scouted by the Rovers! Offered a chance to play for the team I had supported all my life – my dad's team and my grandad's team before him! This was every schoolboy's dream – and, pinch me, but I appeared to be living it.

However, before I could say anything by way of thanks, or make any enquiries about the structure of the trial and the nature of the tests I would be likely to face, and whether there was any additional preparation I could usefully do between now and then, Alf Leeds had already thrust his hands deep into his pockets and set off in the direction of the woods. When he had gone a few yards, though, he stopped and turned round.

'Oh, and son? Don't forget your kit. You'd be surprised how many do.'

'I won't, Mr Leeds!' I beamed, flashing back in my mind, with a guilty wince, to my recent tar episode. That certainly wouldn't be happening again. Once tarred, twice shy, in my experience.

I couldn't wait to get home and break the news to my mum and dad. But before that, of course, I had to play two more youth league fixtures, an U21 friendly over at Cottleborough and then an early evening kick-off in the holding role for Ace Cement Limited against Bessler Freight. I scored hat-tricks in both of the youth league games, poached five in a 7–0 clattering of Cottleborough, and then helped the Ace Cement boys to an edgy 1–0 win, netting with a header from a corner late in the first half and then going in goal for the last quarter of an hour after the Freight's big number nine broke keeper Dougie Stimpson's jaw with an upper cut. Things had looked gloomy for us when the Freight were awarded a dubious penalty in the eighty-eighth minute, but I guessed correctly, got down low and just managed to tip the ball round the post.

I don't suppose anyone has ever cycled the fourteen and a half miles from Hanbrook Public Playing Fields to Sutton Street as quickly as I did that Saturday night. I was standing up on the pedals, not just on Shirley Hill, but virtually the whole way. As I rode, I was imagining my parents' reactions when I told them about the day's monumental development. Mum, I knew, would burst into tears. Dad would most likely nod and turn back to his radio – always keen to manage my expectations and protect me from being built up and then let down.

Almost beside myself with desperation to share the tale, I hurtled up the alley, flung open the back gate, dropped my bike against the wall and banged through the back door.

'Mum! Dad! I've only gone and got a trial for the Rovers!'

Mum burst into tears. Dad nodded and turned back to his radio, keen, as ever, to manage my expectations and protect me from being built up and then let down. I can't overstress the value to a child of predictable, consistent parents.

Then Mum set my tea in front of me and, as I wolfed it down, I told them the whole story: the surge upfield through despairingly lunging defenders, the last-minute goal, the figure in the mac approaching me as I left the field . . .

'He said to go along at eleven on Monday,' I said.

'You'll be needing a fresh set of kit, then,' said Mum, with perhaps just a faint trace of weariness, although, in fairness, it was now getting on for ten-thirty.

In bed that night, staring at the ceiling and hearing the faint thumping noises that so often floated across the way from Mr Hotchkiss's house at the weekends, I mulled everything over. Tomorrow was Sunday, which meant obligations for me at Melbrook Boys Club v. Ibstock Athletic, Cromwelleynians v. Wigmore Hall and Belton United v. Blacktown Wanderers, with the possibility (Dad said he would let me know in the morning) of a cameo appearance off the bench for Sargeant's Plumbing Supplies in some kind of closed-doors five-a-side tournament on a patch of disused ground near the railway arches at Coneydene. And then I was going to need an early night.

Because when Monday dawned it was going to bring my once-in-a-lifetime chance with the Rovers.

'Don't blow it, Roy,' I said to myself, perhaps a touch anachronistically, as I finally turned on my side and closed my eyes. 'Don't blow it.'

4

On Trial

The Monday of my try-out with the Rovers dawned bright and clear, although with the possibility of some cloud moving in later in the day, and the westerly wind maybe bringing one or two scattered showers by the end of the afternoon.

Or at least, that's what the man on the radio was saying over breakfast as I did my best to ignore the butterflies winging around in my stomach and attempted to force down on top of them the plate of food that Mum had placed on the table in anticipation of the ordeal ahead: seven slices of bacon, four tomatoes, three fried eggs, half a pound of sausage substitute, a serving of yesterday's roast potatoes, two thick slices of cold lamb, something dark and gluey which I didn't really recognise (possibly pickled beetroot in some form?) and six rounds of buttered bread. Mum was, in many respects, ahead of her years in acknowledging the importance to the sportsperson of the carb-loaded, protein-intensive and highly fat-saturated diet, which really only came into football properly in the 1960s, and was to remain in vogue until the late 1990s. The easing of rationing restrictions in 1954 certainly played into Mum's hands in that respect.

As I hoisted my kitbag (shirt freshly laundered, socks paired, boots fastidiously blackened and coated with dubbin the night before) onto my shoulder and went out to get my bike, Mum followed me. Stopping me on the back step, she straightened my tie (which didn't need straightening, obviously), brushed at the shoulders of my jacket (which had no fluff on them, clearly) and then cupped my face in her work-scored but still soft hands which, as ever, faintly gave off the homely smells of soap powder, carrot peelings and lard.

'Do your very best, son,' she said, her anxious eyes filling up slightly. 'And we love you, whatever happens.'

'Thanks, Mum,' I belched.

And with that, I wheeled my bike out of the back gate and down the alley and took off for Mel Park and my appointment with destiny, or, more specifically, as it turned out, with Dick Burnleyside from the coaching arm of Rovers' Youth Development Division, or YDD. (The Rovers' back-room operation was even more ahead of its time than Mum was in the kitchen!)

The ride to the ground passed in a blur and I was soon leaning my bike against a boarded-up concession stall on the concrete apron at the front of Mel Park. Ah, the uniquely poignant atmosphere that emanates outwards from a football stadium on a non-match day! It still speaks to me. Indeed, some afternoons even now, I'll put my coat on and wander over there, just to stand on the pavement and experience that atmosphere. In the days before Dad started taking me to matches, I had often cycled across just to gaze wonderingly at the home of the Rovers from the outside, and was always struck by the way that, even empty, the place seemed to be throbbing with history, as if all the noise that the stadium had encased down the years had somehow soaked into its walls and was now quietly pulsing in the brickwork. I can still feel that pulse now – though, of course, these days the club Megastore will be open, meaning that people are coming and going at all times, in a way they never used to be. Plus, obviously, the ground, which was of necessity comprehensively rebuilt in the wake of the great Melchester earthquake of 1986, now abuts the new Eastgate out-of-town shopping centre, with its big branches of Bed World and its drive-through Meaty Burger, so it's a busier part of town generally than it used to be.

Mel Park had been entirely refurbished in the 1930s and, even twenty years later, it retained a shiny, palatial, almost fairy-tale grandeur – or so it seemed to me on the morning of my trial. The white external fascia of the main grandstand was an Art Deco masterpiece, with a pair of giant Rovers badges painted red and set high into the stonework at each end, like pieces of ancient heraldry. The main entrance into the club – distinct from the turnstiles which admitted the crowd – was a set of tall glass doors at the top of a wide white staircase which had handrails of exactingly polished brass. On guard at the summit of those regal steps was a uniformed commissionaire with bright buttons on his epaulettes – an ex-military man, although, of course, almost every man you came across was an ex-military man in those post-war days, with one or two notable exceptions such as my dad. Altogether, you could have been forgiven for thinking you were entering one of the posh Park Lane hotels in London, rather than going into a football ground in humble Melchester.

Barely able to control myself at having a legitimate purpose here at the stadium, I now jogged self-consciously up those steps, my kitbag swinging from my arm, my frequently resoled school shoes clacking on the swept stone. At the top, with the grand old stadium clock showing three minutes to eleven, I presented myself to the commissionaire.

'Race, sir,' I said. 'Roy Race. Here for a trial. Sent by Mr Leeds.'

'Not f***ing here, sonny.'

I was confused.

'But Mr Leeds said I—'

The commissionaire cut me short.

'This is the main entrance. Players and staff only. Which – forgive me if I'm wrong – wouldn't f***ing happen to be you, would it.'

It wasn't a question, but I somehow felt obliged to answer it anyway.

'Er, no, sir.'

The commissionaire looked me up and down, taking in my school blazer and tie in a manner that made me feel about three inches tall.

'Fancy your chances as a Rover, do you, sonny?'

'I would certainly like to give it a try, sir.'

'You'll be f***ing lucky,' he said. 'Hundreds like you, son. I see them all, pitching up – hope all over their spotty faces. And then leaving an hour later, crushed to s***tery, or worse.'

The commissionaire let those words hang in the air for a while, then gave a flick of his thumb over towards the corner of the ground.

'Dick Burnleyside. That's who you'll be needing. There's a black-painted door, just by East Stand, Entrance J. Give it a good rattle, mind. That Burnleyside's a deaf old c***.'

Somewhat shocked, I thanked the commissionaire for his help, if not his encouragement (nor his language), and set off at a jog in the direction he had shown. A couple of years later, as an established first-teamer, and now able to use the main entrance as a matter of course, I gently reminded Buzzer Hawkins (aka Norman the Doorman, aka Attack Dog) of this conversation and my first introduction to life at the Rovers.

'You can f*** off,' he said. 'Don't start on me with your f***ing "I told you so's".'

'F***ing footballers,' he added.

That was old Buzzer through and through, though! A man who seemed to have climbed out of bed on the wrong side more mornings than not! But a good man underneath, and a loyal club servant who always meant well.

As it happened, I didn't need to give the black-painted door a rattle, because it was open and a number of other trialists were already hesitantly passing through, all of us with the same nervous expression on our faces, but not many of them, like me, dressed in their school uniforms. In fact, none of them: everybody else seemed to have turned up already in kit. I recognised a couple of players from various local games I had played in, and we were nodding to each other stiffly, when I suddenly noticed a face that was almost as known to me as my own and a comfortingly familiar flop of black hair above it.

'Blackie! What are *you* doing here?' I cried, with delighted and relieved recognition at the sight of my greatest pal, Blackie Gray.

'I'm having a trial, Roy.'

'Well, obviously – but you never mentioned that Alf Leeds had given you the nod after that possibly pivotal Melchester Grammar match on Saturday morning.'

My oldest friend and neighbour explained that, in fact, Alf Leeds hadn't given him the nod on that occasion, but that the following day, when Blackie was playing for Harbury Athletic in a Sunday League fixture over at Thistledown Grove (he, like me, was setting his stall out at a number of local youth outfits at this time, albeit to a slightly lesser extent than I was), a man called Willy Holmes had taken him aside and asked him to attend today's try-out. (As I explained earlier on, the Rovers' scouting network was a widespread and sophisticated operation.)

'It couldn't have worked out better!' I said. But Blackie was looking anxiously at my clothes.

'I didn't realise we were meant to be in school uniform,' he said. 'Oh, God, Roy, I've gone wrong already! I'm in me kit!'

I told him to relax because, by the look of things, it was potentially me who had got the dress code wrong, and not him.

'But you're never wrong, Roy,' said Blackie, which was good to hear, though not, in fairness, one hundred percent the case, and it was beginning to look like this might be one of those times.

We had no more time to talk about it, though. The black door had taken us into a wide access passage in the corner of the ground, lined with lawnmowers and rollers and various other pieces of ground-keeping equipment. And this passage had in turn led us up and out across the sandy run-off track and (thrillingly, unbelievably) onto the hallowed Mel Park turf. Again, I had that shivery, vaguely guilty feeling of being somewhere that I wasn't allowed to be. How extraordinary it was to feel that luxuriant spongy surface underneath my school shoes. And how dizzying to look up from this privileged vantage point into those towering, empty stands, so high they almost seemed to join above your head, and to imagine them brimming with ecstatically roaring fans. If I hadn't already known for years that I wanted to be a Rover, I would have known it then.

My reveries were cut short by the arrival of Dick Burnleyside. The Rovers' youth development coach was a stout, broad-jawed figure in his sixties, extremely muscular, with a viciously close short-back-and-sides haircut and a pair of gritty sideburns. He was wearing a huge pair of brown football boots, navy blue tracksuit trousers and a dark grey cable-knit sweater, thick enough to drop a slighter man. We formed a loose horseshoe in front of him and for a while he just stood there with his arms folded, looking at us dismissively, much as the commissionaire had.

I was about to ask if there was somewhere I could get changed, but before I could get my hand aloft, Burnleyside, who had said nothing up to this point, barked out an order.

'Right! Press-ups! Twenty-five of them! Off you go!'

I could sense some reluctance, bordering even on dismay, among my fellow trialists, and I guess I was a little startled myself at the abruptness of the instruction. But I was more than ready to comply. Without wishing to seem immodest, twenty-five press-ups didn't seem like much of a demand to me. Even as a four-year-old, during Dad's Sunday morning training sessions over at the fields, I had been easily capable of doing sixty press-ups (and these were the more challenging kind, where you quickly clap between each press) and then, directly afterwards, of jumping up, sprinting 300 yards and making an unassisted jump over a three-foot wall into a bed of nettles.

So, without too much trepidation, I went down on the wet grass with everyone else and began to comply vigorously with the order. But I had only been down there about five seconds when, from up above, came the noise of Burnleyside letting out a rich, croaking laugh.

'Nah, I'm kidding! What do you think this is – the bleedin' army? Stroll on! We're trying to be a football team here at the Rovers. So let's go over to the pitch and play some b****y football, then! Eh? Shall we?'

Everybody now got to their feet and wiped their hands off, a bit sheepishly but with manifest relief and amid some gradual laughter. I stood up too and smiled broadly, but with, I have to confess, slightly mixed feelings. I saw and understood what Burnleyside had done there: he had broken the ice, settled a few nerves in a way that, I'm sure, Blackie, among others, appreciated, and created a positive environment in which the rest of the session could now duly unfold. At the same time, I was a little bit surprised to hear him being quite so dismissive (at least, by implication) of non-ball work. After all, while it's easy to deride it as somehow unsophisticated or brutish, exercising without the ball has its place. As I am always at pains to stress to the youngsters, general conditioning is crucial, and an appropriate, personally tailored workout regimen away from the pitch is an important tool to have in your footballing locker. It certainly didn't do me any harm.

Burnleyside now led us further onto the turf, where some coloured markers had been put down in various configurations, and he set himself to unknotting and upending a giant net of footballs. Again, there was still no time to ask for the changing rooms. No matter. I would just have to wait for an appropriate pause in proceedings and, in the meantime, do the best I could.

'OK,' said Burnleyside. 'I want you to find a partner and play some passes to each other across a distance of ten yards. Simple balls, along the ground, one touch to control, one touch to distribute. Away you go.'

Blackie and I paired up – again, relieved to have each other to fall back on – and I took a ball and we began to stroke it back and forth between us. I could feel us both starting to relax and open up and get into the swing of it. Burnleyside then increased the distance to twenty yards, and left us doing that for a little while. Then he brought us in for a heading exercise and then he split the group into smaller units and had us playing games of two-touch and three-touch, to work on close control under pressure. And then, finally, he divided us into two teams, and we played a match, albeit using just half of the pitch, with a portable goal pushed up to the halfway line.

That, I think, was the point where the trial really started to go well for me, and also, my impression was, for Blackie. I got on the ball a lot, hit a number of constructive passes and made some positive contributions overall. Of course, it was by no means the perfect display, because no such thing is possible. Analysing my performance at home later that night, I concluded that some of my blindside movement at set pieces could have been crisper and that I could probably have encouraged the defence to maintain a slightly higher line during a spell of concerted pressure during the second half which led to a couple of close chances for the opposition.

Nevertheless, there was no getting round the fact that I had scored five goals, one of them a scissor kick from twenty-five yards, and made three, including two for Blackie (who had, in turn, made three of mine). Also, in what turned out to be the final passage of play before Burnleyside called matters to an end, I had broken down an attack on the edge of our penalty area and then set off on a mazy run the length of the (admittedly, half-size) pitch which had ended with me impishly lobbing the advancing goalkeeper before running round him to volley home. All in all, then, I had made a decent fist of it, and indeed, by the time the whistle blew at the end of the session, I had quite forgotten that I was in grey flannel trousers and a purple and yellow striped blazer.

As I left the pitch, loosening my tie, Burnleyside came up alongside me.

'You'll do for me, son. What's your name?'

'Race, sir. Roy Race.'

'Race, is it?' Burnleyside's eyes narrowed. 'Any relation?'

'Billy Race was my grandfather, sir.'

'Was he now? Good player, your grandad. One of the greats.'

'I know, sir.'

'Listen, Race. I'd like someone else to have a look at you. Can you come back Wednesday evening?'

'Yes, sir. I certainly can, sir. Thank you, sir.'

'Be here at seven, then.'

'I will, sir. Absolutely, sir.'

Excitement coursed through me. A call-back! Just like that! As I headed off to collect my bag, I heard Burnleyside shout after me.

'Oh, but Race? Bring some kit next time, would you? You look an utter pillock in that blazer.'

The great news was that Blackie, too, got a call-back for the Wednesday night. This time we cycled to the ground together and once again passed through the black painted gate and out onto the pitch, though now the ground was bathed in floodlights, which only seemed to lend the scene an even greater theatrical romance. What's that saying from William Shakespeare? 'All the world's a stage.' Well, it's a bit of an exaggeration because there are clearly parts of the world that aren't a stage, nor likely to become one any time soon: some of the bits of Melchester down by the river, for instance, not to mention the Berkbeck Estate. But a football ground at night, under the lights? That's a part of the world which is definitely a stage, and the Bard will get no argument from me on that account.

It turned out that what we had been invited back to was a youth team training session which we were asked to join in on. The procedure was much like our original trial – various gradated exercises with the ball, then a match – although the standard of play was noticeably a notch higher. Still, Blackie and I seemed to more than hold our own, and in the match, I set my pal up for a simple tap-in midway through the first half, and, late on, he returned the favour, whipping over a cross that I was able to get on the end of with a fully stretched diving header that turned out to clinch the game, 3–2.

And the man Dick Burnleyside had wanted to see us? Ben Galloway, the Rovers manager!

I was awed, naturally, to be in Galloway's presence, and undoubtedly made a touch nervous by the sight of his familiar, slightly rotund figure watching from the touchline. But he was extremely friendly, and smiled and shook my hand warmly at the end of the session.

'Very nice piece of work, son,' he said. 'Very nice piece of work.'

And just like that, the pair of us found ourselves offered a twelve-month contract with the Rovers on apprentice terms.

Animatedly cycling home together through the dark streets that night, Blackie and I couldn't prevent our minds from spooling ahead and contemplating the future.

'Imagine if it works out, Roy. Two mates from the same street, both playing for the Rovers! What are the chances of that?'

'They must be a million to one, Blackie,' I said.

'Really?' said Blackie. 'That sounds like a lot. But you're the one with the head for figures, Racey!'

I suppose that was true. But even I, at that stage, wouldn't have wanted to assess the odds on the adventures in football that lay ahead for us.

5

Through the Ranks

The arrival in the post of an apprentice-terms contract with Melchester Rovers left me with a decision to make, the first proper decision of my adult life, really, unless you count choosing to decline to join Mrs Creamer from number 42 in the cupboard under her stairs during a street party to mark the Coronation of Queen Elizabeth II in the summer of 1953 – which I don't, and neither, I think, did Mrs Creamer, so the slate was, as I say, pretty much clean at this point in terms of adult decisions.

Basically, the situation was now this: if I was going to take up the club on its generous offer of a twelve-month probationary development period as a junior or 'A team' player (one down from senior level), I was going to have to leave school. In the first heady hours after Ben Galloway and Dick Burnleyside made their intentions clear on that fateful Wednesday night, I would have had no hesitation whatsoever about making that leap. But, over the ensuing forty-eight hours, as the initial excitement abated, and as I began to be able to subject the offer to slightly more level-headed scrutiny, the path ahead didn't seem to be quite so straightforward.

I mulled over the pros and cons and the full extent of the dilemma in a lengthy discussion at home with Dad on the evening after the official paperwork had landed.

'The way I see it, Dad,' I said, 'is that, obviously, professional football has been the dream all along – and accepting this deal would potentially be a major step in bringing that dream to fruition. However, there's also, clearly, education to consider. Both of us know that careers in football are frequently short and not at all secure. Injury or loss of form could curtail your ability to earn a livelihood at any moment. So it's obviously prudent to have some qualifications behind you for the eventual day, sooner or later, when football can no longer pay the bills.

'Now, in that regard, at the moment, I'm holding a respectably broad set of O levels, including geography, history, maths, English, art, domestic science and metalwork. So, all well and good. However, a few more months at school and I could reasonably expect to have the additional security of A Levels to fall back on, which would, in turn, open up the possibility at some point in the future of a university place and, potentially, a tertiary-level degree, which would greatly enhance my prospects in the job market, should it ever come to that.

'Therefore, I'm caught between thinking: is quitting school the thing to do at this point? Should I, as it were, stick with the hand I currently have, and take my chances? Or should I decline Rovers' offer in favour of completing my schooling and banking those A Levels, with the intention of retrialling, and take the risk that they would still look favourably on my application a year hence?

'Or might there in fact be a third way? Might it be worth trying to persuade Rovers to defer my apprenticeship with them until next summer – or perhaps, better still, reach some kind of compromise position, whereby I could play a part-time role at the club, in the evenings or at weekends, say, while staying on at school and continuing to study towards those all-important A levels?'

'Leave,' said Dad, without even having to look up from his paper.

Dad's ability to cut to the nub of the matter never failed to impress me, and I don't suppose anyone could doubt, given the way things turned out, that this was another of those many occasions when his parental guidance proved rock solid.

So, I quit school and became an apprentice footballer. And I have to say, I had never been happier. Every morning, from Monday to Saturday, at 7.25 on the dot, Blackie and I would get on our bikes and, wearing our thick, navy blue, standard-issue Rovers apprentice tracksuits, cycle over to Mel Park. We were so proud of those tracksuits, though, of course, in the style of the day, they were made of wool. If it rained as we cycled, they would retain water and come to weigh in excess of fifty pounds. That could certainly make Shirley Hill a bit of an ordeal, especially into a headwind and in the company of some of the raging horizontal sleet that typified a Melchester winter, and very often a Melchester spring as well! And also, on reflection, quite a lot of a Melchester summer too. But, the way I saw it, it gave us the opportunity to benefit from a bit of extra, stamina-building resistance work which we wouldn't otherwise have been doing.

Once at Mel Park, the fifteen of us who were on apprentice terms would report for roll-call in the tiny, windowless, grey-painted Apprentices' Muster Room (more a storage cupboard, really) in the warren of interconnecting chambers and corridors under the stands. And then we'd be handed out our jobs for the day by the stadium under-manager, Harry Parnell, an unemotional man with a clipboard whose own promising career in the game (according to the legend) had been tragically cut short by an injury on the fields of the Somme. Apparently he had twisted his ankle in a rabbit hole during a family walking holiday there in the summer of 1952. The club, typically, looked after him with an administrative role.

Tasks for us apprentices essentially fell into two categories: there would be kit-work, which might mean helping out in the laundry for a morning or putting in a five-hour shift in the boot-room, chipping the mud off the first team's boots, scrubbing them clean and applying layers of polish and dubbin. Or there would be jobs connected with general stadium upkeep – whitewashing walls, maintaining septic tanks, unblocking toilets, etc.

And, of course, there was football too. On two afternoons per week, at the end of the day, assuming there was time, we would have a forty-five-minute training session, with a further evening session on Wednesdays, if there was no first team home game. And then, once a week, normally on a Thursday, we would have a match against another A side, either at Mel Park or away from home – when, that is, opponents could be found whose schedules allowed for it.

The matches and the training, obviously, were the aspects of the job for which we all lived, when we really felt like we were Rovers – or, at least, like Rovers in the making. Some grumbled about the menial tasks that occupied so much of the rest of our time, and a few even complained, in a roundabout kind of way, that they were being taken advantage of. But I felt that was the wrong attitude. I can honestly say I loved every part of the apprentice existence, and threw myself into it accordingly. Each day seemed to me to be excitingly fresh and different and I didn't see how anyone could ever know a moment's boredom, because there was always a dressing room to be swept, a lavatory block to be disinfected or an area of terracing to be scrubbed with a pad of wire wool and a pan of cold soapy water.

Don't forget that we were paid too: threepence halfpenny a week, handed out to us every Friday afternoon in a small brown envelope by Brian Derwent, the club's wages man, when he remembered to do so. I would hand the threepence to Mum for housekeeping and put the halfpenny in my savings jar, where I was also salting away some of the proceeds from my part-time jobs: my Tuesday evening grocery delivery round, my Thursday night work as bottle-boy and glass washer in the Saracens' Arms, and my Saturday night shift at the candle factory. (Anything I could do to ease the pressure at home.)

It wasn't about the money, though, for me. I would have worked for the Rovers for nothing. The way I saw it, being an apprentice was simply about being given a rare and precious privilege to be one of a small, select group of people allowed access to the very engine room of a functioning, top-flight professional football club, discovering how the operation worked, from the smallest flush handle to the largest ballcock. A football club is a bit like a swan, I guess, in that respect: what the outside world sees is a magnificent, sedate creature gliding smoothly along, but, under the surface and out of sight, a whole army of people is paddling away like crazy, fighting for air, trying not to drown and fixing the toilets.

And, of course, the other great privilege of my new life – the feature of it that made me keep wanting to pinch myself to check I wasn't in a dream – was to find myself, as a matter of course and on an almost daily basis, around the players. In those days, the first team trained at the stadium. (This was long before the development of the club's state-of-the-art, Norman Fosscock-designed training complex over at Fenton Parkway.) As a fan, I couldn't get over the fact that, on the way to the roller-towel cupboard, say, I might suddenly find myself passing Buster Brown, Rovers' first-choice left-half, in a corridor; or that I might have to step out of the toilet cubicle whose walls I was sponging down so that Andy McDonald could use it. McDonald, the team captain, was virtually royalty to my mind, and after he had finally flushed and left, it would sometimes be several minutes before I could bring myself to go back in and resume my work. These were players whose faces had looked out at me from the wall of my bedroom and from the pages of my carefully archived season-by-season scrapbooks. And now here they were, made flesh.

For the most part, the players gave off what seemed to me an almost impossibly romantic aroma of carbolic soap, hair lacquer and tobacco. But mostly tobacco. These days, smoking is something footballers only do in private or while on holiday when they wrongly think there aren't any paparazzi around. Not so in the mid-Fifties. Of the regular Rovers' starting XI in the 1954–5 season, only Tom Dawson, the plucky outside left, didn't smoke, and that was because he was on doctor's orders for six months following an acute pulmonary infection and was therefore temporarily restricted to snuff.

Otherwise, in the dressing room before and after training, or during their rests on the pitch, the players would always be sitting around in a pretty much impenetrable fug of smoke. Sam Higby lit one cigarette off the end of another. Dave Williams, saving time, liked to have two on the go at once. Between cigarettes, Hughie Griffiths, the Rovers' pacy and incisive right-half, was wont to smoke a pipe. It gave off the most pungent stink, as if someone was burning animal hides adjacent to a paint factory. Just to walk through the emissions from that pipe of Hughie's was to experience an almost overwhelming nausea accompanied by a sharp stabbing sensation in the eyes, though Hughie himself seemed blithely unaffected, puffing away happily with his apparently fireproof thumb tamped in the bowl, and pausing only to hawk darkly into the grass.

During practice matches, Len Dolland, the trusty goalkeeper, had a tin ashtray lashed to the rear of the goalpost. He could spark up and take a few restorative tokes while the play was at the other end, and then rest the cigarette in the tray when the ball came his way, only to resume smoking immediately the danger was cleared. Nobody thought this was remarkable. Any stoppage in play was interpreted, unofficially, as a fag break, and on more than one occasion in a full-scale training game, I saw Jim Hallett score, reach into his pockets for his cigarettes as he turned away, light up on his way back to the centre circle, take a rapid set of deep puffs, and then stub the remainder of the cigarette out on the grass at the restart.

Obviously, the science on the effects of smoking on health was inconclusive at this time. Nevertheless, even with those questions aside, you would think Taff Morgan, the first team trainer, might have been concerned to see his players indulging the habit to the extent that they did, simply on the grounds that it occupied so much of their time and attention. Then again, now I come to think of it, Taff smoked constantly too – roll-ups, which he kept in a rusty tin with a picture of King George on the lid, and which he always seemed to be in the process of making, compressing the tobacco's oily straw with his thumbs, licking the paper's gummed edge with the tip of his dark yellow tongue, a lit one clenched smoulderingly between his fingers as he did so.

Of course, as apprentices, we wouldn't have dreamed of approaching the players or venturing near them, even if the smoke hadn't made that complicated. We knew our place, and the rule was very much 'don't speak unless spoken to'. However, sometimes the players would use us to run errands for them. Someone would send you out for, say, a bottle of milk and 240 Capstan. Some of the players had cars and they might ask you to go out to the car park and give them a wash. Others might want you to fill them a bath, or, when they emerged from that bath, fetch them a warm towel and a cup of tea and maybe read to them from the newspaper. I believe the term they used for this kind of thing at boarding schools was 'fagging'. (Nothing to do with cigarettes!) I suppose these days you'd call it a concierge service.

And, of course, we apprentices were more than happy to comply. Indeed, though we probably wouldn't have admitted as much to each other, we yearned to be chosen for these errands and were secretly disappointed when, for example, Dick Stokes, the nippy but always faintly lonely-looking and frequently quiet winger, urgently needed, say, a bottle of drain unblocker, a hacksaw and some strong plastic sacks, and elected to send someone else on the mission.

I think my first summons to play errand boy came from Bob Roberts, the left-back, who sent me out for some shaving cream. Not long after that he trusted me with a slightly more difficult mission to get a specific haemorrhoid application for his wife. (I ended up going to six different pharmacies before I located it.) And not long after that, Roberts had me run over to Crace's breaker's yard at Salcombe Hollow and pick up an exhaust pipe and manifold that he had had set aside for his Austin A30. That was quite a challenging trip, the exhaust pipe proving quite hard to balance across my shoulders over the necessary miles, but it was all worth it for the moment when Roberts ruffled my hair, gave me an avuncular wink and let me fit it for him.

Something else the players liked to get the apprentices to do was place a bet for them – usually on the horse racing. There were no bookies shops in those days – they wouldn't become legal until 1961. But it was widely known among the gambling fraternity that Harry Stout, Melchester's leading underground bookmaker, would sit at a corner table between eleven a.m. and one p.m. on weekdays in the Shepherd's Market Café, a couple of streets away from Mel Park, and surreptitiously do his business from a baggy brown briefcase.

One afternoon, approaching lunchtime, I had just come from regrouting the tiling in the showers when Ted Barker pulled me aside. Barker was a useful left-half, though he was mostly being kept out of the side in this particular season by Buster Brown, who was in a good run of form. Barker had impressively quiffed and always entirely tidy black hair and a thin pencil moustache, which, in tandem with the fashionably wide pinstriped suits that he often favoured, gave him something of the look of a spiv. Had he drawn you into a quiet corner and tried to sell you some knocked-off silk stockings, you would hardly have been surprised! Indeed, that's exactly what he did, in my first week, rather to my confusion, but I muttered something about not needing any at present, and we moved on.

Anyway, Barker now had me buttonholed again. 'Race,' he said. 'Nip out and stick this on Uncle Nobby in the two-thirty at Campdock Park, all right? There's a good lad.' And with that, he pressed a rolled-up piece of paper into my hand.

When Barker had gone, I unrolled the piece of paper and discovered that it was a five pound note. This was quite shocking to me. Five pounds was at that point more money than I had seen gathered together in one place at the same time. It was more money than my dad was likely to earn in a year – or had perhaps ever earned, since his groin injury. The idea that Barker was willing to risk a sum this size on the uncertain outcome of a horse race made me feel very uncomfortable, even a little sick.

The thought that I was going to have to go to the bookmaker on Barker's behalf made me more uncomfortable still. Though I had been an apprentice for more than three months at this point, and had heard the other apprentices talk about doing it often enough, I had never placed a wager with Harry Stout.

Still, an errand was an errand, so I fought down my instinctive reservations, moral and otherwise, and headed over to Shepherd's

Market. The café was a small corner premises, typical of the period, with ruched curtains strung across the lower halves of its windows that may once have been white but were now battleship grey with accumulated dust and grease. The market stalls were packing up for the day and the lunchtime custom was building up. Vapour fogged the room like it was a laundry and there was an overpowering smell of bacon and steamed chicory. Through the mist, though, I could clearly make out a small, bald, suited figure, busily writing at a corner table where a coffee cup and a fat brown briefcase betrayed the temporary office of Harry Stout.

Nodding slightly embarrassedly to the owner behind the counter, I threaded my way across the café, feeling – I suddenly realised – woefully intimidated. But I told myself to get a grip. Other apprentices put bets on for players all the time. It could hardly be difficult. In front of Stout's table, I held out Barker's five pound note and thought back to what Mr Longland had taught us at Melchester Grammar about managing ourselves in public, among adults. Be clear, be confident, but, above all, be polite.

'Uncle Nobby, please.'

Stout's head had risen from his work but he hardly seemed to be listening. His attention seemed to be entirely absorbed by the five pound note. At the first sight of it, his shoulders had visibly stiffened and his eyebrows had risen approximately four inches up his forehead, where they remained. He continued to say nothing, and nor did he move.

I decided to forge on. Clear, confident, polite.

'In the two-thirty at Campdock Park. If I may, sir.'

Stout now managed to wrench his eyes from the fiver and, without changing his expression, looked me up and down, still clearly in an advanced state of disbelief. He then lowered his gaze to the newspaper, open and folded into quarters by his empty coffee cup, and ran his inky forefinger down its closely printed page, until he seemed to see what he needed. Then, with his other hand, he picked up his pen, wrote something in his ledger and tore off a small, square green ticket which he pushed towards me across the table. At the same time, casting quick looks across the café, he reached out slowly and tentatively towards the five pound note, before abruptly snatching it from my fingers and dropping it into his briefcase almost as if it were hot. Then he returned to his writing. Our transaction was apparently concluded, so I turned and left.

'You lumped me on, right?' said Ted Barker, back at the ground.

'Yes, Mr Barker.'

'Good lad.'

I handed him the green ticket, and Barker walked away, happily examining it like it was the photograph of a loved one.

He had got about ten feet when he froze, still hunched over the ticket, and then seemed to sway, ominously, like a tall building in a high wind. There came a sound somewhere between a gasp and a scream and Barker spun back round.

'What the f***, Race? Didn't you check the b****y slip?'

'Do you mean the ticket, sir?'

Barker came pacing back at speed and thrust the square of green paper under my nose. I pulled my head back far enough to be able to focus my eyes. In Harry Stout's scrawling but legible hand were the words, 'If I May Sir'.

My mind spun back to that fumbled conversation in front of Stout's café table. 'In the two-thirty at Campdock Park. If I may, sir.'

Stout had obviously misunderstood me!

My voice seemed to have gone high and thin. 'I . . . I was just trying to be polite.'

'Polite? You've put my money on the wrong b****y nag, Race.

If I May Sir? My a**e! It was Uncle Nobby I said, you b****y dim-wit. Uncle Nobby! Thirty chuffing quid, that little arrangement was going to make me. Easy money! The fix was in. Surest thing I've ever been allowed in on.'

In his fury, Barker seemed to be on the verge of ripping the ticket in half, right there in front of my nose.

'You'll be paying me back for this for the rest of your miserable life, Race,' he said, and then he pushed his face right into mine, to the point where I could smell the faintly lemony lacquer on his moustache, and his voice dropped two octaves and became the kind of noise a dog might make just before a fight.

'And do you know why the rest of your life is going to be misera-ble? Because I'm going to f****ing *make* it miserable. And while I'm thinking up ways to do so, you owe me five pounds.'

Barker twisted on his heels and stormed away.

That afternoon, I was meant to be playing for Melchester A against Carston A at Mel Park, but I was so shaken by my run-in with Barker, I seriously didn't think I had the mental wherewithal for it. I sat in the dressing room before kick-off, not getting changed, just staring ahead of me in an anxious daze.

'What's up, Racey? You look as if you've just received the death penalty,' said Blackie, coming to sit beside me in front of the lockers and referring to the ultimate judicial sanction for murder which remained in force in British law until 1965, when it was replaced by the mandatory sentence of imprisonment for life.

'Funny you should say that, Blackie,' I replied, and then I told him the whole story – about Ted Barker's little errand, the mis-understanding with Harry Stout, how I had ended up inadvertently losing Barker the small fortune of thirty pounds on a fixed horse race, not to mention a five pound wager, and how Barker was thus far failing to see the funny side.

'But how was he so sure that this horse of his was going to be the winner?' asked Blackie.

I explained again that the race had been fixed and that Barker had been let in on it by the people who had been doing the fixing.

'So . . . what? People already knew who was going to win?'

'That's right, Blackie.'

Blackie thought about this for a while.

'Wouldn't have been a very exciting race, then, would it?' he said.

I didn't think Blackie was getting the full picture. However, what he said next did chime with me and, for once, seemed to be a point worth making.

'What you need is a football match, Roy. It's the only thing that can take your mind off the problem – even if only for ninety minutes. While you're out on the pitch, you won't be thinking about anything else. Come on. What do you say?'

My little pal was right. It's how football works. Once you cross that white line and the whistle blows, nothing else on earth matters. The game can be a huge blessing that way – a salve for the troubled soul.

With rekindled resolve, I got changed, ran out and played my part as we soaked up some early Carston pressure. Then, teaming up promisingly with Micky Dinsmore on the left, I began to help us exert a grip on the midfield areas and gradually turn the momentum our way. It was still 0–0 at half-time, but the second half saw me nod in a corner and then add another with a swerving thirty-yard free kick. I then beat five defenders and set up Blackie for number three before completing my hat-trick with a marauding run to the byline, terminating in a bending shot, struck with the outside of my right foot from an almost impossibly acute angle. As I left the field, I was delighted to see that Ben Galloway, the Rovers' manager, had been watching in the stands and was now looking at me and applauding. Galloway seemed to have been coming to see a lot of our A team matches of late.

I left the ground that night in a far lighter mood, but I can't deny that the Barker incident eventually returned to weigh heavily on me, and by supper time at home, I could only sit and pick absently at the food on my plate. 'You're quiet tonight, Roy,' said Mum. 'And you've hardly touched your kidneys.' But I couldn't tell her and Dad what was going on. It would have worried them too much. So I simply muttered something about being tired after the match and maybe needing an early night.

I sat in my bedroom in my pyjamas, racking my brains to try and think of ways I could come up with five pounds. There was nothing I could sell because there was nothing I owned that was worth that much. I removed my savings jar from the bottom drawer of my dresser and upended it on the bed. I counted the halfpennies into piles. It amounted to one shilling and fourpence. That was some way short of my debt, clearly. But it might buy me some time.

I reported for work the following morning feeling utterly desperate, with a sickly anxiety gnawing away at the pit of my stomach. The jingling of twenty-eight halfpennies in my tracksuit pockets as I walked into the stadium could only provide an ironically bright musical counterpoint to the darkness of my mood.

And, of course, on the day when I least needed it, who was the first player I should bump into but Barker?

He appeared to be sizing me up. It was obvious that, at any moment, he was going to pin me to the wall by my throat.

My fears began to be realised when Barker, visibly trembling, stepped in, stuffed his hands under my arms and, seemingly without the slightest effort, lifted me fully two feet off the ground. I was now helplessly aloft above the wily left-half's carefully parted hair and looking down into his upturned face, gingerly inspecting it for some clue to the extent of the violence that he intended to wreak.

Instead, I watched in confusion as, beneath Barker's tight moustache, a smile slowly began to unfurl, which then spread right across his face and rose up to illuminate quite dramatically his suddenly bright green eyes.

'You little beauty, Race!' he said. 'Did you hear?'

I was now completely disoriented – and still awaiting, at the very least, a rabbit punch to the stomach.

'I don't think I did, Mr Barker . . .'

Barker set me back down on the ground, with a muffled chinking of coins, and continued to beam at me mysteriously. I realised he was trembling, not with contained violence, but with its close relation, joy.

'Uncle Nobby fell at the third! If I May Sir's only gone and romped home! Forty to one! I've cleaned up!'

I felt my shoulders rise, as if an enormous iron weight had just been removed from them.

'Also, the police are investigating suspicious betting patterns surrounding Uncle Nobby – and I'm in the clear!'

Barker was almost dancing on the spot in his pleasure.

'Quids in, Race! Quids f***ing in!'

'Well done, Mr Barker.'

I shook his hand and, as I moved, I felt against my leg the somehow reassuring weight of all the halfpennies that I hadn't been required to hand over. So, in a sense, I was quids in too. Or, at any rate, one shilling and fourpence in.

And nor was that the end of my good fortune that day. In a carnival mood, on the back of his brush with Lady Luck, Barker made an extremely generous gesture in my direction. During the afternoon, as a special treat, I was allowed to take a rag and the Brasso out to the car park and polish the chrome trim on his Morris Oxford.

The Uncle Nobby episode became a running joke between

Barker and me from then on. Every time I saw him in the morning, he would laughingly clout me round the back of the head and say, 'How's my little form analyst? Any tips today, Race?'

In all seriousness, if I'd had a tip for Ted Barker, it would have been 'don't gamble'. It's no coincidence, after all, that bookmakers are rich. Apart from Harry Stout, maybe, who was never seen again in Shepherd's Hill Café, nor indeed anywhere in Melchester, after Barker's Uncle Nobby wager. In the main, though, I think it goes without saying that the odds don't favour the punter over the long term, which is why I have never felt able to advocate betting – on racing, football, or any other outcome – or been keen to get involved in it myself. And I had no cause to change my mind about that when, soon after his playing career ended, Barker went in way over his head, accrued a mountain of gambling debts which left him in permanent fear of violent reprisals from the criminal underworld, and was eventually imprisoned following a botched armed raid on a mail train.

So, yes, my tip to Barker would have been 'don't do it'. But it was hardly my place to say anything at that stage. I was, after all, just an apprentice.

Though not for much longer.

6

First Teamer

What you're hoping for, above all, as an apprentice, is to get noticed, and I was fortunate that attention began to come my way very quickly at Melchester Rovers. For instance, within my first fortnight at the club, some of the extensive solo work I had done on the replastering project for the rear wall of the West Stand had attracted a few seemingly admiring glances – and not just from my peers, but also among one or two people further up the club hierarchy. Indeed, one afternoon, the chairman's wife, no less, Jean Chievely-Mason, a flamboyant woman (a former actress, it was said) whose long blonde hair was artfully arranged beneath a strikingly fashionable hat, drove past while I was cleaning off my trowel and beckoned me to her car window.

'Well, you're quite the little plasterer, aren't you?' she said in her low, smoky voice.

'Thank you very much, Mrs Chievely,' I replied.

'You know,' she went on, her voice, if anything, now lower and even smokier, 'I have a couple of surfaces at home that could do with a hand-finish from a young man such as yourself.'

I told her that I would be more than happy to assist, but that my commitments at the club and elsewhere were fairly extensive, so maybe the best way forward was for her to give me a sense of the scale of the surfaces in question, so that I could put some figures together regarding the quantity of materials involved and give her some idea about the likely timescale of the project, assuming she decided to go ahead. She thanked me fairly crisply and drove off, but I never heard anything further, so I guess she must have found someone else to do the job. Still, it was an endorsement, at a very early moment in my time at the club, and one which gave me a lot of confidence, going forward.

Meanwhile, when it came to renewing the damp course in the cellar beneath the ticket office, I had certainly put in a stand-out shift, working overtime on nine consecutive nights to dig out the original footings and get a bitumen layer down in order to prevent a longstanding moisture ingress problem from worsening before the wet weather properly set in. Furthermore, Bill Devlin, the senior foreman in the club's works department, very soon had cause to commend me on my installation of a replacement waste pipe in the groundsman's lavatory. 'You've got a lovely clean seal there, son,' he said, crouching down and reaching behind the bowl to run his forefinger around the joint. 'That's quality plumbing.'

On the pitch too I was working as conscientiously as I could in the time allowed and doing my best to (as the phrase has it) set my stall out – although obviously without ever prioritising my own stall over the stall of the team. I trained with relish, when training was available to us, and was always among the first onto the pitch at the start of the session and the last off it at the end. In the eight months that I had been at the club, I had appeared in seventeen A

Team fixtures, of which we had won fifteen and drawn two. I had scored forty-two goals and been directly responsible for making a further twenty-nine. I had also written and composed a team song, teaching it to the lads during a week of lunch-hours. (It was entitled 'Go, Melchester A,' and posterity should probably be allowed to draw a kindly veil over it! That said, the lads seemed to get a lot out of singing it and handled the three-part harmonies in the fourth and final verse pretty well considering.)

At the same time, I knew I was by no means the complete package: there were plenty of aspects of my game that needed work and I knew that there always would be. Like the saying goes: it's when you no longer believe you have anything to learn that you truly have everything to learn. But I felt I was continually improving, and that was the main thing.

For all that life was moving in the right direction, though, I was completely taken aback one night when, just as I was rinsing off my drain rods and getting ready to leave the ground, Ben Galloway, the Rovers' manager, came up to me.

'Race, been meaning to say: great work on the groundsman's khazi,' said Galloway, who had his overcoat on and his hands thrust deep into its pockets in the pose I had seen from him a million times beside the pitch during Rovers' matches. 'Bill Devlin took me in to have a look at it, and we both agreed – that's some of the most professional workmanship, U-bend-wise, that we've seen from an apprentice in a fair number of years.'

'Thank you, sir.'

'No, but really: it put a lot of other U-bends to shame. Real excellence.'

'Thank you, sir.'

I was ready to walk away, glowing with pride. But Galloway went on.

'That's not what I wanted to say, though. I've been keeping an eye on your performances for the A Team since you came in . . . what is it now, eight months ago?'

'Seven months and twenty-four days, sir.'

'Right. So how do you think it's going for you?'

'Well,' I replied, 'there's clearly room for improvement, but I think the team has begun to put some foundations down that can be built on.' I felt I could risk a light-hearted remark here, so I added, 'And I'm not just referring to the new staff catering block adjacent to the Mel Road entrance, sir!'

Galloway nodded and smiled.

'I like your attitude, Race,' he said, 'and let me tell you something: I think you've got a great future at this club. Furthermore, I think it's time we got that future started. I want you to come into the first-team squad for the match against Elbury Wanderers on Saturday.'

I couldn't believe what I was hearing. I felt like my head was going to spin clean off my neck. First the U-bend compliment, and now this! It was almost too much to take in. Galloway had to prod me into responding.

'Well, do you think you're ready for it?'

'Thank you, sir. Delighted, sir,' I gasped and I couldn't prevent a beaming smile from exploding across my face.

'Excellent,' said Galloway. 'So, tomorrow morning, you'll report for training with the first team. Look forward to seeing you there.'

'Absolutely, sir.'

'And you don't need to call me "sir", Race. You can call me "boss". You're a Rover now.'

I could have leapt a mile in the air after Galloway left. Instead, I dried and stacked away the drain rods, did a bit of tidying up that I had been meaning to do in the metalwork shop, and then prac-tically sprinted outside to where my bike was parked and where

Blackie was waiting for me, ready for the ride home. I was about to tell him my amazing news but Blackie, who was also clearly fired up about something, started talking before I could draw breath and get my mouth open.

'You'll never guess what . . .' shouted Blackie.

'Tell me,' I said.

'I've been asked to train with the first team from tomorrow morning,' said Blackie, actually hopping up and down on the spot with pleasure. 'Ben Galloway thinks I've got a great future at this club and he wants me in the squad for Saturday's upcoming game against Elbury Wanderers.'

Now, some people might have been slightly disappointed to hear an exact replica of their amazing, life-changing news delivered to them just as they were preparing to enjoy unveiling it themselves. Some might have felt their thunder was being stolen. But that wasn't the way I saw it at all. This was Blackie, after all – my closest pal, the person who had been with me, like a shadow, for the whole of my life. Whatever I wanted for myself, I also wanted for Blackie. We had dreamed together, schemed together; and now our mutual dreams and schemes were tantalisingly close to becoming a mutual reality. I wouldn't have had it any other way.

'That's fantastic, Blackie,' I said. 'And guess what? Ben Galloway said the same thing to me! He wants me to train with the first team from tomorrow morning and be in the squad for the game against Elbury Wanderers on Saturday. Both of us! Isn't that absolutely brilliant!'

Blackie went quiet and looked down at the ground. After a little while, I said, 'Are you all right, my oldest friend?'

Blackie was silent for a little longer, and then he suddenly said, 'It would just be nice if for once – for once – I could achieve something, or do something in my life, and not feel immediately overshadowed by you! If I could just feel that . . . you know . . . that my thunder wasn't being stolen all the time.'

I was shocked. I had no idea that Blackie felt that way. I immediately tried to put him right.

'Blackie,' I said, 'that's really not how it is. Really it isn't. You know that. There have been plenty of times when you did things and I didn't overshadow you.'

'Name one,' said Blackie.

Over the next few minutes, I racked my brains to come up with something, and eventually had the eureka moment that I was looking for.

'What about that time, in the first year at Melchester Grammar, when we all had to enter a competition to make a dog's head out of papier mâché? No way was my papier mâché dog's head better than yours. No way! Yours was so much the superior papier mâché dog's head.'

'Yours won first prize.'

'Yes, but yours was better. The judges got it badly wrong. We both agreed on that. Even to attempt a Weimaraner at that level put you out on your own.'

Blackie seemed to cheer up at the memory of this, and the moment passed. Moreover, the subject of any rivalry or ill feeling between us was never again mentioned for the rest of our lives.

Cycling home, the sense that our fledgling careers now stood on a daunting and yet, at the same time, thrilling precipice and that we were about to join hands and leap into the unknown, thrummed in our nerve-ends.

'Just think,' said Blackie. 'In four days' time, we could both be making our debuts for the Rovers, just eight months after signing for the Mel Park-based outfit on apprentice terms.'

'Unbelievable, Blackie,' I said. And it truly felt so.

The rest of that week passed – it's obvious to report – in a euphoric blur. But what certainly remains sharp in my mind's eye is the memory of reporting for training on that first Wednesday morning – daunted, obviously, but at the same time with the pride almost exploding in my chest as I finally, in the role of an official Melchester Rover, got to bound up that spotless white stairway to the main entrance, following in the footsteps of so many heroes, past and present.

'We've been called up into the first team squad,' I explained, as the splendidly uniformed figure of Buzzer Hawkins moved to block the door.

'We're Rovers now!' added Blackie, who was just behind me.

The commissionaire looked at us blankly.

'Yeah, right. And tomorrow's bleeding Christmas in Swaziland. P**s off round the back, like normal, you f****ing Herberts.'

Good old Norman the Doorman! A club like Rovers wouldn't have been half the institution it was without people like Buzzer, who lived for the place and gave everything he had to it.

So, Blackie and I went through the service gate as usual and then walked round the outside of the pitch and down the tunnel, and got in that way. And pretty soon we were nervously entering the hallowed inner sanctum of the home dressing room for the first time as players – though obviously we had entered it plenty of times as apprentices in the afternoons when the players had gone home, and we were intimately acquainted with it. Indeed, I could legitimately say I was familiar with every white ceramic tile on the wall of the communal bathroom, because I had put them all up there myself only three weeks previously.

Andy McDonald, the club captain, showed us to our lockers and introduced us around the room, where the rest of the squad were busy getting changed and chatting animatedly and, of course, smoking even more animatedly. The atmosphere was enormously jovial and everyone was fantastically welcoming. 'Good to have you aboard,' said Sam Higby, offering me a cigarette, which I politely declined. 'Congratulations, Roy,' said Buster Brown, also offering me a cigarette, which I also politely declined. 'It's the tipster!' said Ted Barker and cuffed me affectionately on the forehead. 'Seriously, though,' he added, 'we hear great things. Well done on stepping up.' Then he offered me a cigarette, which I politely declined.

I was issued with a new first-team tracksuit, which couldn't have arrived at a better time. My apprentice's tracksuit was looking decidedly worse for wear and, despite nightly washings by my mum, always seemed to bear a faint sheen of the cement and plaster dust that were now embedded in the wool. Also, I had caught the sleeve in a rotary sander while reconditioning the floorboards in the club boardroom and made a rare old hash of the cuff. It was good to feel properly smart again. You can't overestimate the importance of that kind of thing, to my mind. I often say to kids starting out: keep your kit clean. Be fastidious about cleaning all of your bits and pieces. Clean kit, clean mind.

I had barely finished getting changed into my new things when Taffy Morgan, in a scruffy green roll-neck jumper and a pair of dark track pants more clapped-out, even, than my old pair, put his head round the door and shouted, 'All right, let's get out there.' And the next thing I knew, I was walking out to train with the Rovers.

To start with, we did a loosening jog around the pitch, accompanied by quite a bit of coughing and spitting. And then, when everyone's lungs had begun to settle down, we did some shorter sprints and some stretches. But it was mostly ball-work, in accordance with Rovers' over-arching philosophy. (It was an article of faith with Ben Galloway, the boss, and has long since become the quotation for which he is most famous: 'If God had meant footballers to run up and down all the time, He wouldn't have given them balls.')

Obviously, Blackie and I both experienced the sense of mild bewilderment that everyone has on the first day in a new job. But we got on with it as best we could and the session concluded with an eight-a-side training game in which I acquitted myself OK, scoring seven in a 9–2 victory for the orange bibs – including, to be fair, one which went in off Len Dolland's ashtray, but which was allowed to stand.

Work ended at midday. I still felt a bit pent-up, so I went for a thirty-nine-mile run round Melberry Dyke (one of my favourite routes) and then went back to the club and helped out the other apprentices with a bit of tarmacking in the car park. Old habits die hard, I guess! But I just needed to feel busy.

Would I get picked for Saturday? That was the question I was trying to stop pinballing around in my head. There was no guarantee that I would be selected. Ben Galloway had only said he wanted to call Blackie and me into the squad – not that he necessarily intended to pick us on the day. To this extent we were very much on trial again. And let me say once more: there were no substitutes in matches back then. There was no making it to the bench and hoping to get called on at some stage. You either made it into the first eleven, or you sat in the stands in your suit.

For an eager lad, with all the impatience of youth chafing away in his fibres, the prolonged uncertainty was hard to live with. All I could sensibly do over the course of those three days was get my head down, sink myself in the training sessions and work as hard as possible in the hope of doing something that would mean Galloway had to pick me – a tough call, given the established professionals that I had been thrown in with.

Moreover, I noticed the atmosphere in general becoming more serious as the week wore on. If Wednesday had felt relatively cheerful and relaxed, Thursday was noticeably more earnest, and Friday was more earnest again, the tension beginning to ratchet up, even among the most experienced players, as the weekend's match got nearer. Ben Galloway had also started joining Taff Morgan at the sessions and we had begun to do some work tailored specifically towards our upcoming opponents, Elbury Wanderers, a distinguished side whose line-up boasted Arty Hedlow, a formidable, tough and unsentimental centre forward, regarded as having the hottest shot in the league. The very mention of him seemed to focus a few minds and sharpen a few tackles on the training pitch.

In the middle of this new earnestness and growing momentum, I felt like I was a small child, standing among a crowd of giants and pitifully jumping up and down with my hand in the air. It seemed like a potentially hopeless quest. Still, I continued to knuckle down as best I could, scoring nine goals in the training game on Thursday, and then adding eleven more in the game on Friday, including two from the halfway line. (Ashtray not involved in either case!)

The routine was that, at some point on Friday morning, normally while the squad was getting changed after training, Galloway would pin the team sheet for Saturday on the noticeboard in the corridor outside his office. When our session had concluded, I put on my clothes quickly and left the dressing room, jangling with anticipation, hardly daring to think what I might be about to discover.

But as I turned into the corridor, I saw that Blackie had beaten me to the board and I could tell from the look on his face as he turned back towards me that it wasn't good news.

I felt a terrible pang for my old friend. 'Oh, Blackie,' I said. 'No go?'

'No, I made it. I'm in the team,' he said. 'But . . .'

Now I was worried. With a whole cluster of sinking sensations in the pit of my stomach, I went to the board, ran my eye down the names and numbers on Galloway's somewhat ink-spotted sheet of paper and saw the following written there: '9. Rice'.

'I'm really sorry, Roy,' said Blackie. 'I can't believe he's gone for somebody called Rice rather than you.'

I confess that I did experience a sudden stab of alarm at the sight of this unknown player in the number nine berth, but I was very quickly able to rationalise the situation and put my mind at rest. There was nobody called Rice on Melchester's books. It was obviously a slip of the pen on Ben Galloway's part – and entirely of a piece with the rather scrawled and scratchy nature of the team list as a whole: I had got the nod.

'I think it's all right, Blackie,' I said, the relief flooding through me and waves of excitement suddenly building everywhere. 'He meant to write "Race". I'm entirely convinced of it.'

'Really?' said Blackie. 'Then we're both in! That's absolutely brilliant! But somebody had better tell this Rice bloke. He'll be gutted.'

I knew in my heart of hearts that I was picked to play, but I thought it would be prudent to be absolutely sure, so I went along and knocked on the manager's door.

'Oh, b****y hell, not this again,' said Ben Galloway, who sounded a little cross. 'That's not an "i" – that's an "a".'

'Seriously?'

'Of course it b****y is. Race. With an "a". I know that.'

'It's only that it looks quite a lot like an "i" – you know, with a dot above it? So I guess I felt I ought just to ch—'

Galloway cut me short.

'Listen, people can bang on as much as they like about my literacy skills, but I can pick a team all right, and you're in it.'

I left very quickly, closing the door behind me. It was clear that I had unwittingly touched a nerve, which I naturally felt anxious about. But in the dressing room, the rest of the lads hooted when I told them about it.

'Galloway's got the least legible writing in football,' chortled Andy McDonald, slapping me on the shoulder. 'Famous for it. First time I looked at one of his team sheets, I thought we'd signed someone called McDoughnut.'

'I'm forever staring at that board and thinking to myself, who is this bloke Parkin, then?' laughed Ted Barker, poking me in the kidneys with two fingers.

'And I'm not even going to tell you what it looks like when he puts my name up,' said long-term injury Derek Cant.

Everyone in the first eleven was allowed to collect a pair of tickets for the match from the office on their way home, which we could give to friends or relatives, and I hatched a plan to use those tickets to break the great news about my selection to my mum and dad. I was going to wait until a quiet moment during supper that night, then reach into my pocket, say, 'Oh, by the way . . .' and drop the tickets onto the table. Mum, I knew, would burst into tears and say, 'I don't believe it.' And Dad would probably be out of the house because he tended not to be around all that much on Friday nights.

Sure enough, that night, as Mum and I sat eating together, I pulled out the tickets and said, 'Oh, by the way . . .' And Mum burst into tears and said, 'I don't believe it.' You always knew how it was going to go with Mum! And with Dad too.

Sleep was almost impossible that night. I mostly lay on my back, playing the game through in my head, running through a few matchplay scenarios. 'Visualisation' is, I suppose, the modern term for it, although back then we tended to refer to it as 'getting properly worked up'. I slept only fitfully, if at all. Eventually, soon after five a.m., I gave up and decided to go for a cycle ride to calm my nerves. When I got back at seven-thirty, Dad was apparently still in bed but Mum was up and already hard at work, preparing me one of her extra special breakfasts – all the usual fried goods, soups and bakery products, but with an added beef stew and dumplings component, which I wolfed down.

Players weren't due at the club until one-thirty and the morning stretched ahead ominously. I had no idea how I was going to fill the time and I certainly had no intention of sitting around at home and fretting and growing ever more nervous and maybe being fed more dumplings, delicious though they were. So I decided to cycle over to Mel Park early and spend those hours overhauling the club's electrical generator. This passed the time very efficiently and, before I knew it, the electricity was back on in the admin block and my team-mates were beginning to arrive.

How different the dressing room felt on a match day! It was much quieter, for one thing. People seemed to be talking less, and in lower voices. The carefree ebullience of midweek was now gone, replaced by a purposefulness and even an edginess, as the pre-match nerves began to bite. Even the most experienced players, I noted, were not immune to anxiety, but they each had their different ways of showing it, or trying to conceal it. Tubby Morton, the big centre back, got changed and then sat staring straight ahead of him, oddly unreachable, both his massive legs jiggling almost uncontrollably. Paddy Ryan also sat and stared unreachably, but, rather than jiggling, he was totally still and humming – and not tunes, but one single, continuous, low note.

Others had their match-day rituals and superstitions, which they adhered to religiously. Tom Dawson always had to put his socks on first. Jim Hallett always had to put Dave Williams's socks on for him – and Dave only ever put his shorts on in the tunnel. Buster Brown needed to be the last player to run out onto the pitch. Sam Higby always had to be the second last – unless there was an 'e' in the month, in which case he had to be third from the front, apart from in the case of November, when he needed to be either fifth or seventh, depending on whether it was raining or not. Hughie Griffiths didn't mind where in the line he was, as long as he could run out backwards, patting himself on the head with his right hand and rubbing his stomach with his left.

Absurd? I suppose it could easily sound that way. And I was never one for superstition myself – unless being fastidious about the cleanness of your kit is superstitious, and I never saw it in those terms. The point is, if these things helped other people do what they had to do, and didn't get in anybody else's way, as they mostly didn't, then I couldn't particularly see the harm in them.

With kick-off nearing, the tension throbbing, Tubby Morton's legs now pumping away in a blur and Paddy Ryan humming louder than ever, Taffy Morgan clapped his hands for silence and Ben Galloway gave us his final team talk. He spoke calmly and kept it simple. There was a brief recap of some of the things we had talked about in the week in relation to approaching Elbury Wanderers, with Arty Hedlow once again singled out. 'Hedlow, we know about,' said Galloway, his tone slow and even. 'If you give him space, he's going to punish you. Simple solution? Don't give him space.'

And with that, Galloway raised his voice slightly and said, 'We've worked hard all week – now let's make that work pay. We can win this. Let's go.'

Then, as was his tradition, he stood in the doorway and as each of us passed him on our way out to the tunnel, he shook us by the hand and clapped us on the shoulder and offered us a personal word of encouragement. When it came to me, he winked and said, 'Go out there and play your football, son. You were born for this. Enjoy it.'

'Yes, boss.'

And after that there was the tunnel, and the searing light of a grey and overcast Melchester day at the end of it, and then the explosion of noise as I stepped onto the turf, running behind Jim Hallett, with Blackie behind me, and with Sam Higby behind Blackie, one from the back of the line because it was April and it wasn't raining.

And let me tell you, the noise of a packed Mel Park hits you like a blow to the chest. You can experience the crowd's welcoming roar as a spectator, but until you have stood in the middle of it and felt it coming at you from all four corners at once, you haven't really heard it or measured its full impact.

We had a few moments to limber up, during which I exchanged an encouraging glance and a pumped fist with Blackie. News that Ben Galloway intended to blood a couple of young prospects had made it into the papers and you could sense the goodwill coming off the crowd in the form of personally directed shouts such as 'Come on, the new lads' and 'Do it for the Rovers, son' and 'Hope your a**e is in gear, blondey – it's the big time now.'

Scanning the opposition, my eyes were drawn to the almost lumpishly muscular, surly-faced figure of Arty Hedlow, who seemed to be mouthing something at me and making some kind of hand gesture, though I put that down to paranoia on my part. There was no time to think about it in any case, because the next thing the referee's whistle blew, the game started and my career in professional football was underway.

Any initial nerves died down quickly. I got an early touch – a simple, defence-splitting through ball to Dave Williams who shot narrowly wide – which helped me settle. I began to feel comfortable, acclimatising to the atmosphere and the pace of the game. I was getting into gear and moving relatively freely, observing the patterns as they developed, and tentatively working the spaces for openings.

Then in the twenty-second minute, it happened. Blackie, who had also quickly shaken off his nerves, had gone on a marauding run down the right-hand channel, almost to the byline. With the defence expecting a cross, his cut-back ball to the edge of the penalty area found me arriving late and unmarked. I just had time to think to myself, 'I could hit this . . .'

I've got to say, the power I managed to generate surprised even me. The ball seemed to detonate off my swung boot and the goalkeeper could only watch it fizz past his right shoulder and into the top of the net.

'A rocket', the match report would call it the following day – the first of my career. 'The crowd went mud,' the reporter added, though I think that was a misprint. Unless Ben Galloway had found his way up into the press box!

Heading back upfield for the restart, and stressing to my delighted team-mates (in tandem with team captain Andy McDonald) the importance of holding our shape and building on this lead, I passed Arty Hedlow, who had his hands on his hips and an unpleasant sarcastic leer on his lips.

'You jammy little f****er,' he said.

Perhaps the possessor of the hottest shot in the game sensed a rival and felt piqued – I don't know. Whatever, I chose to ignore him, but I can't say I was impressed by his gracelessness. And neither, clearly, was Buster Brown.

'F*** off, Hedlow, you poxy s***stick,' said the clearly aggrieved left-half.

I suppose I wasn't too impressed by that, either.

Still, we kicked off again, and ten minutes later, when Hughie Griffiths added a second, once more from a cut-back cross, but this time delivered by me, things were looking very promising indeed. Two–nil – and Hedlow hadn't even been in the game yet.

'The points are as good as in the bag,' said Charlie King, as we celebrated with Hughie.

'Let's not be complacent,' I said. 'There's still an hour to play and football has a way of turning around on you when you least expect it.'

'Fair point, Roy,' said Charlie.

And indeed, my words were more prescient than I knew. In the very next passage of play, Charlie went into a strongly contested fifty-fifty challenge with one of Wanderers' centre backs and the Melchester man came off worse, shattering both of his hips in the incident, which effectively ended his career.

I went over to Charlie to console him as he left the pitch on a stretcher, but he was one of those really valuable, irrepressible types that football seemed to be full of in the Fifties, and he merely grinned up from under the blanket. 'It's all in the game, Roy,' he said. 'I'd been thinking about getting out and opening a sweet shop in any case. Just make sure you hold on for the points.'

I felt sure that we could, but I knew it would be an uphill task. With Charlie on his way to hospital, we were down to ten men and Arty Hedlow, hitherto merely a brooding presence, now smelled blood. Barrelling through our still reorganising defence, he pulled a goal back for Elbury just before half-time. Ten minutes into the second half he wrestled himself free at a corner and scored again. And just like that, our lead was gone, Elbury were on the front foot, and my glowing debut was threatening to turn to cold ash in front of my eyes.

Anxiety was rippling from the stands to the team, and from the team to the stands. 'Keep calm, lads,' Andy McDonald insisted. 'We can hold on for a point and send the capacity crowd home at least part way satisfied.'

We were under siege though. For more than twenty minutes, we clung on. I have no idea how we did so for that long. The attacks were coming in waves and Elbury were getting chance after chance, most of them falling to the instinctively dangerous Hedlow, who twice rattled the uprights and once put a free header fractionally wide.

Yet still our exhausted defence held firm – until, in the eighty-seventh minute, agonisingly, the ball fell loose in the penalty area to Hedlow, who, with Len Dolland wildly exposed, only had to hit the target . . . and somehow got under it, scooping the ball against the top of the bar and sending it out harmlessly for a goal kick.

Relief washed through Mel Park like a tsunami (as it happens, one of the few natural disasters not to have afflicted the stadium down the years – but we'll come on to that). 'I reckon that's it,' said Hughie Griffiths. 'They won't get a better chance than that.'

But he reckoned without Hedlow. We just needed to retain possession for the final moments, so Len sensibly played the goal kick short to Bob Roberts, who was standing out wide on the left, midway in his own half. Immediately under pressure from the hungry Hedlow, Bob elected to knock the ball square across the pitch, at about waist-height, in the direction of Dave Williams, who had dropped back to the edge of the centre circle to receive it.

What happened next was to become the subject of some lasting controversy. What's beyond doubt is that the advancing Hedlow extended an arm, the ball came into his possession, and the next thing he was running in on goal and shooting under Len Dolland's despairing body.

Was it hand ball? Let's just say, you've seen them given. Certainly the grin on Hedlow's face as he jogged back upfield, with poor Bob Roberts running after the referee to protest, didn't suggest that the Elbury striker's conscience was too bothered either way.

Still, I don't think there was any cause to raise doubts over the integrity of the match official, Mr FR Pollen from Gormsbury Bay. The referee has to call it as he sees it. If he was genuinely unsighted and the linesman was also in no position to make a clear call, then the ref had no alternative but to let play continue and allow the goal, even if it meant that my debut, which had started so promisingly, was now completely ruined.

Or was it?

We lined up again. I could sense the despondency in a few of the lads' body-shapes, some of whom had dropped to the floor in the wake of Hedlow's strike, the air sucked right out of their lungs.

But, of course, it's the oldest verse in the football bible: it isn't over until it's over.

Accepting Jim Hallett's tapped kick-off, I sent the ball right to Blackie, and then sprinted off up the pitch on a slightly diagonal line across to the left. I was just outside the Elbury penalty area when I turned back to see Blackie's long, pumped pass falling out the air. I took it down on my chest, turned back inside to go past the centre half and, from just inside the D, unleashed a curling left-foot shot which started out wide of the post but then began to bend in . . .

. . . and bend in . . .

. . . bending just enough to . . .

. . . hit the post! Aargh!

But the inside of the post! The ball spun inwards to ripple the back of the net for 3–3!

Pandemonium! The next thing I knew, I was under a pile of screaming team-mates and the crowd was going nuts – in so far as I could hear them, with one ear glued to the turf and the other repeatedly blocked and unblocked by Sam Higby's bouncing shorts, giving everything a strange wowing effect.

'Brilliant, Racey!' said Andy McDonald, after we'd all stood up again.

'I got a bit lucky with the rebound, Andy, to be fair,' I said. 'If I'd caught it a bit more sweetly it would have bent further and gone straight in.'

'We'll forgive you!' said Andy. Which was good captaincy on his part.

'Thanks,' I replied. 'It's something I'll have a look at on the training ground on Monday.'

The referee didn't even have time to restart the game. It was over. My debut had ended all square, and the Rovers had snatched a draw.

During the post-match handshakes, I found myself confronted by Arty Hedlow, who looked as though he had just swallowed an entire jar of pickled eggs. I reached out my hand and was about to congratulate him on a hard game, well fought. But before I could open my mouth, Hedlow, whose hand was not extended, said, 'Enjoy your day out, sonny? You'll be back in the f***ing reserves next week.'

I didn't know what to say to this and had just concluded that it was probably better if I said nothing at all, when Buster Brown chipped in on my behalf.

'Shove it up your a**e sideways, Hedlow, you classless t**t.'

'Toss off, Brown,' replied Hedlow, 'you useless f***ing knobhead.'

'Yeah, p**s up a rope.'

'W***er.'

Which, I suppose, felt a bit crude and slightly worrying to me at the time and perhaps not the sort of exchange I had expected to hear in the upper echelons of the game. Even in matches for the notoriously aggressive Butcher's Hook pub side into which Dad had inveigled me from time to time, I hadn't witnessed players talking to each other in this way, albeit that I did once see a disappointed centre half attack a part-time referee with a tyre tool following a marginal offside decision. (My view? As above, with FR Pollen: the referee is always right, even when he's wrong. And you should never attack him with a tyre tool. That's a message I try to get over to today's youngsters as strongly as I can.)

But I eventually realised that the words shared by Hedlow and Buster were just a bit of banter – the kind of harmless to-and-fro that went on between players, and between managers, and between managers and players, and between spectators and players, and between managers and spectators, and between everyone and referees, all the time. It didn't mean that the people concerned didn't have the utmost respect for each other, deep down.

The home dressing room after a draw would commonly be a slightly subdued place, but the nature of that day's result – the point ripped at the last gasp from the jaws of defeat, rather than lamely surrendered – meant that the outcome was treated more like a victory and the atmosphere expanded accordingly.

And what a reception awaited me there! I found myself repeatedly whacked in celebratory fashion on the back and punched affectionately on the upper arms, by players and squad members and back-room staff alike. Andy McDonald tousled my hair for what felt like two whole minutes, until I was sure it would start coming out in clumps. Then Hughie Griffiths took hold of my cheeks between his fingers and thumbs and twisted and shook them for ages while simply shouting 'Waaaaaaay!' directly into my screwed-up face. Then both Dick Stokes and Sam Higby jumped onto my back and rode me piggyback-style for a while, whooping the whole time, until I collapsed onto the floor. Then Tubby Morton pulled me upright, got me in a headlock and towed me, bent forward at the hips, all the way around the dressing room, bringing his knees up high in an impish, madcap dance. Finally released by Tubby, I staggered head-first into the lockers, where Ted Barker spun me around, cried 'You beauty, Racey,' and cracked me expertly in the testicles with a knotted towel, roaring with laughter as I doubled up on the muddied, boot-strewn floor for a few minutes to recover.

I couldn't have been happier. To have scored twice on my debut and earned my team a deserved draw, and to have been accepted by my team-mates, so thoroughly and so quickly, was simply amazing.

Soon after, Blackie and I lay back in the communal bath, our wet heads wreathed in steam, listening to the shouts, the laughs, the brags and the gags – the sheer inescapable maleness that inevitably arises when eleven men are naked together in soapy water. And as my head swam with elation, I realised that something had tilted forever in Blackie's and my relationship with these particular naked men, and with all this. We were still juniors, yes, with a lot to learn and everything to prove. But we were one of them now. There was no divide. We were part of the team.

I towelled myself dry and got dressed and went out into the corridor to rejoin my parents. Once again, I was pretty sure I knew how they would both react. Mum was going to burst into tears and say, 'I'm so proud of you!' while sobbing, and Dad wasn't going to be there because he would have been sore about the dropped point and would already have gone to the pub!

And, of course, I stepped out into the corridor, and there, exactly as predicted, was Mum, who burst into tears and said 'I'm so proud of you!' while sobbing.

And there was Dad.

Who just stood and looked at me. And I looked at him. And it felt like one of us probably ought to say something and I reckoned it probably wasn't going to be him, so eventually I said,

'A Rover, eh, Dad?'

And he carried on looking at me and nodded very slowly.

And then, quite quietly, I said, 'I owe it all to you.'

His eyes had filled with tears and his mouth didn't quite know what to do with itself and I thought for a minute he was going to step forward and hug me. But instead he laid his hand on my arm and very gently squeezed it.

Mum and I went home, and Dad went off to the pub, where I guess he must have had time to digest the result more fully because later that night he was arrested for pulling a police patrolman off his motorbike.

But that's the story of football for you. The emotions it stirs! Always has, and always will.

And now I was, without question, a part of it.

7

Confrontation

There are no guarantees in football. I can't stress that firmly enough. The way the game is, you can never take anything for granted. Arty Hedlow's words to me about finding myself back in the reserves within a week might have been intended to rankle, but they had a core of truth in them that it wouldn't have been wise for me to ignore. All I could hope was that I had done enough on my debut, with the last-minute equaliser and the other goal, and the assist, and my performance and conduct generally, on and off the ball, over the course of the ninety minutes, and while helping hand out the teas and orange segments at half-time, to give Ben Galloway cause to pick me again the following weekend.

It was a discussion I had with Blackie in the days after our debut.

'I reckon we'll keep our places, don't you, Roy?' said Blackie. 'I played a blinder. And you played an even bigger blinder. Plus you helped out with the teas.'

'We can't take it for granted, Blackie,' I replied. 'Nobody should ever regard themselves as an automatic selection. Complacency is the enemy. As the saying goes, you're only as good as your next performance.'

'Yeah, but that *will* be our next performance, won't it? Stands to reason, surely,' said Blackie.

So I explained a bit further about the importance of a footballing mindset which regards nothing as written in stone, and feels that everything is still to be proved at every point, making every single game an audition for the next one – a mentality which I think I can say I adhered to as closely as I possibly could throughout my forty-four-year playing career, and indeed, still take with me onto the golf course and into the charity five-a-side fundraiser, even today.

Anyway, fortunately, Ben Galloway did think I had done enough against Elbury Wanderers, and he did pick me for the following Saturday, and he kept on picking me for the rest of the season, at the end of which I won the Young Player of the Year award.

In the meantime, though, there was one thing I felt confident about in the heady days after the Elbury Wanderers game; and that was how happy I was that I wouldn't be seeing Arty Hedlow again for a little while. I looked at the fixture list, taped to the wall above my bed, and we weren't due to go to Elbury for the return league fixture until well after Christmas. I was certainly happy to wait (assuming selection). It wasn't just what Hedlow said as we left the pitch. It was also his demeanour throughout. There was a surliness about him and a pent-up aggression that seemed to follow him everywhere like a black cloud. It seemed incredible to me. Here he was, playing football at the highest level and getting paid to do so – a dream outcome for most men his age. Yet the game clearly brought him very little pleasure beyond the opportunity to wind up other people or score points in entirely irrelevant personal battles of his own. I wondered how his team-mates put up with him.

I certainly knew that I couldn't have done so. Ah, well. Thankfully, I could put him out of my mind for a while.

On the Wednesday morning, I walked into the dressing room ahead of training and found Ben Galloway looking extremely pleased with life.

'Roy, I want you to meet our new record ten-thousand pound signing.'

'All right, young 'un?' said Arty Hedlow.

My heart sank. I had just identified this man in my own mind as the enemy of football and as an all-round nasty piece of work – and now I was being told that he was a new team-mate, someone I was going to have to work with, play with, share the highs and lows with, even bathe with. I felt like the sun, which had been shining so brightly and so warmly, had just gone in on my life at Melchester Rovers.

But almost as soon as I had had that thought, I tried to banish it from my mind. Who was I to prioritise my personal feelings, such as they were, over the needs of the team? Arty Hedlow's prowess in front of goal spoke for itself. The man had scored twenty-four goals in thirty-six appearances for Elbury Wanderers in the previous season. If Ben Galloway thought this player could bring a missing ingredient to the team (and, moreover, was prepared to pay a club record fee in order to secure his services), then that was good enough for me, or certainly ought to be. Everything else was irrelevant.

I extended my hand. 'Welcome to the Rovers,' I said.

'Thanks,' said Hedlow, though he didn't shake my hand.

Over the next couple of days, as we trained, I felt I began to see another side of Arty Hedlow. OK, so he never smiled and he seemed to be permanently on the verge of potentially violent anger. And OK, he was prone to call me somewhat patronising things such as 'junior', 'new boy', 'young lad' and 'little tosspot'. At the same time, you had to concede that he hadn't, as yet, actually been violent – either to me, or to anybody else. And his qualities on the pitch – his strength, his ability to find space and create scoring opportunities and, it goes without saying, his finishing – were beyond rebuke.

Come Saturday, both of us were picked for the league match away at Cobdale, a fixture which brought me, for the first time in my career, up against the Cobbers' notoriously aggressive centre half, Norman Porter, a six-foot-four, eighteen-stone mountain of muscle who was famously reckless in the tackle and was alleged to keep a running tally, notched onto his bedhead with a penknife, of legs that he had broken. The tally was said to stand at seventeen, although there was some argument about whether or not he was inflating the figure for effect by including legs he had broken in fights outside pubs and nightclubs. (The purists maintained that only legs broken within the field of play and without the use of improvised weaponry should be allowed to rank. It's a point of view.)

'Any preference for which one I snap, new boy?' enquired Porter in his surprisingly high, strangely feminine voice as we came alongside each other for the first time. I did my best to smile quietly and ignore him.

Porter was quite a hard person to put out of your mind altogether, though. The game was only three minutes old when the vast and uncompromising centre back presented me with his greetings card – a two-footed, studs-up dive into the backs of my calves, dropping me onto my knees and sending shooting pains the length of my spine and down my arms to the palms of my hands.

'Ref!' protested Andy McDonald.

'Play on,' shouted the ref, Mr E.F. Hewdean from Potterage Bay. 'It was shoulder to shoulder.'

I could see that Mr Hewdean was one of those refs who likes to encourage the flow of the game, and I realised that I probably wasn't going to get much in the way of protection from him. So I simply took the decision to knuckle down and get on with it. It's a lesson I had learned very quickly as an eager nine- and ten-year-old in some of the pub and works team games that Dad had got me involved in: the worst thing you can do in those kinds of ultra-physical contests is to lose your nerve and start pulling out of challenges. That's when the injuries occur.

Indeed, this had really come home to me one evening while playing in midfield for Drexlar Plastics in a hot-blooded encounter against a pick-up side from J.R. Bishop's Meat-Rendering Services, behind closed doors in a warehouse over at Drayton Bec. At one point I was obliged to go for a fifty-fifty ball with the carcass-flaying outfit's compact but formidable right back, who was swinging a bike chain above his head at the time. If I had gone in anything less than wholeheartedly, I would probably have come off quite badly. As it was, I stayed firm, rode the tackle, ducked the bike chain, and fed the ball into the channel where our inside left was able to punish some sloppy defending with a clean finish. If it's between a goal and a trip to Casualty, I know which one I'll always take!

So, against Norman Porter, I summoned all the physical resolve that I could. I knew that if I could get the ball down on the ground and use my pace to go round him, the worst I would be leaving with was severe bruising and possibly some light friction burns and a few blisters, along with some minor tendon damage. Sure enough, as the game wore on, all of my essential bones were still reassuringly intact, I was getting more and more change out of Porter, and we were beginning to cause Cobdale some problems.

The trouble was, I seemed to have another formidable opponent on the pitch in this encounter: Arty Hedlow. Our new striker had been on at me since the referee's whistle to pass him the ball and openly bawling me out in an enormously hostile, spittle-flecked way when I didn't or was unable to.

For instance, about twenty minutes into the game, I managed to retain possession, despite Norman Porter's attempts to shake me off it by piling into the small of my back with both his knees, and was advancing to the edge of the Cobdale penalty area, when I heard Arty Hedlow shout, for the umpteenth time, 'To me, Race! I'm unmarked.'

But Hedlow wasn't unmarked. He simply hadn't noticed the right back arriving efficiently at his shoulder, ready to shut him off immediately. Instead, I worked the ball to the left to give myself a yard of room and shot narrowly wide.

Hedlow's face was almost molten with anger.

'Jesus wept! I'm playing too, Race. All ten thousand pound-worth of me.'

Not much chance of me forgetting, I felt like replying, but I held my tongue.

Only minutes later, I once again lost Norman Porter, this time by flicking the ball over his head, hurdling his waist-high challenge, landing with a somersault and springing up before latching onto the ball again. And then I moved quickly forward into the final third, where I surveyed my options.

'Now, Race!' shouted Hedlow, bursting towards the area.

But Hedlow had gone fractionally too early and was slightly ahead of the last defender. Had I played him in at that point, the linesman would have flagged him offside. So, I dummied the man now advancing to close me down, and unleashed an arching shot which thudded against the bar and was wildly lashed away for a corner.

And there was Hedlow in my face again: 'F***'s sake, Race. Am I invisible or something?'

All too visible to the linesman, I felt like saying, but there wasn't time to explain my reasoning.

There were at least two other episodes, very similar to these, with Hedlow feeling he was well placed to score and with me deciding that I had no option but to go it alone, so that, with half-time nearing, Rovers' new record signing was almost in flames with fury.

The mood didn't exactly improve when Cobdale went ahead, three minutes before the interval.

Back in the dressing room, Hedlow didn't hold back.

'What's your problem, Race? You didn't listen to me. You hogged the b****y ball and then every time you came up against their centre half, you funked it.'

It was one thing to find myself being lectured by a team-mate in this way – quite another to have to listen to an accusation of funking it.

'I funked it?' I replied, feeling myself redden with affronted anger.

'You funked it.'

'I did not funk it.'

Hedlow now pushed his face into mine and I could smell the cigarettes on his breath, as well as something else which might have been whisky, or possibly lighter fluid.

'You did funk it. You're a funker. A funk. A funking funker who funks it.'

Even now I wince to remember what happened next. I'm not proud of it – quite the opposite. But something about being accused so nakedly of something as awful and as alien to my nature as funking, in combination with the notoriously inflammatory scents of stale tobacco and (possibly) alcohol, seemed to cause all the resentment I had been nurturing towards Hedlow since our first encounter to come boiling to the surface at once.

There's no other way to put this: I lost control.

It was the only time I ever threw a fist in the dressing room – except to knock down that bank robber-turned-arsonist whom I discovered, midway through a friendly against Austrian side Flaudermitz, excavating the stash he had hidden under the dressing room floor. But we'll come on to that story in due course.

It was certainly the only time I ever threw a fist in the dressing room and followed it up immediately with a furious knee to the groin.

As Hedlow lay on the floor, clutching at his shorts and pitifully mewling, did I feel any kind of surge of pleasure or vindication? Memory fails me here, but let me tell you that if I did, it was momentary, swallowed immediately by an enormous wave of remorse and a sense of profound disbelief at what I had just done, the stain of which seemed set to be with me for the rest of my career. I had responded to provocation. I had struck a fellow professional – moreover, a member of my own side, which offended against so many of the game's fundamental ethical ground rules. I had let myself down but, far more importantly, I had let my team-mates down and, beyond that, I had let football down. Having helped Hedlow to a winded but relatively comfortable recovery position and having fetched him a glass of water, I went round the room to apologise to everyone individually and express my mortification.

'You're all right, Roy. Serves the s***ty f***er right,' said Buster Brown – a view which seemed to be pretty much the consensus, inasmuch as it could be established. But that wasn't the point. I hadn't gone on a tour of the dressing room to gather support; I had done it, perfectly humbly, to express contrition. The truth was, I had erred and fallen well short of the standards that I set for myself. The fact that I wasn't yet, at this early stage in my professional career, a role model to millions of young kids is irrelevant. Bad behaviour is still bad behaviour, even if it doesn't get into the newspapers. I think we sometimes lose sight of that today.

When we went back out for the second half, I was still consumed with guilt and shame at what I had allowed to happen. The only way that I could see to begin to patch up the damage was to make it up to everybody with my performance on the pitch – particularly to Arty Hedlow, who was now both sullen and silent, which was almost worse, in a way, than when he was sullen and noisy. If I could have created even a single goal-scoring opportunity for Hedlow in that second half, it might have gone some way towards resolving the ill feeling that inevitably hung between us and making him feel better about the black eye. But Cobdale had very effectively shut up shop, and the chance simply would not come.

The game was in its dying seconds, with Rovers facing defeat to that solitary first-half strike, when, just to compound my misery, Norman Porter again clattered me – a variation, this time, on wrestling's 'scissor' move, flying in horizontally so that both his legs wrapped around me and took me down at just above the knees. 'Ref!' protested Andy McDonald. 'Play on,' shouted Mr E.F. Hewdean from Potterage Bay. And fair enough: you could argue that the ball had been there to be won.

In fact, wait a minute . . . the ball was *still* there to be won, just beyond our tangled limbs. I realised that if I could just stretch out my now almost entirely numb left leg . . .

. . . and keep stretching it . . .

. . . and stretch it as far as it would go . . .

. . . I might just be able to toe the ball . . .

. . . into the path of Arty Hedlow, who ran onto it, cut into the penalty area and cracked it past the despairing Cobdean keeper for 1–1. There wasn't even time to restart the game. Mr Hewdean from Potterage Bay immediately blew for full time and Rovers had salvaged a point.

'Nice goal, Arty,' I said as we left the pitch.

'Good ball, Race,' he replied. And he extended his hand.

Our dust-up in the dressing room was never mentioned again and Arty Hedlow and I developed a sympathetic and productive working relationship which lasted for the rest of our time together at the Rovers. Which wasn't very long at all, as it happened. I was as saddened as anyone when, just a couple of games after this, Hedlow suffered a career-ending injury – not on a football pitch, ironically enough, but at home in a fight with his wife – and disappeared from football altogether.

8

Two Farewells

There was more sad news at the start of the 1957–8 season when Andy McDonald announced that this would be his last year at the club. He had learned that an opportunity was going to come up in mid-1958 for someone to run a sub-post office over in Churleigh Manor – a part of the world that Andy knew well and loved – and Andy had decided to give it one more season and then take the job and move there with his wife Eileen.

He had our blessing in that, of course, but Andy had, at that point, captained the Rovers for twelve years, and I think many of us found it hard to imagine the place without him. He was a man of exceptional integrity, a sensational centre back, a leader and a true inspiration – to me and to everyone who came into contact with him. True, those twelve years had been entirely trophyless – an extended barren period of a kind that would soon be anathema to the club and its supporters. But then there's always a temptation, in football, to measure the worth of a player's career in terms purely of medals won and honours gained, and in my opinion, it's a temptation to be resisted.

Trophies, after all, are the exception rather than the rule. You think of some of the great names who lastingly distinguished themselves on the pitch without coming anywhere near major prizes: Micky Kershaw of Everpool, for instance, a great little midfielder throughout the Eighties and a mighty competitor, on and off the pitch, who never won anything; or Eastoke's Robbie Dunbar, whose performances impressed themselves indelibly upon the mind during the Nineties, yet who couldn't even buy a trophy, it seemed. Indeed, he was accused of trying, and failing, to do just that in the 1997–8 season, when despair about being a serial loser seemed finally to have got the better of him, though the allegations were never proven.

All of which is just another way of saying that Andy McDonald would have deserved to be ranked as a great player and a truly valuable club servant even if he had won nothing at all, which almost happened.

And the reason it didn't happen is the story of the 1957–8 season – one of the most extraordinary in the history of Melchester Rovers to that date.

If Andy McDonald's announcement was sad, I don't think anyone would necessarily have said they were surprised by it. The press had been retiring him in writing for a couple of seasons before this. Andy was forty-six now, after all, and the accusation was that he had lost a yard of pace. In fact, that summer, Taff Morgan, Rovers' trainer, measured it in pre-season fitness tests and discovered that Andy had lost 3.4 yards of pace, season on season, and perhaps as much as 14.7 yards of pace in the last three years alone. If the press had got hold of that information (as these days, no doubt, they would), they would have had a field day. But then, I was never sure how much faith to place in those calculations of Taff's, which were often done, quite literally, on the back of a cigarette packet. Better, I always feel, to measure a player's worth in terms of the tangible things that he brings to a side, both on the field and off it.

In that regard, even as he slowed down and occasionally found himself fighting for breath, McDonald was a constant innovator who always had the club's best interests at heart and was continually looking for ways to maximise our advantage. He was a proven 'thinker outside the box', even in a time when the box had yet to be invented, let alone the concept of thinking outside it.

For instance, it was Andy's idea, in 1956, that the club should have a mascot – and, what's more, that that mascot should be a live goat.

'They have them in the military,' McDonald explained to us one day, in the dressing room after training, growing quite misty-eyed about it. 'And I always find the sight of a goat on parade moves me enormously. Think of the intense surge of pride we would all feel, coming up the tunnel behind a goat.'

There was a brief, meditative silence while we all digested this thought.

'Can I just mention that I'm allergic to cat hair?' said Paddy Ryan.

'I don't think we should get a cat,' said Buster Brown. 'They're fiercely independent and almost impossible to train.'

'My aunt's got a cat,' said Blackie.

'I think a goat,' said Andy McDonald.

'I like the notion of having a mascot,' said Len Dolland. 'But I wonder what message we'd be sending by choosing a goat. Why don't we go for something that makes a bigger statement about who we are as a club – something like a puma, say, or a lion?'

'I think that could be prohibitively expensive,' argued McDonald. 'And possibly quite dangerous.'

'And I'm allergic to cat hair,' said Paddy Ryan.

'Tuppence,' said Blackie.

'What?' asked Dick Stokes.

'The name of my aunt's cat,' explained Blackie.

'The advantage of a goat,' said Andy McDonald, 'quite apart from the established and potentially inspiring military associations, is that they are reliable, relatively easy to acquire, good with children, provided it isn't the rutting season, and extremely low maintenance. They eat absolutely anything.'

There was another pause while everyone continued to reflect.

'Here's a thought,' said Dave Williams. 'I'm just throwing this in, and forgive me if it seems a bit outlandish, but I'm thinking about the maintenance aspect: if goat is the way we're deciding to go with this, why don't we get someone to dress up as a goat, in a kind of big, padded costume, and have them walk around the pitch before the match, waving to the crowd? It would be cheaper, there's no upkeep involved, and it would give the fans a bit of fun and something to identify with, thereby providing all the benefits of a live animal mascot, but with a fraction of the complication.'

Everyone agreed that was a terrible idea.

'Definitely a goat,' said Andy McDonald. 'And definitely a real one. I'll get one of the apprentices onto it immediately.'

So a goat it was. And the goat in question was called Billy. Billy was procured (from his uncle's farm, apparently) by a seventeen-year-old apprentice named Kenny Blackwick, a promising, quick-witted winger, enormously exciting to watch, who seemed to have the world at his feet at this point in his life. Indeed, his ability to source a goat with just two days' notice obviously impressed the club's hierarchy because he was immediately offered professional terms. Alas, before anything could develop, Kenny got caught up with some Polish immigrants in some kind of cattle-stealing scam and his career died a death. As I'm always telling the youngsters: it happens.

Billy the goat, though, became a fixture. His tough white hair was coarse to the touch and he always seemed to smell slightly of compost, but he was surprisingly friendly when you got to know him and learned not to put your fingers too close to his mouth. To be honest with you, his eyes slightly spooked me. They had a pinkish hue which I found a little troubling, though apparently that's natural. They also had a habit of fixing on you from the other side of the dressing room, unblinkingly, for very long periods of time, the head utterly still – often as the prelude to a charge. Those horns can certainly hurt when they hit you at speed, especially if you happen to be getting changed at the time and therefore partly or completely unclothed, so you quickly learned to move when you felt Billy's eyes upon you and realised that he had gone still. (When he stopped chewing and his jaws ceased moving, that was the clue.)

Billy also seemed to have an insatiable appetite, even by the generally recognised standard for goats. We were all encouraged to bring in vegetable peelings from home and pile them into Billy's tin bowl by the dressing-room door. And though Billy tucked into these offerings heartily, they never seemed to sate him and he always appeared to have room afterwards for a shoe or a coat or, on one famous occasion when he was left unattended during a team meeting, for three footballs and a treatment table.

During training, Billy had free run of the Mel Park pitch. This was to encourage him to eat his fill of grass and therefore dissuade him from consuming people's personal property – which worked up to a point, though you were just as likely to find him chewing the advertising hoardings or gnawing on the roof of the dug-out. It also meant he was frequently in the way during practice matches. I remember one occasion in particular when I burst past three defenders and entered the penalty area, only to find my way blocked by Billy, grazing. Really, though, in situations like that one, it's all about improvising. I played a quick one-two off the goat's flank and tucked the ball away for what turned out to be a decisive strike. On the subject of improvising, Len Dolland suggested attaching an ashtray to Billy's back, so that, in addition to his symbolic purpose, he would have a permanent practical function as he moved about the place. This might have worked, except that no way could be found to attach the ashtray securely enough to remain steady as Billy roamed, and the project was eventually abandoned.

Andy McDonald, I should say, was utterly delighted with Billy. The captain – a ceaseless innovator, as I stated – made him a little blanket in club colours and a bow tie, also in club colours, to go around his neck. He decided that Billy, thus attired, should be paraded around the Mel Park pitch on a leash before kick-off, and that he should then be brought to stand at the entrance to the tunnel, meaning we could all pat Billy for good luck as we ran out at the start of the game. A football dressing room, as I have already mentioned, is a place where superstition has very little difficulty taking root, so there was a lot of enthusiasm for this idea among many of the lads.

Unsurprisingly, before long, several players had worked up their own personal variations on the 'patting Billy' ritual. Tubby Morton, the big centre back, always had to touch Billy with his left hand – unlike Jim Hallett, who always had to touch him with his right hand. Andy McDonald, meanwhile, always liked to touch Billy with both hands. Paddy Ryan would only ever touch him with the tip of his forefinger, but I think that had more to do with worries about allergies than about superstition.

It also seemed to matter to people *where* they touched Billy. Tom Dawson always patted him on the back, whereas Dave Williams was a diehard behind-the-ears man. One time, very early on in Billy's career, we were at home to Shermall United ('the auld enemy', as the fans referred to them; also 'the scummers'), and the traditionally feisty derby atmosphere, which had, as ever on these occasions, turned Mel Park into a cauldron of noise, clearly got to Billy, who was frisking and bucking slightly against his leash as we ran out. The consequence was that, as Sam Higby reached to pat Billy's back (his preferred spot up to that time), the goat twisted through 180 degrees, so that Sam ended up touching him just below the base of his tail. We went on to win 5–0, with Sam netting twice and me securing a hat-trick (still the biggest home victory over Shermall in Rovers' history), and from that point on, convinced that the act had brought this good fortune upon us, Sam would only touch Billy just below the base of his tail – which Billy didn't always seem to want Sam to do, so there would often end up being quite a tussle between the two of them, sometimes with Buster Brown getting involved and helping to shuffle Billy into position.

To be honest, I looked at all this goat-petting with some scepticism. Yes, I patted Billy on my way past (on his head with my palm, for the record) but only because it was the captain's wish that I should do so, and because not to pat Billy might have seemed stand-offish – like I was setting myself apart from the team, which I would never do. At the same time (as I made clear to Blackie, and also to Andy McDonald, in a private conversation soon after Billy arrived), I didn't believe that what happened on a football pitch had anything to do with when and where you had touched a goat. What happened on a football pitch was about how hard you had trained and how well you managed to put your training into action, according to the unfolding patterns of the game, which were never entirely predictable. And no goat, in my opinion, was ever going to be able to help you with that, no matter how well you tamed it. Still, as I said about players and their superstitions earlier, if it worked for them, and if it wasn't upsetting anyone else – nor, in this case, the goat – I didn't think there could be any harm in it.

The presence of Billy certainly didn't seem to have an adverse effect on the Rovers' form in 1957–8. On the contrary, the desire to send Andy out on a high note seemed to have a galvanising effect on everybody in the squad, resulting in the most consistent and plausible league campaign from a Rovers side in living memory. The team were never out of the top three from September onwards and entered the title run-in on the back of a sixteen-game unbeaten streak. The only thing that stood between us and the club's first ever top-flight championship was Brookleigh Wanderers, who had unfortunately chosen this, of all seasons, to rise to an unprece-dented level of invincibility and were entirely unbeaten, home and away. Inevitably, our visit to Brookleigh, just three weeks before the season ended, had 'title decider' written all over it. Brookleigh only needed to avoid defeat to be all but certain of the honours.

What happened in that game will live with me forever. Things certainly did not go according to our plan. We had no experience of competing for the title deep in the season – no idea of the kind of mentality involved, the sheer bloody-minded, blinkered will to win that you need in that phase, the ability to shut out the external noise, damp down the mounting pressure as the finish line comes tantalisingly into view, and simply grind out the results and bank the points. Accordingly, at Brookleigh, the occasion quite simply got to us.

The nerves had been plain to see on the coach to the ground, where a surprising number of players were whistling extremely loudly, and in the dressing room beforehand, where an eerie silence obtained, and for those first forty-five minutes we played worse than we had done at any point in my time at the club. Just twelve minutes into the game, Tubby Morton, receiving a square pass mid-way inside our half, and under no real pressure at all, somehow managed to let the ball squeeze under his foot, and then slipped in the process of trying to regain control, letting in Rob Denselow, Brookleigh's fleet-footed centre forward, who gratefully ran round Len Dolland to slot home. Four minutes later, we somehow lost Denselow again at a corner, and he powered in an unmarked header for 2–0. Utter collapse. Another moment of defensive uncertainty allowed Chippy North to add a third just before the interval and we went in 3–0 down – not just defeated, but crushed. A whole season's worth of hard labour had fallen apart in forty-five minutes of floundering. We had blown the title.

Ben Galloway did his best to rouse us with his half-time team talk, but you could tell that a light had gone out inside him. He had come so close to delivering the first championship of his managerial career, only to trip at the last big hurdle. When he had finished speaking, the room felt flat.

And then Andy McDonald stood up, and he too addressed the room. His voice was very quiet at first, and slightly faltering, though it gradually rose in volume and certainty as he spoke.

'It's all right for you,' Andy began. 'All you other players. You're all coming back. Other seasons, other matches, other chances. Not me. This is it, as far as I'm concerned. It's retirement after this for me. Over. I'm done. What will you be doing, this time next year? Playing football, likely as not. What will I be doing, this time next year? Selling b****y stamps in Churleigh b****y Manor, that's what. Letting Mrs b****y Miggins take ten shillings and sixpence out of her savings account. "All right, dearie? Turned out nice again, hasn't it? I said, TURNED OUT NICE AGAIN . . ." That's me, from here on in. And, oh, yes, I smile and tell Eileen I'm happy and that I can't wait and that I'll be content as anything up there, just her and me, little bell tinkling every time the door opens, weighing parcels and saying "First class or second? Inland or overseas?" I b****y won't be, though. Do you know what all that sounds like to me, really, in all honesty, here and now? Let me tell you: it sounds like death.'

McDonald paused here to gather himself. The room virtually throbbed, it was so hushed. And then he began again.

'So that's me, then. And all I'll have is the past. Seriously. That's it. No future. Just the past from now on. These next forty-five minutes of football – well, they're just forty-five minutes of football for you. Not for me, though. These next forty-five minutes of football are the rest of my life. The rest of my b****y life. So I'm asking you this – because it's up to you now, it's not up to me. And this is my question: am I going to be a sub-postmaster who never won anything, a nearly man of the sub-post office business, living with nothing but his regrets and his maybes and his might-have-beens forever more? Or am I going to be a championship-winning sub-postmaster, a sub-postmaster who actually went there and did it and has the medal to show for it – a medal he can pull out of his pocket and say, "yeah, well, look at THAT, Mrs b****y Miggins"? Eh? Am I?'

At this, there was an almost involuntary, animal-like roar from the rest of the team and suddenly everybody seemed to be infused with that visceral, face-reddening, eye-popping resolve which is very close to anger. And suddenly Paddy Ryan was on his feet and shouting, 'You're going to be a championship-winning sub-post-master!' and Dave Williams was on his feet, too, and shouting 'Championship winner!' and Sam Higby was up and shouting, 'Let's do it for Andy!' and Buster Brown was up and shouting, 'F*** you, Mrs Miggins!' and we stormed down the tunnel, still shouting.

Brookleigh quite simply didn't know what had hit them. We tore into the opposition from the whistle, wrenched them out of shape. After eight minutes of relentless, terrier-like hounding, we got the breakthrough, Blackie floating over a cross which I caught first time and stuffed into the roof of the net. Recent French signing Pierre Dupont, who signalled his exotic foreign-ness off the pitch by wearing, at all times, a pair of crimpingly tight trousers and a camera around his neck, played me in for goal number two. Then I picked out Blackie with a forty-five-yard cross-field pass and watched, ecstatic, as my little pal rounded the goalkeeper for the equaliser.

'A draw won't do, lads,' I cautioned as we headed back upfield for the restart. 'It's both points or nothing.'

Yet, probe and press as we might, that fourth and potentially decisive goal simply would not come. Blackie, Pierre Dupont, myself – we all came close, only to be denied by the frame of the goal or the goalkeeper's outstretched fingers. And so the game wore on, and the exhaustion, mental and physical, began to creep in, along with a growing sense of anxiety, so that the air itself felt thick, until there were surely only seconds remaining – seconds between Brookleigh and the title, seconds between Andy McDonald and a life of subservient, dead-end misery, lying to his wife in a one-horse, know-nothing village . . .

Somehow that thought was enough to kindle a final spark of energy in my bruised and weary body. I was going to drag us over this line if it was the last thing I did. Picking up the ball just inside the centre circle, and expecting to hear at any moment the three shrill blasts of the whistle that would signal the end of our title challenge and the end, effectively, of Andy's useful life, I went route one, directly down the middle of the pitch, riding at least three heavy challenges along the way before reaching the edge of the penalty area, dropping my shoulder to lose the centre back, drawing back my left foot with a view to curling the ball into the top right-hand corner and . . .

Clump! I landed on my back on the turf – taken down from

behind by a despairing, last-ditch challenge as the referee's whistle blew to end the game.

But no! Not to end the game! To award Rovers a free kick on the edge of the penalty area. Which there would just be enough time to take.

As I stood up, Andy handed me the ball.

'You know what to do, Racey,' he said. 'One last blast.'

'No, Andy,' I said. 'You take it. Do it for Eileen and your future together in that godawful sub-post office.'

'But I never take free kicks,' said Andy. 'I've never taken one in my entire and soon to be concluded career.'

'You're taking this one,' I said and ran off to start making a nuisance of myself in the wall.

I don't know how long it was that Andy McDonald stood over that ball, waiting to make his one kick for destiny. It felt like two hours. The ground had fallen completely silent so that you could hear, incongruously, birdsong.

And then the thump of Andy McDonald's boot on the ball, and the sight of the ball rising through the air, sweeping over the defensive wall, dipping violently, just beyond the outstretched glove of the diving keeper, towards, surely, the crossbar – but no! Into the net!

There was no time to restart the game. The referee signalled the end. Rovers had won 4–3, dealing a blow to Brookleigh's title challenge from which it would never recover. We won our three remaining games and were confirmed as First Division Champions after a 5–0 trouncing of Dalebrook United at Mel Park.

Champions!

Heady days. It was the first top-tier championship in the history of Melchester Rovers, and the first major honour, also, of my career, although I will always think of it as Andy McDonald's title.

At his retirement dinner, I was proud to be selected as the player to present Andy with a scrapbook containing clippings from the newspapers about his career – though not, obviously, some of the more recent stuff about him running out of puff. Andy's parting words to me that night were that if I ever needed any stamps or an application form for a passport, I knew where to find him. I was extremely touched by that.

As for Billy the goat, who knows how long he might have served with the Rovers if he had successfully managed to battle his demons, eating-wise? The following season, after we had drawn 1–1 in a fractious league encounter with Seaford Athletic, Billy got into the referee's room while the ref was showering and ate, not only the ref's discarded kit but also every other scrap of clothing in the room. This left the referee in question, Mr J.D.E. Barlow of Herston Green, with no option but to go home in a towel, an outcome which hardly pleased him, given that it was November and he was using the train. The Football Association took a dim view and fined the club fifteen pounds and suspended Billy for three matches. When the club subsequently appealed, the FA increased the ban to four matches. Some thought that was harsh but in my view Billy got off quite lightly. The referee's dressing room is strictly off limits, after all, and when a referee officiates at the highest level he deserves, at the very least, the security of knowing that his trousers will be where he left them before the match. Otherwise the game collapses into anarchy.

Alas, if Billy had been walking a tightrope, discipline-wise, things turned properly sour for him just before a fourth round League Cup tie at home to Gorsley United in 1960, when he ate Dave Williams's sponge bag. Whether it was the hair lacquer, the extra large container of talcum powder or the badger-hair shaving brush, we were never able to ascertain, but Billy was never quite the same after that, and, however much he was encouraged to do otherwise, would only put his head on one side and walk in small circles, very quickly.

It was obvious that Billy would have to retire from his duties but nobody quite knew what to do with him in the circumstances, and things were looking a little bleak for the mascot for a while. Fortunately, Andy McDonald's sub-post office had a decent garden space out the back, where a traumatised goat could spin around to his heart's content, so Andy was able to take Billy in and the pair of them lived out a companionable retirement for many years after.

9

Captaincy

With Andy McDonald retired, speculation turned, inevitably, to the question of who would succeed him as captain of Melchester Rovers for the 1958–9 season. If you had told me that Ben Galloway had me in mind for the role, and that the manager was on the verge of making me the youngest captain in Rovers' history, I would have shaken my head in disbelief and accused you of having a laugh. I would have pointed out that I had only just turned twenty and had barely been at the club for two full seasons. I would have gone on to say that, promising though many of my performances thus far had been, and despite all my valuable contributions in terms of goals scored and goals created, and last-ditch defensive lunges made, and important strategic decisions taken in the heat of the moment and implemented at key points in crucial matches etc., I was still very much a work in progress, both as a player and as an on-field influence. And, by way of conclusion, I would have laughed lightly and explained to you that not even in my wildest dreams was I expecting to be entrusted with the holy grail which is the captaincy at this extremely tender point in my career.

And I would have been right, because Galloway appointed Hughie Griffiths.

'I thought it should have been you,' said Blackie, as we sat in the Shepherd's Market café on the afternoon of the decision, having a cup of tea and a thick slice of the patron's buttered fruit loaf. (We loved that loaf, which was deep black and almost tar-like in its consistency. Even now the smell on a petrol station forecourt can bring the taste of it back to me.) My oldest pal was being loyal, as ever. I told him that Galloway was a top-class manager and that we had to trust him to do what was best for the club, even if his reasoning seemed opaque or hard to comprehend at first. Moreover, I went on, it wasn't just about the player who was captain; it was about everyone in the team. By the way we carried ourselves, we could all be leaders on the pitch.

'Yeah, but there's only one actual captain, and it's not you,' said Blackie. 'Plus, if Griffiths stays in the role for as long as Andy McDonald did, it's not going to be you for another twelve years. Which is a very long time to wait. A *very* long time. Shall I order another round of fruit loaf?'

I said I thought that was a very good idea, and when it arrived I spent quite a long time silently buttering it.

Eventually, there was no more butter, so I put down the knife and said, 'Between you and me, Blackie, I think there's a tendency in English football to overestimate the importance of the captaincy – to fetishise it, even. I don't know whether it's the two wars, or what it is, but we seem to bestow this talismanic, almost religious value on what is, when push comes to shove, a mostly symbolic and ceremonial role. The fact is, to set all this store by the notion of a central authority figure, from whom all power and direction emanates, is to overlook the way in which the best football teams are, in effect, a network of individual responsibilities wherein the various burdens inherent in actioning the given game plan on any specific occasion are equally shared. Under that analysis, beyond the privileging inherent in the toss of the coin and the preliminary exchange of pennants, the captain becomes a player like any other, no more or less significant.'

'I still think it should have been you,' said Blackie.

After another long silence, he added, 'Don't get me wrong – I like Hughie. But he's got nothing about him. Say you were in the trenches with him, and he said, "Right – I'm going over." Would you follow him? I'm not sure I would. I think I'd leave it a few minutes and see what happened.'

I was just thinking about this when the café door opened and Ben Galloway walked in.

'I thought I'd find you two here,' he said. 'Listen, Roy. I've just had a conversation with Hughie Griffiths. He's come to see me about the captaincy. He's given it some thought and he's uncomfortable with the idea, doesn't think he's the right man at all, thinks the additional responsibilities would affect his game adversely. He says he'd like to be vice-captain, and he told me I should consider a younger player for the leadership role. Actually, he specifically said you. And, on reflection, I agree with him. So. What do you say?'

I could hardly believe what I was hearing.

'Are you offering me the captaincy, boss? Of Melchester Rovers?'

'Well, I can hardly offer you the captaincy of Cobdale United, can I?' said Galloway and exchanged a raised-eyebrowed look with Blackie, who was beaming all over his face.

'Well, then: yes, boss. I'm pleased and proud to accept. It will be an honour – an absolute honour.'

I realised that I had risen to my feet as I said this. Somehow to accept the captaincy of Melchester Rovers while sitting down hadn't seemed right – least of all while sitting down in front of a plate of over-buttered fruit loaf!

'Good,' said Galloway. 'We'll crack on tomorrow, then.' And he turned and left.

'What a turn-up, Roy!' said Blackie, extending me his hand. 'Congratulations, skipper. You're the right man at the right time.'

Well, I guess we would see. In the end, only the trophy cabinet would be the judge of that.

The FA Cup has always had a special place in English football. It's the oldest club knock-out competition in the world, so obviously it has a historic status. But its value transcends mere longevity. The meaning of that old silver pot, and all that goes with it, soaks down deep into the fabric of our culture. We grow up, all of us, boys and girls alike, dreaming of leading our team out at Wembley, of scoring the winner in the FA Cup final, of climbing the steps to the Royal Box, of lifting the trophy to the roar of the grateful fans. The FA Cup is, quite simply, the fount of the game's most vibrant and most precious and most widely experienced dreams.

I've been fortunate enough to win the FA Cup eleven times and, take it from me, the magic never diminishes. Not even around the third and the fourth of those times. Not even around the fifth and the sixth. Not even around the seventh, the eighth and the ninth. Not even around the tenth and the eleventh. Those eleven winners' medals – all of them fundamentally the same, but all of them unique at the same time – sit proudly in my trophy cabinet at home, just as my grandfather Billy Race's FA Cup medal sat on his sideboard and enthralled me as a child, albeit that I've had to stack a few of mine up at the back of the shelf to get them all in.

Still, winning the FA Cup was the furthest thing from my mind when I took over the captaincy of Melchester Rovers. All my thoughts in the autumn of the 1958–9 season were concentrated on understanding and making the best of my new role. There is no rule book for being a captain – nothing you can take home and mug up on. Everybody makes the job their own and does it in their own style, according to their own instinctive sense of how it should be. What does the manager want from you? What can you bring to the players? How can you best act as a conduit between the manager and the players, and the players and the manager? Where can you most efficiently work as an ambassador for the club? These are the questions a captain must engage with and on which he must some-how arrive at his own position, and the result is, there are probably as many different ways of being a captain as there are captains.

I remember sitting down with Andy McDonald before he retired, when I was new in the team and eager to learn everything I could and benefit from the experience of the players around me, and ask-ing him what he thought was the single most important thing he had learned through more than a decade of carrying the responsi-bility of captaincy at Melchester.

'Tails,' he said.

'Come again?' I said.

'I always call tails. At the toss. Never heads. And do you know what? More often than not, I'm right.'

But that was Andy. You could ask the same question of another captain and they would say 'heads'. And they wouldn't necessarily be wrong. That's just the way the job is.

My first step along the way to becoming the captain that I hoped to be was to organise my day. I started going into the club at five-thirty a.m., long before anyone else was there, in order to have two or three hours completely on my own to reflect and refresh, mull over any problems surrounding team selection, maybe consider specific tactical issues. Those were productive hours. When the place was quiet, I found I could get a lot done.

Ben Galloway would arrive at eight-thirty and find me waiting for him outside his office with suggestions about possible new training routines or approaches to an upcoming match. Ben was a great believer in dialogue and always seemed to appreciate my input, although, very soon after my appointment, he changed his routine and started coming in an hour later, just before training started, so I would have to find moments at other points in the day to squeeze in those conversations with him, as and when the opportunity arose.

With captaincy, the pastoral aspect is also important. You're responsible for the spirit of the team and that inevitably means taking care of the players' general well-being. It sounds obvious when you say it, but footballers are humans, just like anyone else. They may play football for a living, which can seem to set them apart, but when they come off the field they have lives, and issues within those lives, the same as everyone. I think we lose sight of that these days, with the money and some of the behaviour. Anyway, I went round everyone in the squad individually and assured them that if anything was on their minds and troubling them – be it on the pitch or off the pitch, at the club or at home – then they shouldn't have any hesitation about coming to see me. The message from me was: my door is always open. Not that I had a door, but they knew what I meant. As it happened, certainly in those early seasons, no one did come and see me with a personal problem. But then, this was the late 1950s. People didn't really have personal problems in those days, or, at any rate, not that they would tell you about. Personal problems would come later, with a lot else, in the 1960s.

So, the season got under way – but not exactly with the fireworks that I suppose I had been quietly hoping for. Our league form was solid but unspectacular. We dropped a couple of points that we should have held on to at home, and struggled on a few occasions away, and basically spent the winter hovering between sixth and ninth place in the table – disappointing for a side that was reigning champions, albeit one that was adjusting to the retirement of its captain and making a number of other necessary personnel changes. Nowadays you'd excuse it as 'a period of transition', but then we just thought of it as not playing particularly well.

For example, one of the most pressing problems within the team – and one that kept me awake at night in those first few weeks – related to Tubby Morton. Now in his twenty-fourth season at the club, and for so long the very heart and lungs of our central defence, Tubby was a true Rovers legend, a real gentle giant such as the game sometimes produced in the Thirties, Forties and Fifties, who had always given, and continued to give, everything to the cause. Everything about Tubby was extra large: his courage, his commitment, his smile, his shorts. And the food that man could eat! Tubby was capable of putting away an entire fruit loaf at the Shepherd's Market café, without comment, just for a snack – and did so, most mornings before training. Once, at breakfast, when the team was staying at a hotel in Eastingham, I saw Tubby carry the domed silver salver of scrambled egg from the buffet sideboard to his place at the table, and then consume its entire contents with a spoon. Then he moved on to the sausages. It goes without saying that everybody loved him – the players, the fans, everyone at the club. It's funny to reflect, but none of us knew his actual name. I don't think it ever even occurred to us that 'Tubby' was a nickname. To us, Tubby was, quite simply, Tubby.

Still, at the start of the 1958–9 season, something about Tubby could not be ignored. Hard as it was for any of us to admit it, form was deserting him. Pace had never been his main attribute, but he had always managed to compensate for that with an acute positional awareness. Now, though, even his canny feeling for the best places to stand wasn't enough. This was partly to do with the fact that the game was becoming quicker in those post-war years, and also because Tubby had ballooned to thirty-four stone over the summer, largely, he admitted, as a result of eating an awful lot of clotted cream on a ten-day holiday in Cornwall with his lovely wife, Milicent. Nearly all players put on a bit of weight over the summer months, but Tubby's case that year was exceptional and pre-season training just couldn't shift those excess pounds. Accordingly, in matches, the stress on his heart and lungs was increasingly visible, especially as games wore on, and sometimes even before that. Centre forwards were finding it increasingly easy to turn him and we were unhelpfully vulnerable to the long ball played in behind for the attacker to run onto.

There was also, on the third weekend of the season, an unfortunate incident involving Dave Turton of Everpool, when Tubby accidentally sat on him during a goal-mouth melee, sadly ending the wiry winger's career. This definitely affected Tubby – though not as much, obviously, as it affected Dave Turton. (Dave eventually came out of the casts, thankfully, and went on to be a sales rep for a greetings card company in Bradwick, so it all turned out well.)

The truly painful aspect of all this, from the bystander's point of view, was that Tubby knew he was in decline. Players, as they age, can often be in denial about the waning of their powers, but for Tubby, as another striker eased past him or as he once again made it back to the penalty area, red-faced and puffing, while the opposition celebrated, the evidence was too strong to ignore. Tubby knew he was on borrowed time and he frequently wore the expression of a haunted man – worse than that, a breathless, haunted man. The sight of him shaking his head and sorrowfully and sincerely apologising was more than any of us could bear to witness.

The solution came to me out of nowhere in the dressing room after a much-needed 3–2 home victory over Kerslake United in early December. Tubby had been implicated in both Kerslake's goals and, at half-time, with Rovers trailing 0–2, was as low as I had seen him. Fortunately, I was able to pull one back shortly after the interval before equalising in the sixty-fifth minute and then banging in a winner from forty yards just as the referee was about to whistle for full time. Accordingly, in the elated aftermath, Tubby's earlier errors were forgotten and a celebratory atmosphere prevailed, leading to the usual team horseplay, in which Tubby, as ever, played a part.

So it was that I entered the dressing room – after a quick post-match debriefing with Ben Galloway – to find Tubby, naked and braced across the doorway to the showers, with his back to the room, blocking the entrance. Meanwhile, from the other side of the treatment table, a bunch of the lads were trying to get items from their sponge bags past the centre back's spreadeagled figure and into the shower room beyond. It was one of those raucous, impromptu dressing room games which I rarely joined in on, but which I was always happy to see going on because I know how important this kind of thing is for bringing people together. Shaving brushes, tubs of Brylcreem, combs, pots of talcum powder, razor blades, packets of cigarettes, even just occasionally a whole sponge bag – all of them were flying across the room. But here was the thing: all of them were bouncing back, with various slaps, pops and cracks, off Tubby's naked rear. It was extraordinary to witness: practically nothing got through.

It was then, as I sat to one side, smiling gamely, that the light bulb came on in my head.

I took Tubby aside as soon as I could. 'What do you think about becoming a goalkeeper?' I asked.

He looked understandably confused and doubtful. But I persisted.

'It would be perfect for you. It's the job you were born for. Or certainly the job you've grown into.'

'Do you think?'

'I don't just think: I know. I'll have a word with the boss about it.'

'But what about Len Dolland?' Tubby asked. 'He's just won the championship off the back of a nineteen-game unbeaten streak. He's probably not expecting to get permanently replaced as custodian by his own out-of-form centre back.'

'Don't worry about Len,' I said. 'I've got a plan for him too.'

I rushed off to communicate the scheme to Ben Galloway, catching him up in the nick of time after he had run to his car, jumped inside it and quickly fired the engine. Galloway was immediately intrigued. 'It's not a bad idea. I'll think about it,' he said, through the closed side window.

The following day at training we organised a try-out. Tubby was issued with the largest pair of gloves we could find (they were actually Bill Gobb the groundsman's lawn-mowing gauntlets with the seams cut), and then he went in goal while I kicked balls at him from a variety of ranges and Galloway watched. As I thought, Tubby proved as handy at keeping balls out of a goal, face-on, as he had been at keeping toiletry items out of the shower cubicle with his backside. He could narrow the target to vanishing point simply by turning slightly. The shots he couldn't drop onto he could invariably block by sticking out a thick leg. His place-kicking, meanwhile, was tremendous – an offensive weapon in itself – and his kicking from the hand was no less impressive.

'Looks like we've found us a new sticksman, Roy,' said Ben Galloway. 'But how are we going to break it to Len?'

'Leave that to me, boss,' I said.

I wasn't worried about telling Len Dolland about this potentially career-stunting development because, although he could be a quiet, dark and hard-to-read man at times – as well as a man who was constantly, almost obsessively washing his hands and anxiously inspecting his fingernails – I also knew Len to be a thorough professional and a person who would always set personal interests aside in the interests of the team. But I also had a treat up my sleeve that I knew our soon-to-be-reserve goalkeeper would be delighted about. I told Len that he would be playing in the reserves from now on, but that, by way of consolation, I was putting him in charge of the Tuesday bingo evenings that I was planning to institute for the team in the new year, word of which had already got out, creating a fair bit of anticipation among the players and back-room staff.

'I really appreciate that, Roy,' said Len, 'and the loss of regular first-team football will be more than amply compensated by the opportunity to call the numbers on those eagerly awaited club social evenings.'

So it was that Tubby Morton went from being Melchester Rovers' first-choice centre half to being Melchester Rovers' first-choice goalkeeper. What's that saying about how there are no second acts in American tragedies? Well, there are at the Rovers! The press, who tend to be instinctively conservative, were initially unsure about the idea, but they changed their mind when they saw how it worked. With Paddy Ryan at centre half in place of Tubby, we were an altogether more mobile defensive unit. As for Tubby, he amply justified our hunch about him by keeping three clean sheets in his first five games.

Nevertheless, the team still wasn't firing properly in all areas and we continued to drop silly points and were drifting in mid-table when the new year opened. But then the FA Cup started, bringing the injection of optimism which is its yearly gift, and slowly what looked like turning into a season of under-achievement began to take on an altogether rosier hue.

In the third round of the Cup we beat Dunbeck Athletic 2–1 in a fairly routine game, distinguished only by the thirty-five-yard scissor kick with which I secured our victory in the eighty-ninth minute when a replay back at their place was beginning to look inevitable. We were then drawn to face third division Portdean at home – a tie that, on paper, would have seemed more or less a formality, given the humble status of our opponents. But, of course, the Cup is famously a great leveller. And so too is a viral stomach infection, a particularly aggressive example of which struck our club on the eve of the fixture, taking out no fewer than six first teamers and leaving Ben Galloway with a selection headache, and also an actual headache, because he too had picked up the virus, the other symptoms of which included mild fever, diarrhoea and projectile vomiting.

The illness was by no means restricted to the first-team squad: it went right through the organisation and out the other end. On the Friday afternoon before the game, the ground felt like a post-apocalyptic war zone. Heading for Ben Galloway's office from the changing room, I passed no fewer than four apprentices and a woman from admin, all sitting against the wall in the corridors looking ashen, and Bill Gobb, the groundsman, crouching unhappily over a bin of grass clippings. Ben was sitting uneasily at his desk, taking aspirin and staring disconsolately at a team sheet with only the bare bones of a side sketched on it, plus some other marks which I didn't like to think about too hard.

'The problem is in defence, Roy,' said Galloway, gingerly. 'Hughie Griffiths and Buster Brown are out already. Bob Roberts only trained for three minutes this morning before he had to run off and sort himself out. And Paddy Ryan just came in to see me and, before he could say anything, threw up in the waste-paper basket.'

'Can I suggest something?' I asked.

'You probably will,' said Galloway, gently massaging his temples with his fingers.

'Why don't we bring Tubby out of goal and back into the centre of the defence? It's where he used to play, after all, and I'm sure he's still got enough, in terms of positional sense and fitness, to handle the kind of threat that Portdean are likely to muster – without, by any means, wishing to underestimate Portdean or imply that they're not capable of pulling off a shock at the home of one of the giants.'

'Fine, but then who's going to go in goal?' asked Galloway. 'Len Dolland was vomiting for three and a half hours yesterday afternoon. He looks pale and sweaty, even by his own standards.'

'My notion would be to take Dick Stokes off the wing, where we've got cover in the shape of Ronnie Howard, who's only been sick twice so far,' I said. 'And then we put Dick in goal. Obviously, Dick's not as big as Tubby. But then, who is? The point is, Dick goes in goal quite a bit during training and he's not bad. I think he's up to it, given that we're only talking about Portdean – no disrespect, and no desire to imply that this isn't a tie that has got "banana skin" written all over it.'

Galloway's eyes widened, his skin abruptly reddened, and he was furiously sick all over the desk.

'So, you're not keen on the idea, then, boss,' I suggested.

'On the contrary, I think it's a really clever solution,' said Galloway, inefficiently mopping the surface of his desk with a newspaper.

So, for the Portdean tie, Tubby was duly switched back into his old outfield position, with Dick Stokes given the gloves. Somehow we managed to patch up the other positions, but to say it was a makeshift Rovers side that emerged from the tunnel that Saturday afternoon is an understatement. I seemed to be the only member of our team who was fully fit. Blackie hadn't been able to keep anything down for three days and was clearly weakened, Tubby had a mild fever and Bob Roberts came into the game off fifteen consecutive disappearances into the bathroom that morning alone. The chances of us getting to the end of the game with a full complement of players, let alone remaining in the hat for the fifth-round draw, looked highly remote. Our best hope was that lowly Portdean would be overawed by the occasion and that our superior experience would eventually tell. (No disrespect.)

With ten of our players suffering to some degree with a virus and Portdean not wanting to catch it, the game was, inevitably, a cagey affair with very few chances at either end. Late in the first half, a space opened up promisingly for Hughie Griffiths but he ended up vomiting at precisely the wrong moment, and the opportunity went begging.

When Eddie Davis went off to the lavatory in the seventy-first minute, we were temporarily down to ten men. When Buster Brown, Jim Hallett and Tom Dawson joined him, we were temporarily down to seven. Portdean took due advantage and went ahead, Derek Housego lashing past a badly exposed and green-faced Dick Stokes.

Calamity. With the clock continuing to run down and the lower league minnows now content to get bodies behind the ball, we were on the verge of one of the biggest cup upsets in the history of Melchester Rovers. Worse still, I didn't know whether it was psychosomatic, or whether I was genuinely beginning to come down with something, but I had begun to feel a little fragile myself and was increasingly haunted, in particular, by the memory of the fried liver paste and mushroom sandwich that Mum had cooked me for breakfast that morning. (Mum always referred to it as her 'match day special', and with good reason.)

Still, I swallowed hard and tried to put the thought behind me. When Bob Roberts brought the ball out of our defence, only to clutch at his buttocks with both hands and drop quickly to his knees with a look of intense alarm on his face, I took the ball from him, played a one-two with the well-positioned Tubby and continued on up the centre of the pitch. Evading four challenges of growing desperation from Portdean's panicked and skittish defence, I finally found myself one-on-one with the goalkeeper, slotting it under his body for an equaliser.

I think the crowd, at that point, and most of our team, and certainly Bob Roberts, would have happily settled for the draw, followed by the opportunity to go to bed for a few days and recover in time for the replay.

Not Tubby Morton, though.

I still, to this day, don't know where the big man found the energy. What I do recall is the fixed stare of determination in Tubby's fever-tinged eyes as he stormed forward to regain possession after Portdean's restart with a shattering challenge that left two players on the floor. And I also recall the way he then stubbed the ball to me, standing square of him on the right, prior to continuing his barrelling charge upfield.

I knew I needed to hold the ball up to give him time to arrive. I moved out wider, watching Tubby's wobbling back, biding my time, worrying slightly about the clock. Would the referee allow enough time for this? Weren't the ninety minutes almost up? Unable to gamble any longer, I released the ball, hitting a high, arcing crossfield pass, designed to meet Tubby's run at the point at which he entered the penalty area, assuming he ever got there.

The ball was in the air for what felt like an age, slowly falling, falling . . . and surely landing too far ahead of the charging former stopper.

But no – because at this exact moment, with the goalkeeper coming off his line to clear up the danger, Tubby literally threw himself towards the arriving ball. His horizontal form seemed to pass through the air and into the penalty area like a very slow torpedo, fired underwater. As my pass dropped onto his forehead, he instinctively and brilliantly jerked his neck. The header flew up and over the goalkeeper and dropped just beneath the crossbar. The crowd exploded, and Tubby finally came to rest, landing face-down and sliding with a slightly sickening crunch across Portdean's desperately fleeing left back. (Blessedly, it turned out to be a strain rather than a break, and the player was only out for two months.)

The referee didn't even have time to restart the game. Melchester Rovers had won 2–1, an FA Cup embarrassment had been averted and we were through to the Fifth Round – and all thanks to the heroics of our centre half-turned-goalkeeper-turned-centre half!

We would have chaired Tubby off the pitch if we hadn't all been feeling so ill and if he hadn't been so big. Instead, Dick Stokes limped up to me as we left the pitch. 'You're a tactical genius, Roy,' he said.

'It's not about me, Dick,' I replied. 'It's about the players we've got at our disposal.'

And not least among them, of course, the legendary Tubby Morton.

Incidentally, a couple of years later, I finally got to put to Tubby the question I had been meaning to ask him for ages.

'Tubby, tell me: what *is* your actual first name?'

To which he replied, 'Tubbert.'

Apparently it's an old Norman name that his parents took a fancy to and which, in the way of names, very soon got abbreviated. Funny, the little stories the game throws up.

10

Wembley Bound

Luck appeared to favour us again in the draw for the Fifth Round, which paired us up with second division Carnbrook at home. You could feel a growing sense of anticipation around the club, with people starting to think 'maybe this is our year' – a phenomenon which always worried me, as a player and as a captain, because, while you want and need your team to believe in the possibility of victory, you also want them to feel that they are the ones controlling their destiny, rather than being controlled by it.

'I think the fans are beginning to wonder whether our name is on the trophy, Blackie,' I said, rather anxiously, as the two of us left the ground after training one day, before taking the bus uptown to the Melchester Picture House and watching the matinee screening of Alfred Hitchcock's recently released *Vertigo* with James Stewart and Kim Novak, at the price of fourpence per ticket for the stalls. (My handsome new professional wage of £3.10.06 extended to such luxuries, even after I had given Mum £3.10.00 for my housekeeping.)

'Wouldn't they have put our name on the trophy when we won it those times back in the Thirties?' Blackie replied. 'Engraved it around the bottom?'

'Well, yes,' I replied.

'The fans can put their minds at rest on that score, then,' said Blackie.

I was about to explain what I meant, regarding a gathering sense of destiny possibly leading unhelpfully to fatalism, but the bus came.

As it happened, the tie against Carnbrook – not unlike Hitchcock's *Vertigo*, in a funny kind of way – was itself a firm reminder that you can never take anything for granted. Unhelpfully casual during the first forty-five minutes, we went in 2–0 down at half-time and received a very solid talking to from Ben Galloway. Our approach was much crisper after the interval and I had managed to pull both goals back just before the hour mark. Carnbrook, however, perhaps with one eye on a potential money-spinning replay, now decided to sit deep. It looked like we would have to settle for the draw until, with time running out, I rushed on to a Blackie through ball and steered home for 3–2. The referee didn't even have time to restart the game. We were through to the quarter-finals.

This time we were drawn away at Bronton City, who made life extremely difficult for us until my second consecutive FA Cup hat-trick put the tie beyond their reach.

'Blimey, Roy,' said Blackie as we left the pitch that day, 'you don't suppose . . .'

But I immediately hushed him. 'Let's just take it one game at a time, Blackie,' I said.

Our semi-final opponents were Brampton United and the game took place, as is traditional, on a neutral ground – specifically Villa Lane, home of Deanwick Villa, which is an impressive stadium, with a huge capacity and a fantastic atmosphere. But the rain lashed down throughout the match that day and quickly turned the pitch, which was patchy and exhausted after a long, hard season, into a quagmire. We fell a goal behind early on in the muddy confusion, and spent almost the whole of the rest of the match camped in the opposition's half, pressing wetly for an equaliser. No joy, though. The ball simply wouldn't go into the net. And sometimes it wouldn't even go along the ground, such was the extent of the mud and slurry.

And then disaster: we were caught on the break. A booted clearance found Stanley Hogg, Brampton's veteran centre forward, alone in the centre circle. He turned and began to splash forwards into our half. Paddy Ryan, realising with a flash of horror that he had lost his man, followed in sodden pursuit. Hogg was always ahead of him, though. The striker waded energetically through the babbling brook which now ran across the edge of the penalty area at our end and was shaping to shoot when Paddy Ryan, still at least four yards in his wake, decided to make one last, despairing effort. The always committed stopper launched his impressively muscular body feet-first into a last-ditch sliding tackle. Mud flew as Paddy ploughed a gradually deepening furrow diagonally across the pitch. But that kind of challenge is almost impossible to time correctly in wet conditions and Paddy missed the ball entirely. Worse than that, he also missed Hogg entirely, and ended up wiping out Clive Perrymuir, the little Brampton inside right, taking the legs clean from under him and prematurely ending his career. Our centre back was lucky to stay on the pitch – literally, I mean, because his slide continued well beyond the clattered Perrymuir and was halted only when his recumbent body struck the corner flag.

Hogg, partly blinded by the horizontal rain, had eventually shot hopelessly over the bar, but the referee had no option but to bring the play back and award a penalty for dangerous conduct. My heart sank. With less than ten minutes remaining, a second goal would probably decide the match, we would be out of the Cup for another year and my first season as captain would end up dwindling away to nothing – except, obviously, inasmuch as it offered a set of important experiences to build upon, because if there is one thing that we know in football it is that there is no negative so negative that it cannot be made to yield a positive.

Paddy Ryan, who was now so muddied that he appeared to have been recently dredged from a river by police frogmen, was distraught at his error and stood ashen-faced on the edge of the area while Hogg readied himself to take the spot-kick that he had indirectly won – although the spot had long since been washed away and the ref had to improvise another by digging around with his foot in the sludge. Here again, though, the conditions were to play a decisive part. As Hogg limped up, he lost his footing, went up in the air horizontally and landed on his back, whereupon he didn't so much kick the ball as prod it forwards with his studs. The ball rolled stickily towards the goal, where a grateful and absolutely sopping Tubby Morton advanced six yards, bent down and picked it up. Spared!

In the modern era, Hogg would have been obliged to see this hapless moment replayed countless times on the television, with various wry commentaries, until he developed psychological problems potentially severe enough to require long-term residential treatment. In that largely camera-free era, though, the only people who witnessed his trauma were the 179,877 spectators crammed into the ground. I think we can agree that it was a much more forgiving time to be a footballer. And, in fact, probably as many as a couple of hundred of those spectators had gone home in obedience to the flood warning issued over the tannoy at half-time, so let's call it 179,500 people, all told, who saw Stanley Hogg fall flat on his back in a puddle and fail to take Brampton United to Wembley for what would have been the first time in their history. The chances are he was over it by the time the team bus left the car park. Certainly the autobiography he eventually published – *The Whole Hogg: Days of Glory in the Brampton Number Nine Shirt* – makes no reference to the incident.

Anyway, this lucky escape seemed to galvanise us. From Tubby's throw-out, Blackie marauded down the wing, skipping various puddles and fording one fairly sizeable lake, and fed me on the edge of the penalty area, where I was able to side-foot an equaliser into the bottom right-hand corner across a fast-flowing stream. Then, with time fast running out, Dick Stokes regained possession and punted a hopeful high ball into the area which, by running, sliding and, at one point, swimming, I was able to get onto the end of, nodding home past the goalkeeper's drenched fingertips.

There wasn't even time for the referee to restart the game. Rovers had won 2–1. We were going to Wembley.

'Blimey, Roy,' said Blackie as we left the pitch. 'You don't suppose . . .'

But I cut my friend off. 'We haven't won anything yet, Blackie,' I said.

My reservations seemed more than justified when we returned to the dressing room and discovered who our opponents would be.

'Everpool!' groaned Dick Stokes as news of the result in the other semi-final came over the Bakelite wireless. 'They've already run away with the First Division title this season and will therefore be looking to complete a League and Cup double at our expense.'

'There's no question that we will need to be at our absolute best on the day to have any chance of bringing the silverware back to Mel Park,' I replied.

Nevertheless, however daunting your opponents are, the days leading up to an FA Cup final are a wonderful time to be around a football club. Excitement takes hold of the whole place, affecting not just the players but also the back-room staff at every level of the organisation, from the groundsman to Margaret the office charlady, who took to doing her rounds with a rosette and a scarf attached to her trolley and added to her usual range of tea-time treats a plate of rock cakes in club colours.

'How do you get the colouring so bright, Margaret?' I asked, through a large and slightly complex mouthful.

'Enamel paint,' she explained.

Even Buzzer Hawkins, the no-nonsense commissionaire and lifelong club servant, was not entirely inoculated against the party atmosphere.

'Up for the Cup, Mr Hawkins?' I asked, as I passed his splendidly uniformed figure in the entrance one morning that week.

'Up your a**e, more like, Race,' said Buzzer, but with just a hint of playfulness in his tone, I felt, suggesting that he, too, was gripped by Cup fever in ways that he simply preferred not to articulate.

All across Melchester, too, you could see the enthusiasm taking hold. Houses were draped with flags and favours and messages of goodwill ('Up the Rovers!', 'Rovers for the Cup!', 'You Can Do It, Rovers!' and so forth). Businesses in the city centre turned their windows over to displays of support. Beckridge the baker's had created a range of 'Rovers Rolls'; H.G. Arnslow, the local butcher, was offering 'Award-Winning Wembley Bangers'; and Hesketh's the funeral parlour had a casket draped in club colours in its window and was doing a 'Cup Final Special, Rovers Til I Die' 2-for-1 offer on cremations. Just to walk around the place as the big day neared was to realise how much it meant to people.

Talk of tickets seemed to be on everyone's lips: whether you had one, whether you knew someone who had one, whether you knew someone who could get hold of one . . . The shout I was constantly hearing from people in the street was, 'Hey, Roy – can you get us a ticket?' I would smile and turn my empty hands outwards. We players were given two tickets each and I guess it's obvious where mine went: my mum and dad. I laid these precious pieces of paper out on the kitchen table one evening. 'Doing anything on Saturday May the fifteenth?' I said. Mum went saucer-eyed and I began to wonder whether she might fall over backwards. Dad quickly snatched his off the table and thrust it into his wallet. Again, you saw how much it meant.

Golden times, then, and a great time to be a footballer in a football-mad city, although I have to say the build-up to the biggest game of my career so far was badly spoiled for me personally when I got kidnapped.

I've been kidnapped nine times in my career, including seven times while on club tours abroad, which remains a record in top-flight English football, and each time it's been a new and slightly surprising experience. I suppose it's a bit like winning the FA Cup in that sense. You certainly don't get bored of it! Except inasmuch as it's inherently tiresome, obviously. Put it this way: I'd rather be winning the FA Cup for a ninth or tenth or even eleventh time than getting bundled into the back of a truck at gunpoint for a seventh or eighth time in a despotic South American state, and that's for sure!

On this occasion, though, I wasn't in a despotic South American state. I was in the garden of the four-star Friars Grove Hotel near Wetteringham, which is one of the places where teams have traditionally chosen to stay on the Friday night before a Wembley Cup final – as a reward and because the magnificence of the occasion seems to demand something a bit special. With its long drive and green lawns, its mock Greek portico and its quietly spoken staff in waistcoats, the Friars Grove was certainly special. It was the poshest hotel I had ever stayed in, and the same went for Blackie. I still remember my old pal from Sutton Street emerging from the little en suite bathroom and asking, in a tone of wonder, 'Is this soap actually free?'

To which, of course, the answer is, 'No', in the sense that, although use of the soap incurs no additional charge, its cost has been factored in to the price charged by the hotel for the room. And, OK, the club was picking up the bill, but even so, the point is still a valid one: there is no such thing as a free bar of soap. There is no such thing as a free pot of shampoo, either, for the same reason – nor a free disposable plastic shower cap, nor a free waxed shoe-polishing cloth, nor a free cotton earbud. But I didn't get into this at the time with Blackie, as he delightedly spread this treasure trove out on the bed, because I didn't want to spoil his obvious delight as a young, working-class lad, on the eve of his first FA Cup final, being given a taste of the high life that he could never have imagined for himself when he was growing up. I left him to enjoy the perceived gift of toiletries.

When the team used hotels, you had to share a room with a team-mate, and I always roomed, of course, with Blackie. On this occasion, though, we arrived to find that there had been an administrative error and the hotel was overbooked. As a result, Blackie and I ended up sharing, not just with each other, but also with Tom and Marion Howarth, a middle-aged couple from Haresbrook, who had come down for their daughter's wedding followed by a reception at the Friars Grove the following afternoon. They weren't football fans, as it happened, but they were very nice people and we got along perfectly well and all budged up and made the best of it in the solitary double bed that was available to us. Would that happen these days? Perhaps not. But I think people were far more willing to share then than they are now. It was something to do with the communal experience of the war, I'm sure, still fresh in everybody's minds, even though it was fourteen years ago at this point. If you had known within your lifetime the terror and deprivation of aerial bombing raids and rationing, then being required to share a hotel room with two footballers on the eve of your daughter's wedding felt like a challenge you could more or less rise to.

The Howarths seemed content enough, anyway. 'Is this soap actually free?' asked Mrs Howarth, putting her head round the bathroom door.

'Technically, no,' said Mr Howarth. 'It's been factored in to the price charged for the room.'

Blackie looked suddenly crestfallen. But I swiftly moved the conversation along, and he soon cheered up.

In truth, though, the room was wasted on us. Sleep proves almost impossible the night before a Cup final – and also the night before a daughter's wedding. You lie in bed and your mind is racing and your limbs just want to get out on the pitch, and Mrs Howarth's uncommonly pointy elbow is in your back, so you're incredibly restless. Thinking about it, in total, that's eleven nights of lost sleep that the FA Cup has cost me over the course of my career – the best part of a fortnight, which, in other circumstances, would be regarded as torture and a violation of human rights sufficient to earn a rebuke from Amnesty International . But in football, it's just part and parcel, and I wouldn't have had it any other way.

Eventually I got up and started pacing around the bed, only to meet the silhouette of Blackie coming the other way, also pacing. Mr Howarth obviously couldn't sleep either, because he eventually got up and started pacing around the bed too. Soon after that, Mrs Howarth got up and started pacing as well. So, back and forth the four of us went, silently, for most of the night.

In the morning, the tension ahead of the game continued to rise. You could see the worry etched on people's faces. At breakfast

many of the lads were just picking at pieces of toast and marma-
lade. Knowing that it was my duty as captain to set an example
and deliver a calming atmosphere of normality, I managed to get
down a few sausages and some grilled tomatoes, along with some
fried bread and mushrooms and a bowl of porridge, but I've got to
admit that even I found the tension slightly suppressed my appetite. No problems in this area for Tubby Morton, of course, who
helped himself to a mountain of kedgeree from the sideboard and
persuaded the waitress to fry him up a plate of faggots to go with it.
And then he had bacon and eggs followed by smoked salmon and
a pair of pork chops and, after that, some vanilla ice cream with
raspberry sauce. It was reassuring to see him tucking in as if this
was just a normal day.

After breakfast, we were encouraged to go for a walk in the hotel
garden to settle our nerves a bit and, in Tubby's and my case, to
settle our stomachs. And that's when this glorious day went wrong.

It happened so quickly. One minute I was walking with Blackie
in our club blazers along a gravel path to the south of the property;
the next, my arm was twisted up between my shoulder blades and I
was being shoved through a beautifully trimmed box hedge towards
the car park with the point of a knife held in a leather-gloved hand
against my throat.

'If you don't struggle, you won't die,' hissed the voice in my ear, as
the gravel crunched beneath our feet. 'Are we clear?'

There's a feeling you quite often get, when you're being kidnapped, which is that, despite the disguises (the balaclava, the
nylon stocking or, in the low-budget operations, the paper bag with
the eyeholes cut in it), your captor is familiar to you. I had that
distinct feeling now, about the hooded figure wrestling me towards
the back of a large black car, while his accomplice wrestled Blackie
in the same direction: that this was by no means the first time we

had encountered one another. But the feeling, as it so often does, proved elusive, and in any case my meditations were brought to an abrupt halt. I was forced up against the side of the car, my wrists were tied tightly behind me and I was gagged with a foul-tasting rag. Then my captor pushed me into the trunk, on top of Blackie, and slammed the boot lid.

'Ith mth erth?' asked Blackie, through his gag.

'Grth shth rth,' I replied, as calmly as I could.

I don't know whether you've ever been driven anywhere in the boot of a car – maybe to make room for an extra passenger inside, or perhaps during a stag or hen night that got out of hand – but it's an uncomfortable and disorientating experience. Very few saloons in the late 1950s had interior lights in their boots, unlike today, when superior electrics and switch-gear, even across the non-premium brands, have made getting kidnapped an altogether brighter experience. In the pitch darkness, you lose all sense of direction very quickly. As the car pulled away, I tried to keep track of where we were going – attempting to monitor the journey in my mind, from memory – but within four or five turns, I was badly confused. Wherever we were headed, I was fairly sure it wasn't Wembley. By which I mean, if it had been me going to Wembley, I would have gone right at the end of the hotel drive, then left onto the A42, coming off at Evesmere for the Caledonian Road and going straight in from there. You could come off the A42 further down, at the Clandon Gyratory, but with the traffic on Cup final day, that would be madness. We, however, appeared to have gone left from the hotel, heading out to Copwood on the B439 before picking up (presumably) the B685 at Dipton Beeches and then going south, after which, to my frustration, I lost track.

Misery momentarily overcame me. It just seemed so unfair: I was meant to be leading my team out beneath the fabled Twin Towers in an FA Cup final – fulfilling the dream of every man and woman who ever lived, irrespective of race or creed or place of birth. Instead, I was hog-tied in the boot of a Humber Hawk, heading down the B305 (possibly) with Blackie's knees in my face and what felt like a car jack, or perhaps a bag of spanners, against the base of my spine.

Who were these kidnappers? What did they want? Where were they taking us? And would I be back in time to execute my all-important pre-Cup final responsibilities as team captain? (I had arranged a general knowledge quiz and a game of charades for the coach journey into Wembley – just something to help settle the lads down. I hated to think that would be wasted.) All of these questions revolved in my mind over the two-hour journey which ensued.

I realised, though, that, whatever the answers to the above, the most important thing was not to give in to despair. It was only mid-morning and the game didn't kick off until three. Maybe someone had seen us being bundled into the car at the hotel and had raised the alarm. Maybe help was already on its way. All manner of things could yet transpire and save the day – both for us and for the Rovers. In the meantime, I just needed to keep calm.

'Schth dth cth shthd?' asked Blackie in the darkness, above the engine's burble.

'Thtth shth bth shth,' I replied, which seemed the only sensible way of thinking about it in the circumstances.

Eventually, after a long period of constant travel, the stops and starts and the twists and turns became more numerous until finally the car halted altogether and the engine went dead. I remember being sharply aware, above the silence, of the crying of seagulls. Then the boot lid swung open and I was abruptly blinded with sunlight. Dazed and stiff, Blackie and I were hauled from the car and frog-marched across a patch of stony concrete. I glanced around as much as I could to try and get a sense of our whereabouts. By the sea, clearly. In what looked like a fairly major harbour. Portsea? Possibly. That would make sense, in the context of a two-hour drive in a roughly southerly direction from just north of London. But what now?

We were led along a metal gantry and forced to board a medium-sized wooden fishing boat. Once on deck, we were pushed roughly down some steps and into the boat's windowless hold. It was hot and smelled of wood, engine oil and cod. Here we were obliged, at knifepoint, to lie on our sides on the floor. Our wrists were left tied and, in addition, our feet were now bound. Then the captors went up on deck. The boat's tiny outboard engine sputtered into life and we set off to sea.

'Crth thpeth,' said Blackie.

'Prth thpth,' I replied, trying to mean it.

We hadn't been going for more than five minutes when the engine stopped again, leaving the boat tipping and tilting silently in what felt like strong tidal water. Our hooded captors now came down the steps again, knives in hand. I felt an instinctive surge of panic for my own safety. Would they kill us, here, with – what? – three and a half hours to kick-off? But this time they cut loose our gags. Our feet and legs, though, were still bound.

'You'll never get away with this,' I said, mostly in the hope of provoking the kidnappers into saying something further and possibly giving us the opportunity to identify their voices. But they were smarter than that and remained silent in our presence. I still had the dim sense that I knew one of these men in particular, but, again, before I could put my finger on it, they left us and went back up on deck. From outside – directly through the wood beside our heads, it felt like – came the noise of a speedboat engine, revving, turning away and then gradually diminishing to nothing. We were alone.

For a while, Blackie and I just lay there on the floor, looking up at the wooden ceiling, feeling the boat rock and hearing the slap of the water against its sides. I realised, with a sickening feeling in my stomach that wasn't entirely to do with the motion of the sea, that we had been left to drift. We would simply continue to float, at the mercy of the English Channel, until we ran aground in France or, further down, in Spain, or, even further down, in Africa, or until the boat broke up, or (worst thought of all) was ploughed under by an unseeing container ship. And none of these potential outcomes were likely to lead us back to Wembley in time for the three o'clock kick off.

Sadness washed over me. I thought of Mum and Dad, proudly readying themselves to see their son play in a Cup final, Mum no doubt choosing her best dress – and at first confused and then frightened by my non-appearance. I thought of my team-mates, possibly destabilised by the abrupt loss of their captain. I thought, for some reason, of Mrs Howarth and her pointy elbows. I thought of all the questions I would never get to read out in the team quiz on the bus to Wembley. I thought of Ben Galloway, suddenly and puzzlingly bereft of two first-choice players and probably electing to bring in Dudley Hughes, switch Brian Cattermole into the centre, and move Dick Stokes further out wide to help annul Everpool's threat down the left-hand side, which is, at any rate, what I would have done.

'It could be worse,' said Blackie eventually, breaking the solemn silence. 'Fire could have consumed the dressing room at Mel Park, leaving me in hospital with severe burns and with the finger of suspicion pointing at me, entirely groundlessly, as the arsonist.'

'Actually, that's next season, Blackie,' I would have said, had I known. (We'll get to that story in due course.)

A few more meditative moments went by and I was beginning

to resign myself to fate – something I had taken a vow with myself never to do – when suddenly, my eyes alighted on a bright object on the floor at the bottom of the steps.

'A knife!' I said. 'It must have fallen from the pocket of one of the kidnappers as they hurried from the boat!'

'That's a pity,' said Blackie. 'If we weren't tied up, we could run after them and give it back.'

Ignoring Blackie, I edged across the floor, alternately squeezing and unfurling myself like a caterpillar, and got myself into a position where I could gather the knife into my bound hands. Then, by twisting and folding my fingers, I managed to use the blade to saw at the rope. It took a few minutes and was agonising work, but finally there was a 'thock' and my wrists were free.

I quickly unbound my legs and then untied Blackie and we both scrambled up the steps to the deck. The May sunshine bore down hungrily from a cloudless sky. The waves chopped and foamed. There were no other craft anywhere within hailing distance and the coast was now merely a wafer-thin line on the horizon.

But at least we could still see the coast. All we had to do now was work out a way to get back to it in the absence of oars, sails or an engine (our captors had taken the key), and without any means of drawing attention to ourselves, such as flares or a radio.

There was only one solution.

'We're just going to have to paddle with our hands, Blackie,' I said.

'Whatever you say, Roy,' said Blackie, rolling up the sleeves of his club blazer.

I did the same, and we stationed ourselves at the back of the boat, on either side, and leaned into the water. Then, on the signal from me, both of us began thrashing as hard as we could with our palms. Slowly, as we flapped and smacked and windmilled, the boat gathered a little momentum and began to edge forwards. We had managed to propel ourselves about twenty yards in the approxi-mate direction of the harbour when the delayed wash from a Navy frigate, passing in the far distance, sent us thirty yards back again.

'Don't give up,' I shouted, above the noise of our furiously slap-ping palms. 'There's an FA Cup final at the end of this, Blackie.'

'Name on the trophy, Roy!' shouted back Blackie.

'Not the way I prefer to think of it, Blackie, as you know,' I hol-lered. 'But let's at least get there and find out!'

'Fair comment, Roy,' shouted my trusty friend.

Our faces were etched with salt spray, our palms were red and raw, our club blazers were bleached by the sun. Yet within only slightly more than an hour we were paddling into Portsea Harbour and guiding the boat into the first free berth we could find. We then climbed ashore and sprinted through the streets to the British Rail train station where, luck would have it, we had enough money on us for two third-class tickets to London and where, luck would further have it, the 12.38 service was just about to depart from Platform 4.

'If the train gets in to Waterloo at 2.07, as advertised, and we jump directly into a taxi, we may still make it to Wembley in time for kick-off,' I said.

One problem: we now had no money to pay for a taxi. But I felt sure that, if I explained the situation to the driver and took an address from him, I could arrange to get payment to him later. With this in mind, we jumped off the train almost before it had come to a halt and dashed to the front of the rank at Waterloo.

'You're Roy Race, aren't you?' said the cabbie through the win-dow. 'Aren't you meant to be at Wembley?'

I explained to him that Blackie and I had been kidnapped by unknown and hooded assailants in the garden of the Friars Grove Hotel, bound and forced at knifepoint into the boot of a Humber Hawk, driven to Portsea and set adrift in a medium-sized fishing boat, where we had managed to cut ourselves free, paddle back into the harbour and catch the 12.38 London train, arriving Waterloo at 14.07, and that we were, indeed, due very urgently at Wembley. I also explained about the money.

'Well, you're right out of luck,' said the driver, 'because I'm an Everpool fan.'

Blackie and I looked aghast.

'Only kidding!' said the driver. 'I'm Rovers through and through, me. Hop in – we've got a Cup final to win.'

As we headed across the Thames and north past some of London's most famous landmarks, including the Monument, the Houses of Parliament and the dome of St Paul's Cathedral, but not yet the Shard, the Gherkin or any of those other really tall buildings, our driver made a number of interesting points regarding Melchester Rovers, the managerial shortcomings of Ben Galloway, some of my own performances in recent weeks and the future of football, as he saw it. His theme was what he perceived to be the dangerous stagnation of the sport in the land of its birth.

'The thing is, English football – and I'm including Rovers here – has been caught cold by the tactical development of the game in other countries,' the driver said. 'Consider some of the advances made by the Hungarians, for instance. There's an openness to new ideas there which you simply don't see with English coaching methods. And something needs to change, and to change soon, or we're at risk of being left behind altogether on the world scene.'

As fascinating and insightful as all of this was, I confess I wasn't giving the driver my full attention, being rather distracted by watching the clock on the dashboard as it ticked relentlessly towards three p.m. Still, the London traffic was surprisingly light and we seemed to be eating up the distance. Indeed, many of the streets we drove along were virtually deserted.

'Where do you suppose everyone is?' asked Blackie.

'My guess, Blackie,' I said, 'is that they're at home getting ready to watch the Cup final on the television.'

'Lucky them,' said Blackie.

As the taxi driver continued to expound his views on the virtues of the Hungarian 'total football' system, I looked out of the window and caught my first glimpse of Wembley's fabled Twin Towers, as they were then, squat but noble against the skyline – football's dream palace.

It was a view to stir the heart. True, I had hoped to see that view a couple of hours earlier, from the team bus, soon after asking a question about the date of the Battle of the Boyne (1690, but I would have accepted anything five years on either side of that). But seeing it now, from the back of a taxi, after a tricky morning in which my life had several times been at risk, did not in any way diminish its impact.

This close to kick-off, even the traffic bearing people to the ground had conveniently thinned out and our cab was able to bring us to an intersection, three quarters down the length of Wembley Way.

'And another thing about those Magyars,' began the taxi driver, but Blackie and I were already leaping from the cab and sprinting for the players' entrance, our words of thanks trailing behind us.

The sight of Blackie and me dashing around the outer walkway in our club blazers certainly caused a few double-takes from the last few straggling fans entering the stadium.

'Hey, Roy – can you get us a ticket,?' shouted one of them.

I smiled and turned my empty hands outwards.

At the players' entrance, an expressionless steward blocked our way. I explained to him that we were Melchester Rovers players, but that we weren't with the rest of the team because we had been kidnapped by unknown and hooded assailants in the garden of the Friars Grove Hotel, bound and forced at knifepoint into the boot of a Humber Hawk, driven to Portsea and set adrift in a medium-sized fishing boat, where we had managed to cut ourselves free, paddle back into the harbour and catch the 12.38 London train, arriving Waterloo at 14.07.

The steward eyed our blazers suspiciously.

'All right then,' he said, and opened the gate.

Boundlessly grateful, Blackie and I bolted up the tall-ceilinged, echoey passageway and virtually fell through the door of the dressing room where the clock on the wall read three minutes to three.

'Roy!' said Galloway. 'Thank God! Where have you been?'

'It's a long story, boss,' I said as I peeled off my shirt and pulled on my strip. 'But, essentially, we were kidnapped by unknown and hooded assailants in the garden of the Friars Grove Hotel, bound and forced at knifepoint into the boot of a Humber Hawk, driven to Portsea . . .'

'Look, why don't you tell us later,' said Galloway. 'Dudley? Brian? You're no longer playing in the Cup final. Dick? I want you to come in more central, as previously planned. Roy and Blackie? You know what to do. Now: let's go out there and win this.'

My head ached from being shut in the boot of a car for an hour and a half, and my arms ached from paddling a medium-sized boat across several nautical miles of choppy sea water, and my stomach ached from the gritty British Rail cheese and onion sandwich that I had consumed just outside Nailborough on the 12.38 from Portsea to London. All things considered, it wasn't the best of preparations for an FA Cup final. Then again, if emerging from the tunnel behind the goal at the home of English football and walking out into the welcoming roar of 100,000 scarf-waving, rattle-twirling fans doesn't lift you and make you set to one side the thought that you were recently kidnapped at knifepoint and set adrift on the sea, then nothing the game has to offer you ever will. As we proudly lined up on the red carpet in front of the Royal Box for the presentation of the teams to Her Royal Highness the Duchess of Marwick and Bert Wetherseed, the chairman of the Football Association, the morning's ordeals were – with the exception of the onion from the cheese and onion sandwich – a dim and distant memory.

Alas, the first half didn't go our way. Everpool took control from the start and their pressure was rewarded with an opening goal in the twenty-fourth minute, followed by a second, right on the stroke of half-time – a devastating blow, psychologically, after a spell of ten minutes or so in which we had finally begun to look as if we might get back into the game.

The dressing room at half-time was, understandably, a fretful place. Mr Mason, the supermarket mogul and owner and chairman of the club, came down from his seat, which was always an indication that anxiety was running high. As Ben Galloway addressed us, reminded us of our duties and pointed out one or two areas where some of us had fallen a bit short, Mr Mason stood to one side, nervously chewing on the inside of his cheeks and jingling the change in his pockets.

After Galloway's team talk, we had five minutes to compose ourselves over a cup of tea. Seated in front of his locker, Blackie was struggling with a knotted lace on one of his boots. 'Has anyone got anything I could cut this with?' he asked.

'Here,' I said, remembering the knife so carelessly dropped on the lower deck of the boat by our fleeing captors, and retrieving it from the pocket of the blazer hanging on my peg.

As I held out the knife for Blackie, Mr Mason, with a curious look on his face, suddenly grabbed my wrist and turned my hand towards him.

'Wait a minute,' he said. 'I know that knife. Why, I'd recognise it anywhere. It belongs to Ted Smith, the chauffeur I recently had to fire, despite fifteen years of otherwise dependable service, following a regrettable and entirely avoidable incident involving misuse of my car.'

Ted Smith! Suddenly it all made sense. That's why I had vaguely recognised the hooded figure who had grabbed me at knifepoint. It was Mr Mason's chauffeur, sacked as recently as a month ago – and perhaps understandably so. Unbeknown to Mr Mason, Ted had used the car at the weekend to help his brother-in-law shift a load of garden manure. Mr Mason's suspicions were aroused when Ted collected him on Monday morning and he climbed into the back of the car to find the interior smelling strongly of horse and rotting vegetables and coated with flecks of straw and worse. Mr Mason demanded an explanation and, understandably disappointed, sacked Ted and insisted that he hand over his peaked cap on the spot. This was Ted's revenge – to sabotage Melchester Rovers' FA Cup chances by removing two of its key players on the morning of the match.

'And he would have got away with it too, if he hadn't been careless enough to drop his knife, Mr Mason,' I said.

'I think the police are going to be very interested in this little item,' said Mr Mason, leaving the dressing room to initiate the due legal process which would see Ted Smith arrested on suspicion of abduction with intent to harm and, following trial, imprisoned for twenty-seven and a half years.

I don't know whether it was the satisfaction of having the mystery solved, but we were a different team in that second half. I scored two stunning goals to put us back on terms and then, with the referee right on the verge of blowing his whistle for full time, a third stunning goal to clinch the match. There wasn't even time for the game to be restarted. Rovers were the winners and the fans were going wild.

It's true what they say about those Wembley steps: after ninety minutes of football, that climb up to the Royal Box really takes it out of you, irrespective of whether or not you have spent the morning traversing the Solent by hand. I'll say this much, though: I had enough strength in those arms to shake the cream-coloured cotton glove of the Duchess. And I had enough strength in them, after that, to lift the FA Cup.

11

Fire

Over the summer of 1959 we bolstered the squad by signing Ken Harcombe as a utility sub on a free from Baswick Albion, hit the ground running when the season started, and went into the Christmas period two points clear at the top of the table. It was, then, in terms of established momentum and the spirit at the club, a disappointing moment for the stadium to burn down.

The first I knew of the now famous Mel Park Fire was on Christmas Day in the afternoon. Mum, Dad, myself and Mr Sexton from next door were sat around the front parlour in that wonderful dazed silence which so typifies the traditional family Christmas. Mum had really gone to town with the dinner that year, serving up a hind leg of beef, stuffed in a goose, stuffed in a turkey, stuffed in a pig, with stuffing, so all of us were feeling cosily replete and, by the looks of Mr Sexton, a little faint. Dad was quietly soaking up the festive atmosphere in his favourite armchair with its back to the room, which he always loved to do. The crackers had been pulled, the paper hats were on, the Queen, heavily pregnant, had addressed us briefly over the wireless to reassure us that we had her constant interest and affection, and I was about to get us all going on the quiz that I had written for the team's Cup final day bus journey, that previous spring, and hadn't yet had the opportunity to use.

'Question one,' I began. 'In what year did King Leopold the Second of Belgium . . .'

At that very moment, the door burst open, and into the room came Blackie, his hair wild, his clothes singed, his cheeks and forehead comprehensively splattered with oily soot.

'Roy!' he gasped. 'The ground's on fire!'

And with that he dropped to his knees and passed out on the floor with his face in a bowl of entirely untouched Brazil nuts.

Leaving Mr Sexton to arrange for Blackie's immediate transportation to the hospital, I jumped on my bike and set off for the ground. It seemed odd to be pedalling down those rapidly darkening streets, past the windows of humble houses, lit for the season, while entertaining vivid visions of disaster. The closer I got to Mel Park, the more the air grew acrid and smoky and the harder my heart beat with anxiety. However, my worst fears – of finding the entire stadium reduced to smouldering ash – were far from realised. By the time I arrived and eased my way through the crowd of curious onlookers who had gathered on the concourse – some, like me, still in paper hats, and clearly abruptly drawn away from their festive celebrations – the fire brigade had contained the blaze. Hoses, now dormant and dripping, lay across the soaked concourse in the blinking blue lights of the fire engines, and the firemen, in their thick black woollen uniforms, were beginning to pack away their equipment.

The fire had apparently started in the home dressing room and the damage had been restricted to the underside of the West Stand, but one glance through the door there immediately revealed an unrecognisable and deeply depressing vista of charred and sodden wood. I hurriedly sought out a senior fire officer and asked the first question anybody in my position would have asked in the circumstances.

'What about tomorrow's Boxing Day fixture at home to fourth-placed Shermall United, who are going into this one off the back of a decent run of results and may fancy themselves for a point?'

'I'm afraid it's going to have to be postponed, Roy.'

'Drat it! And was anybody hurt?'

'Thankfully, nobody.'

'Well, I suppose that's something, at least. And what do you think caused the blaze?'

'We'll know in due course, Roy. But there's something rum here, I feel sure of it.'

Indeed there was. Published three days later, the investigation of the fire brigade in conjunction with the police immediately discounted the obvious explanation: a cigarette butt left in an ashtray. It also entirely ruled out the possibility of an electrical fault, the report stating that the electrics in the affected area were found to be 'sound in every regard'. I had done a lot of that wiring myself as an apprentice, under the tutelage of Reg Murphy, the builder that the club like to use for major structural projects, so it was nice to be commended officially on some solid work.

However, the report's conclusion was deeply troubling. The investigators found that, prior to ignition, the dressing room area had been 'widely and liberally soaked in a combustible material, most likely petrol'.

In other words: arson.

'Unless,' I suggested to Ben Galloway, a couple of days after this, while he was setting up a temporary office in the groundsman's tool shed, 'one of the lads went in there on Christmas Day, quite coincidentally, with a can of petrol, not knowing that it had a leak, and walked around a bit, inadvertently leaving a trail of flammable liquid, and then dropped a cigarette as they left, little knowing the conflagration that they were about to cause, meaning the whole thing was just an unfortunate accident.'

'Doesn't sound particularly likely to me, Roy,' said Galloway distractedly, placing a framed photograph of his wife Bunty and a ceramic pen-tidy on top of a lawnmower.

'Fair point,' I said.

I was clutching at straws, and I knew it. The thing was, admitting to myself that it had been arson meant entertaining some highly uncomfortable thoughts. What kind of person would do a thing like that? Who hated Melchester Rovers enough to deliberately – not accidentally, but deliberately – set fire to their ground?

And most alarming of all: what might such a person do next?

On the way home from Mel Park, I had taken a detour to the hospital and found my old chum Blackie, recently transferred to the ward and now lying significantly bandaged around the head, arms and legs. But he was his usual indomitable self.

'Nah, it's just a few third-degree burns, Roy. I'll be right as rain in a minute or two.'

'But Blackie, one thing slightly puzzles me,' I said. 'What on earth were you doing in the ground on Christmas Day?'

Blackie explained that his Christmas present for his mum that year had been a bottle of Yardley English Lavender perfume, a case of which Ted Barker had been touting around among the squad in the run-up to the holiday season. Come Christmas Eve, though, when Blackie went up to his bedroom to wrap this gift, he couldn't find it anywhere. That was when he realised, with a natural pang of disappointment, that he had left it in his locker in the dressing room.

'But we don't open presents until the afternoon in our house,' said Blackie. 'So I popped down there to get it after lunch.'

Blackie explained that, as he had headed along the corridor towards the dressing room, he had noticed a growing warmth and a bitter taste in the air. He had then opened the dressing room door to be confronted by a raging conflagration. He had battled bravely to overcome the flames for as long as he dared but had grown worried when a pot of liniment exploded and the treatment table went up while, simultaneously, lit rafters began to fall out of the ceiling and crash onto the tiled floor around him.

'That was the point at which I decided to give up and go,' said Blackie. 'I didn't realise that fire could be so . . . hot.'

I shook my head slowly in sympathy.

'What a terrible thing,' I said.

'I know,' said Blackie. 'That perfume cost me one shilling and fourpence.'

I told Blackie to get some rest and then headed home. Mum brought out the Christmas cake and buttered some turkey, goose, beef and pork sandwiches with stuffing, and the three of us sat with Mr Sexton in the front parlour, talking over the day's unforeseeably dramatic developments.

'What about tomorrow's game?' said Dad.

'It's off,' I said.

'B****r and s***,' said Dad. 'You serious?'

'Yes,' I replied.

'That's bad luck, Roy,' added Mum.

'Yes, really bad luck,' said Mr Sexton.

'And was anyone hurt?' asked Mum.

'No,' I said.

'Well, there's plenty of consolation there, at least,' said Mr Sexton.

'That's easy for you to say,' said my dad, who then left to spend the rest of the evening in the pub, if pubs opened on Christmas Day in those days, which I'm assuming they did.

The best estimates were that the interior of the West Stand, including the dressing room area, would take a month to rebuild and refit. After the structural examination had been carried out, though, and the initial clear-up completed, the ground was able to reopen for matches, albeit with the West Stand now cordoned off and out of action.

Meanwhile, the police inquiry continued. Who had taken it upon themselves to attempt to burn down Mel Park in the innocent quiet of a Christmas Day, traducing that festival's global message of peace, joy and not setting fire to things that aren't yours to set fire to? Who had the means? And, more pressingly, who had the motive?

Imagine my shock when, going in to visit Blackie in hospital after training one afternoon, I should pass three police officers going the other way, with extremely grave expressions on their faces.

'What did your visitors want, Blackie?' I asked, placing a bag of grapes on the bedside cupboard beside the glass jug of water, the plastic, kidney-shaped sick bowl and the three other bags of grapes.

'Oh, just a chat, Roy,' said Blackie, wincing as he adjusted his pillows. 'They were very nice. Wanted to know what I was doing in the dressing room at Mel Park on Christmas Day when it was on fire.'

'And what did you tell them?' I said.

'I told them I was looking for a bottle of my mum's favourite perfume,' said Blackie. 'Are those more grapes?' he added.

I didn't admit it to Blackie at the time, but the direction in which the police's enquiries seemed to be leading them was a source of enormous worry to me. Not that I believed, for even one fraction of a second, that Blackie was responsible for the fire. I considered it beyond doubt that he had gone to the ground, as he said, to retrieve the present that he had accidentally left there. I knew that he wasn't clever enough to make up anything as complicated as that. No disrespect.

I also knew that my oldest friend had no reason whatsoever to want to burn down Mel Park, which he, like me, regarded as his second home – in fact, quite simply, his home. Furthermore, even if he had wanted to burn down Mel Park, he wouldn't have had the first clue how to go about doing it. No disrespect.

My worries by no means diminished when I visited Blackie with more grapes the following afternoon and noticed a new bag of grapes which hadn't been there the day before.

'Who brought those?' I asked.

'Oh,' said Blackie. 'A very nice detective superintendent called Farley. Or Farling? Something like that. Came in this morning, outside visiting hours, just to say hello and ask me how I was coming along. Lovely man.'

'Did he ask you about anything in particular?' I said, trying to sound as unbothered as possible.

'Actually, you'll love this, Roy, because it was a bit like a quiz, which I know you're partial to. He asked me what my mum's favourite perfume is. And, of course, I told him it was Yardley's English Lavender. And he said, "What if I told you it wasn't?" And I said, "What do you mean?" And he said, "What if I told you your mum's favourite perfume was actually Chanel Number Five?" And I said, "You're kidding me! How do you know that?" And he said, "Because I asked her." And I said, "Why didn't I think of that?" Unbelievable, Roy! We both laughed fit to burst! I'd only gone and got her the wrong perfume! One shilling and fourpence! And if I'd only checked up by asking her, like the police did, I wouldn't have wasted my money. But I guess that's why they're the police and we're not, eh, Roy?'

It seemed to me that Blackie's alibi, never entirely solid from a subjective outsider's point of view, was rapidly turning to dust in his hands, and without him knowing it. He had sustained extensive injuries fleeing the scene of an act of arson on Christmas Day and had subsequently justified his presence, alone at the source of that fire, by claiming he was attempting to retrieve a bottle of perfume that it turned out his mum didn't even use and almost certainly didn't want. However, there was one positive thing: his injuries, ironically enough. I figured that, for as long as Blackie remained in hospital, recovering from his burns, he was safe from arrest on suspicion of the crime. What I needed to do was hope that the mystery was solved and that the real Mel Park arsonist emerged before Blackie was discharged. Otherwise I sensed that things were likely to grow very uncomfortable for my old pal, very quickly.

Discussions about the arsonist's identity were, inevitably, rife among the players in those first days after the incident. With the reconstruction work underway – Reg Murphy was once again in situ with his men – we had been forced to establish a makeshift dressing room in Margaret the charlady's small, low-ceilinged kitchen under the South Stand. As we washed and got changed after training, conversation would invariably turn to the ongoing mystery, with some of the players expressing scepticism about the work thus far of the police.

'Those Melchester busies couldn't catch a cold,' said Paddy Ryan, vigorously towelling off. 'They still haven't arrested anyone in connection with that raid on Melchester National Bank which was all of, what – nine months ago?'

That story had caused a big buzz in Melchester at the time. Capitalising on weakened levels of security while the bank was having its windows renovated, raiders had entered one night and made off with the entire contents of the vault.

'I'm sure they're doing their best,' I said, stripping off my muddied kit and standing in the sink to wash myself down. 'But the force is terribly overstretched, especially during the Christmas period. I'm backing them to get to the bottom of it eventually.'

'The fuzz couldn't get to the bottom of my bottom!' joshed a naked Jim Hallett, who then bent over and pointed to the bottom of his bottom with both his forefingers to underscore the point.

'All the evidence indicates an inside job,' said Tubby Morton, unknotting his jockstrap and then stretching and crouching to relieve his tired thigh muscles.

'Or it could just have been a prank by kids that got out of hand,' said Margaret, opening a catering box of KitKats and loading a number of them onto her trolley. 'And if you must sit on my Formica surfaces, could you at the very least put your pants on?'

Speculation was clearly mounting. Later that day, I was on my way from the kitchen to the groundsman's shed for a word with Ben Galloway when Dick Stokes stopped me.

'Word in your ear, Roy?'

'Always, Dick.'

'Ken Harcombe,' said Dick and winked very slowly.

'What are you saying, Dick?'

'Look no further,' said Dick, glancing furtively to either side as he spoke. 'Harcombe's your man.'

'What makes you think so, Dick?' I asked. 'All the pointers are that Ken has settled in well since his arrival on a free from lowly Baswick Albion.'

'But it's Harcombe who stands to profit,' hissed Dick.

'In what sense?' I asked.

'With Blackie out of the way, the former Baswick utility player gets a clear run at a place in the first team.'

This much was true. Ken was almost certain to be selected

in Blackie's place for the upcoming away fixture at Lipton Wanderers.

'But the arsonist didn't try to burn down Blackie in the first instance, Dick. He tried to burn down the ground.'

'You say that,' said Dick. 'But who's currently in hospital with burns?'

'Well, Blackie, obviously. But that's just because he unfortunately happened to be in the wrong place at the wrong time.'

Dick merely raised an eyebrow. Eventually he lowered it again.

'Ken Harcombe,' he repeated. Then he did the slow wink again, and then he walked away.

Later that morning, not all that long after my conversation with Dick, Ken Harcombe himself came up to me.

'Roy,' he said. 'Word to the wise?'

'Of course, Ken,' I said.

Ken looked around uneasily. Then he leaned in close.

'Dick Stokes,' he said.

'What about him, Ken?' I asked.

Ken looked around again. Then he leaned back in.

'Arsonist,' he said.

'What makes you think so, Ken?' I asked.

'Look at his eyes,' said Ken. 'They're the eyes of an arsonist.'

'No firmer evidence than that, Ken?'

'Mark my words,' said Ken meaningfully. 'Dick Stokes.' And with that, he walked away.

I was growing worried. The suspicions that were beginning to fester in the dressing room clearly had the potential to divide the squad and fracture our team spirit at a potentially pivotal moment in the season. How long before our league form began to suffer? The sooner the mystery of the Mel Park arson attack was resolved, the better for everyone at the club.

Fortunately, a happy distraction was in the offing with the visit to Melchester in early January 1960 of Austrian side Flaudermitz for a friendly. European football and foreign players in general are so much a part of the domestic game's culture nowadays that it's very hard to convey exactly how exotic the prospect of a visit by a team from the continent seemed to us back then. Don't forget, too, that this was not a world in which people travelled abroad the way they do now. (I, for instance, at the age of twenty-one, was still two months away from getting shot out of the skies on my first foreign plane trip – but we'll come to that.) Many people in Melchester had never seen Austrian people before, let alone Austrian footballers, so our visitors were the objects of widespread and genuine curiosity. Wherever they went, over their two days in the city, a crowd would gather and simply stare at them, silently.

The night before the match there was a gala dinner at the town hall hosted by the Mayor of Melchester, Councillor Don Hardiment, and his wife Tonya, who wasted no time in extending the very warmest of welcomes to the Flaudermitz coach, Oscar Stomppel. I was seated next to the visiting captain, Dieter Bomschrift. I had no German and Dieter had very little English, so conversation was a little tricky, but we got along famously.

'You are liking the hotel, you and the team, Dieter?'

'Ya, Roy!' said Dieter. 'Izt ver gutt!'

'And you are liking Melchester?'

'Ya, Roy!' said Dieter. 'Izt ver gutt!'

'And is this in England your first time that you come?'

'Ya, Roy!' said Dieter. 'Izt ver gutt!'

'Could you pass the pepper?'

'Ya, Roy!' said Dieter. 'Izt ver gutt!'

It was my first personal experience of that enthusiastic, continental can-do attitude and I found that I warmed to it straight away.

After the dinner, the Mayor made a speech celebrating the friendship between our two countries and expressed how much our city was looking forward to the match, and the players of both teams were presented with an engraved solid silver cigarette lighter in honour of the occasion. (I kept my lighter proudly on display at home for a number of years until, as a toddler, my son Roy Jr set fire to the sitting room curtains with it. I'm not quite sure what happened to it after that.)

We were all changed and about to listen to Ben Galloway's pre-match team talk when who should march – or rather edge – into Margaret's kitchen than Blackie Gray!

'Blackie!' I cried, delighted to see him, but immediately worried. 'You're meant to be in hospital.'

'I've discharged myself,' said Blackie. 'Well, I was hardly going to miss this one, was I?'

'But what about your burns?' I exclaimed.

'Completely healed,' said Blackie. 'At any rate, with the exception of a couple of slightly weepy areas.'

'Well, it's good to have you back,' said Ben Galloway. 'Kcn? You're no longer playing. Blackie? Get changed.'

'Mind where you go putting those weepy areas,' said Margaret, who was washing up in the sink.

What a crowd it was that we ran out to! The records show that the official attendance that night – and this is with the West Stand out of action, remember – was 213,455. However, unofficial estimates put it at closer to 300,000, with the spectators spilling over the hoardings on three sides of the ground, and standing right up tight against the touchline, such was the eagerness in Melchester to get a glimpse of the touring Austrians in their pomp.

What's beyond doubt is the extent to which we were outplayed in the first half – dominated by Flaudermitz to a degree that I don't suppose a Melchester Rovers side on its own turf had ever been. True, one of their players hadn't recently discharged himself from hospital after suffering third-degree burns in an act of arson. Even so, their application, their close passing, their comfort on the ball, even under pressure, was an object lesson. We were chasing shadows a lot of the time.

Flaudermitz scored after twenty-four minutes, and again after thirty-seven minutes. After that second goal had gone in, I jogged back upfield for the restart with Tom Dawson.

'A sophisticated showing by the Austrian visitors, eh, Tom?' I suggested. 'They seem to be passing to each other with a pace and accuracy which the English game has yet to consider.'

'Incredible levels of imagination and intensity in the final third from those Flaudermitz boys,' said Tom. 'And when you consider they don't even speak English . . .'

I'm not making excuses for my own performance in those opening forty-five minutes, but I don't think it helped that I found myself distracted by thinking about Blackie, who, by leaving the safety of the hospital, had unwittingly rendered himself – in my view – vulnerable to arrest. My feelings about this by no means diminished when I noticed, during the game, with a sinking in my stomach, that an unusual number of policemen had gathered by the temporary tunnel in the corner by the South Stand. Blackie, it occurred to me, was going to find his freedom curtailed sooner rather than later, with embarrassing and potentially complicated consequences for himself, not to mention the fact that it would potentially take us down to ten men for the whole of the second half, and, with Flaudermitz already two goals to the good, I wouldn't have fancied our chances of coming back into the game from there.

Worse still, Blackie – completely impervious to the developing situation – had, despite the extensive bandaging, been just about our best player in the first half, dropping back to help soak up the pressure and then sprinting forward again tirelessly to provide a valuable out-ball on the very few occasions when we managed to break. We really couldn't afford to lose him.

Something else was preying on my mind too. Fifteen minutes or so into the game, a desperate hoofed clearance by Dave Williams had cannoned off the overlapping Flaudermitz full back, sending the ball flying down the temporarily disused tunnel in the closed West Stand. I dashed in ahead of the ballboy to retrieve it, in the hope of taking advantage of a quick throw-in, only to hear, as I gathered up the ball, the distant but distinct sound of drilling coming from . . . where exactly? The building site in the old dressing room? This had struck me fleetingly as odd: yes, there was a tight deadline for the renovation work, but surely none of Reg Murphy's builders would be working in there on a match night – not when they could have been watching Austrian maestros Flaudermitz.

Even as I dashed back to the touchline to take the throw-in, two and two were coming together in my mind to make four . . .

I needed a plan – and fast.

When the referee signalled half-time, and the players began to head towards the temporary tunnel in the corner, I made sure I was right on Blackie's shoulder. Sure enough, as we got to the touchline, I noticed the policemen start to come away from the tunnel where they had gathered and move towards us, with intent expressions on their faces.

I pulled my old pal around and began to sprint away from the corner, up the touchline in front of the abandoned West Stand, almost dragging him along behind me.

'What are you doing, Roy?' shouted the confused and at best partially recovered burns victim.

'Just stay with me,' I pleaded.

Flicking a look over my shoulder, I saw the arresting officers, abruptly concerned, quicken their pace and then break into a run to follow us, clutching on to their cumbersome police helmets to hold them in place. On I ran to the centre line, with Blackie trustingly on my heels, and then I veered right and entered the tunnel.

Blackie sensed where I was headed. 'But Roy,' he said, 'the dressing room is closed pending a refit following the fire damage. We got changed in Margaret's kitchen, don't you remember?'

Ignoring him, I continued to run between the tunnel's darkened walls where the depressing stench of charred wood was slowly being replaced by the more optimistic smells of fresh cement, soldered piping and newly applied undercoat. The dressing room door was shut but the glow of a workman's arc light around its edges betrayed its occupant.

I didn't bother to knock.

And there, turning round in shock with a shovel in his hand, was the man I had expected to see, doing exactly what I had expected to see him doing.

'Working late, Reg?' I enquired nonchalantly.

'Why, you . . .' spat Reg Murphy the builder, and, to my startled horror, he began to come towards me with the shovel raised.

I decided it would be prudent to get my blow in first.

'Take that, you treacherous builder and decorator,' I shouted, and threw my right fist against the thieving workman's jaw.

It was the second and last time I ever punched anyone.

The dressing room now filled with panting police constables.

'Here's your man, officers,' I said, pointing at the dizzied figure on the floor.

'Why, it's Reg Murphy the builder!' exclaimed one of the policemen.

'The very same,' I said. 'And right where he was digging when

I came in, I don't doubt you will find a tin trunk containing the missing money from the Melchester National Bank raid. Remember how the bank was having its windows done at the time of the robbery? The builder on that project, I don't need to tell you, was Murphy. He took advantage of his position to fake a raid on the bank, and then interred his ill-gotten gains here, under the dressing room floor, while doing his next job – the underfloor heating. And then, at Christmas, he set fire to the stand in order to be re-employed at the club and to be able to excavate his ill-gotten loot unobserved.'

'And he would have got away with it if you hadn't discharged yourself prematurely from hospital, Blackie,' I added.

'I'm not following this at all,' said Blackie.

'Never mind – I'll try and explain it again as we walk back to the kitchen,' I said. 'Now, if you'll excuse us, everyone – we've got the second half of a football match to play against the leading Austrian side of their generation.'

Back in Margaret's kitchen, news that the arson mystery had been solved was greeted ecstatically. It was as if a dark cloud that had been hovering over all of us had abruptly lifted. All the needless suspicion that had hung in the air evaporated at a stroke and I even saw Ken Harcombe, in his tracksuit, give Dick Stokes a grudging nod of reconciliation, which Stokes returned.

We were a side transformed in that second half. With seventy-two minutes on the clock, Blackie played me in to reduce the deficit, and then, ten minutes later, I played in my bandaged pal for the equaliser.

However, try as we might, a winner simply would not come – until, deep into the ninetieth minute, I dropped back to pick up a pass from Dave Williams and looked up to survey my options. They were limited, to be frank: Flaudermitz had our players efficiently covered in all zones of the pitch. But then, out of the corner of my eye, I noticed the goalkeeper, right out of his goal, almost on the edge of his penalty area.

Advancing into the centre circle, I flicked the ball up with the toe of my right boot and then volleyed it, as hard as I possibly could, with my left. There was an audible intake of breath from the stands as my shot arched through the floodlit sky, and then dropped under the crossbar, just above the fingertips of the hastily retreating Flaudermitz keeper: 3–2 to the Rovers!

But no! There was a sharp whistle-blast.

'Offside,' shouted the referee, Mr. D.G. Bird from Whittleham.

I was never one to query a referee's decision – never had been, never would be – but even I had to raise a quizzical eyebrow in Mr. D.G. Bird from Whittleham's direction at this disallowance. You can't, after all, as everybody knows, be offside in your own half.

Mr. D.G. Bird of Whittleham came over and spoke quietly near my ear.

'Diplomatic reasons, Roy,' he explained. 'Trade relations, global entente and so forth.'

'Entirely with you on that, ref,' I replied. 'Believe me: for as long as I'm captain here, anything that football and Melchester Rovers can do in that "bigger picture" regard will always be done.'

There wasn't even time to restart the game. The final whistle sounded and the crowd unleashed a long and heartfelt demonstration of gratitude for the feast of football which they had just witnessed. On the pitch, I exchanged shirts and shook hands warmly with Dieter Bomschrift.

'Quite a team you've got there, Dieter,' I said, 'but a draw was probably just about the right result at the end of the ninety.'

'Ya, Roy!' said Dieter. 'Izt ver gutt!'

What an extraordinary season 1959–60 was turning out to be

for Melchester Rovers! We'd had the early run of results which had lifted us to the summit of the league, the Christmas Day arson attempt, Blackie's injuries, the subsequent visit of Flaudermitz and the solution of the Melchester Bank raid mystery – and it was still only January. We hadn't even been shot down over the jungle yet.

12

Shot Down

We had barely waved goodbye to our exotic visitors from Austria when we were off on an exotic trip of our own. Melchester Rovers had agreed to participate in the inaugural International Club Cup, a fledgling attempt to found a competition for the best domestic sides around the globe – a World Cup for clubs, if you will. The local press had largely derided the concept as 'a money-spinner' and had taken exception to Rovers' willingness to disrupt our league schedule in order to 'ponce about in Bongo-Bongo Land', as one of the more vocal columnists had put it. I thought that was a little narrow-minded, though. The way I saw it, the competition granted a welcome opportunity to take English football abroad – to carry into remote and perhaps less fortunate places than our own the flag for this great game which, after all, we had invented, and to be ambassadors for English football and for English ways in general. We might even learn one or two things ourselves. So, it was in a spirit of high optimism that the passports were acquired, the bags were packed, the club suits were dry-cleaned and pressed, and we were all set for the nineteen-hour flight to the war-torn South American country of Beltigua.

'Blimey, Roy,' said Blackie, as he and I pored over an atlas in his mum and dad's parlour one night. 'It's even further than France. Do you suppose they speak English there?'

'I'm sure some of them do,' I said, reassuringly. 'And we can always teach them to, if they don't.'

'Are you worried that you might miss home?' asked Blackie. A good question. This was, after all, for both of us – and for quite a number of the lads, in fact – our first trip abroad.

'Not nearly as much as I'm worried about postponing those league fixtures against Portdean and Hamwick Albion, Blackie,' I replied. 'This International Club Cup represents an exceptional learning opportunity for everyone at the club, but there's no doubt that, upon our return at the end of January, we'll be facing a substantial fixture backlog which could have serious consequences for our tilt at the title.'

Though I didn't mention it to Blackie, I was also worried about the developing political situation on the ground in Beltigua where, according to news reports that I had heard on the radio, a civil war was raging between the state-controlled army and rebel forces loyal to the deposed president, Huevos Di Santador.

'I think I'm going to miss cheese,' said Blackie. 'I can't imagine they'll have cheese, that far away. Especially if they don't speak English.'

It was a highly excited and also slightly anxious party of fifteen (a squad of thirteen players, plus Ben Galloway and Taff Morgan) that gathered at the airport on the appointed morning. As we waited in the departure lounge, we talked about our various 'offerings'. I had asked the lads to pack into their suitcases something that they felt was quintessentially English and which they might give to one of our hosts at some point as a token of friendship. 'Remember,' I said, 'these are people who, in all likelihood, don't have much in the way of material things and will probably be grateful for almost anything.'

Having thought about it for a long time, I had decided, for my own part, to take several packs of playing cards with a portrait of the Queen on the rear of them. I figured they would be a nice, simple thing to hand out, potentially useful as a conversation starter, and easy to carry too. In a similar vein, Jim Hallett said he had brought Tuesday's edition of the *Melchester Evening Chronicle*, complete with the used cars classifieds section. Paddy Ryan had brought a leg of lamb. Dick Stokes had brought a table lamp which he and his wife had bought on holiday one year in Salport Bay and which, he said, always reminded them of the town and the beach there. And Dave Matthews had brought a book token to the value of one shilling and sixpence. 'I didn't know what to get them,' he explained. 'I'm sure that will go down very well,' I said. 'I'm sure everything that we've brought will.'

In those days there were none of the extravagant security checks, body searches and evacuations of liquid which have made modern aeroplane travel such a challenge, and before long we were climbing the steps to the vast white Boeing 707 that awaited us at our gate. It felt impossibly glamorous. Getting on and off planes was something you had seen movie stars do. It was hard to believe you were doing it yourself.

The thrills continued on board. Many of the lads were delighted to discover that the arms of their seats contained ashtrays, and they lit up as soon as they could in celebration. There was much experimental tipping backwards and forwards of the reclining seats. 'Look, Roy!' said Blackie. 'Overhead lockers! Lockers that are actually overhead!'

Meanwhile, a stewardess in a crisp white blouse introduced herself as Shirley and kindly leaned across me to help fasten my seat belt. She smelled of perfume and make-up and, as she tightened the strap across my thighs, she said, in a voice that was almost a whisper, 'If you need absolutely anything at all in the course of our flight, Mr Race, I most sincerely hope you will let me know.'

I thanked Shirley very much and later was glad to be able to call upon her a couple of times for a glass of water.

We landed at Dos Pedros International Airport at three a.m. and then transferred for the internal flight to San Angino, scheduled to leave shortly after dawn. If the Boeing 707 had been comfortingly large and well equipped, the plane for the next stage of our flight was the opposite. It was a tiny, propellor-driven sixteen-seater which looked more like a balsa-wood model of an aeroplane than the real thing. With some concern, I observed two members of the ground crew stooping under the wings to wedge our numerous suitcases and kitbags into the cramped cargo hold.

'Do you think it will ever get off the ground?' asked Jim Hallett.

'I hope my table lamp's all right,' said Dick Stokes.

We climbed aboard, bending almost double to get through the door, and then bending again in order to get down into the rows of narrow seats. When we were all buckled in, our pilot entered, wearing a white short-sleeve shirt with navy epaulettes stitched unevenly onto its shoulders. He too was bent double and he seemed to be rocking somewhat unsteadily as he addressed us from the front of the plane. He appeared, from his accent, to be Australian, although his voice was slightly slurry so it was difficult to be sure.

'Good morning, everybody. My name's Stu. And just so's you know, I've flown one of these before, and I only crashed it twice.'

He paused to allow a wave of horror to freeze the cabin.

'That's a little joke, by the way,' he added. And, just to underline it, he emitted a sharp, barked laugh. 'Hah!'

We all laughed uneasily.

'Now, strap yourselves in,' continued Stu, 'and we'll see if we can get under way. And if you need anything during the flight, feel free to come up and tap me on the shoulder. Helps me stay awake.'

Another pause.

'That's another little joke, by the way. Hah!'

Stu then turned and dropped into the pilot's seat, where he fumbled his way into a pair of headphones and began flicking switches on the furiously busy cockpit panel in front of him and making notes in pencil on a clipboard. Outside the window, the propellors began to rotate, causing a rumble that shook the whole of the craft, and then we jolted and bumped and puttered out to the runway. There was a brief pause, while Stu muttered inaudibly into his headset. And then, with no warning at all, the plane threw itself forward down the tarmac, amid the whine of hysterically straining engine parts and the buzzing of loose screws, lifted slightly, bounced three times, made an ominous cracking sound and then finally, implausibly, and by no means in a straight line, rose into the air.

I was seated directly behind Stu, next to Ben Galloway, the plan being that the two of us could take the opportunity at some point to run over a few last-minute tactical points prior to the match, but I thought we might hold off on this when I swivelled and cast a look around the cabin at my team-mates. Those who weren't white with terror were green with airsickness. I gave an encouraging smile and a thumbs-up, because that's the captain's role at times of duress such as this, although, inside, I too was marginally concerned for our safety and trying to draw as much reassurance as I could from the sight of the plainly unperturbed, but possibly quite hung-over, Stu.

Things settled down a bit once we were airborne. Or, at any rate, they remained unsettling, but consistently so, which was something of a relief. Where our mighty Boeing 707 had journeyed nonchalantly and imperviously above the clouds, as if in its own world, our current vessel was flying unignorably low over the densely jungled mountains. I could sense the nervousness continuing, even among the seasoned travellers in the squad, some of whom seemed to be whimpering and possibly even praying. I decided that, from a morale-boosting point of view, this might be the time to produce my Cup Final Day team quiz, still unused after my interrupted attempt to present it at home at Christmas. I twisted round and knelt on my seat to face back down the cabin.

'Question One,' I began. 'In what year did King Leopold the Second of Belgium . . .'

At that exact moment, a hail of machine-gun bullets tore into the fuselage. The plane tipped to one side with the impact of the blow and then righted itself, only to tip again as a second volley of bullets smacked into the right-hand engine. Through the porthole, I could see flames lick briefly around the propellor and then black smoke entirely engulfed the wing.

Behind me, the lads were panic-stricken. Some were shouting and screaming and clutching their heads in horror. Others were rendered entirely frozen by fear. Ahead of me, Stu was wrestling madly with the controls.

'What is it, Stu?' I shouted.

'No worries,' Stu shouted back, continuing to wrestle. 'I'm gonna stick it down in that clearing. I mean, what's the worst that can happen?'

'That's just a little joke,' he added. 'Hah!'

Were we flying or falling? Was Stu in control of the plane, or was the plane in control of Stu? It was hard to tell. As the fragile and overloaded craft plummeted towards the treetops, I looked at

Ben Galloway beside me. Ben's jaw was tight and his eyes were perfectly round and staring fixedly ahead. His bottom lip appeared to be quivering. I was a little surprised, but also quite touched, to feel his hand close over mine on the armrest and squeeze tight.

Through the window, the scenery grew closer and closer and then there was the noise of the wings ripping and clattering through foliage and then a huge crump as the belly of the plane grounded in the grass and began to drag, juddering the cabin so violently that, for a few wild seconds, everything blurred. And then there was one final resounding crunch. And then silence.

'I hope my table lamp's all right,' said Dick Stokes.

I couldn't, at this stage, speak for Dick's lamp, but clearly the plane, at least, was in one piece. I leaned forward to congratulate Stu, who was still gripping the plane's rudder control and breathing heavily. Ben Galloway, recovering his self-possession, now released my hand, stood as best he could and turned to face the team.

'Has anyone picked up a niggle?'

Ken Harcombe raised a hand, wincing. 'I'm feeling my hamstring a bit, boss.'

'That's all right, Ken,' said Galloway. 'I wasn't going to be picking you for the San Angino game in any case. Anyone else? Any knocks?'

Fortunately, with the exception of a bit of bruising to some shoulders and knees, the rest of the squad was unscathed. Stu opened the side-door and, one by one, relieved to be alive but still stunned by the rapidity with which everything had happened, we abandoned the stricken vessel and jumped down onto the grass.

The first thing you noticed was the heat – clammy, intense and almost suffocating, especially if you were wearing a wool-mix club suit and a knotted tie, as we all were.

The second thing you noticed was the buzzing and chirruping of the insects, almost comically loud.

The third thing you noticed was the army of machine-gun toting rebels, emerging from the jungle to form a ring right around the aircraft.

'Hands up! Hands up! No funny business! Hands up!'

'They do speak English, then, Roy,' said Blackie, raising his arms. 'That's a relief.'

The rebel who had done the shouting stepped out of the pack and began to walk towards us. He wore ripped khaki shorts and a torn and dirt-blackened shirt. He also seemed to have some sort of handkerchief on his head in place of a hat. A cigarette dangled from his lip and an ammunition belt was slung across his shoulder. At first his expression was aggressive, but as he drew closer, his eyes narrowed inquisitively, and after looking us up and down for a short while, he rested the tip of his machine gun against the club crest on my blazer pocket.

'Melchester Rovers?' he asked, in a strongly accented voice.

'Melchester Rovers,' I replied, as calmly as I could with a gun at my chest.

The leader lowered the machine gun, turned and said something in Portuguese to the rest of the men who became suddenly animated and drew in closer. Within their chatter, I could pick out one or two words of English. 'Mel Park . . . Roy Race . . . FA Cup . . . late winner against Everpool . . .' Relief flooded through me and I stepped towards the rebels with my hand out.

'Well, if we're all football fans here . . .' I began.

'SILENCE!' screamed the rebels' leader, spinning back round and jabbing me repeatedly with his machine gun. 'NO FUNNY BUSINESS! HANDS UP! HANDS UP!'

I jumped back into the group and stood, shaken, with my arms raised.

The leader now shouted some instructions in Portuguese.

Some of the men went to the plane, pulled open the cargo door and began to haul out our luggage. Others surrounded us, prodding us into a line with the butts and tips of their guns. Then they marched us, hands aloft, across the clearing and down a path into the jungle.

Under the trees, the sun couldn't reach us, but the air was still thick and wet. Exotic blooms and giant shiny leaves lined our path. A parrot abruptly burst out of a bush in an explosion of colour and noise and flew away, chattering. My shirt was itchy around my neck and my blazer was heavy. I felt a long way from Melchester.

After about an hour, the path widened into another clearing, dotted with tents. Smoke curled from small bonfires and bands of resting brigands looked up from their seated positions on the ground at our arrival. We were led across the compound and shut inside a crude wooden cage. Stu immediately lay down in a corner and went to sleep. The rest of us sat against the fencing or paced around within the enclosure's limited confines and wondered what was coming next.

We had been in the cage for about half an hour when a guard entered and gestured to me with his gun.

'You! Captain! Come!'

'Where are you taking me?' I asked.

'To the Colonel,' he replied.

I was marched to the heart of the compound where a large tent stood in the shade of a tree. The guard lifted the flap and pushed me through. It took my eyes a while to adjust. The air smelt spicy and the floor underfoot was carpeted. The room was dark except for the faltering yellow glow coming from something in the corner that I eventually recognised as Dick Stokes's table lamp. The light was enough to make out a chair, and in that chair I could gradually discern the Colonel's broad, thickly bearded face and his narrowed but unwavering eyes which fastened on me appraisingly and didn't move.

'So,' he began, speaking slowly in a voice that was deep and rasping and only mildly accented. 'The great Roy Race of Melchester Rovers. On his way, no doubt, to the fledgling International Club Cup Competition, and coming off the back of a decent run of form in the league. Do you think you can sustain that title challenge until the end of the season, Mr Race?'

'I'm hopeful that we can be there or thereabouts in May, Colonel.'

'Portdean are looking strong, though. And they have the experience.'

I was impressed by the Colonel's intimate knowledge of the English First Division, but not entirely surprised by it. English football is, after all, a global obsession – an international language, almost.

'Portdean do indeed have the wherewithal,' I replied, 'but I think there are still one or two questions over the depth of their squad. Plus we still have to go to Port Park Lane in late April for a match which has already got "four-pointer" written all over it.'

'Any news on Charlie Skipton?'

The Colonel was referring to the young, up-and-coming Carslake inside left, who had picked up an ankle injury over the Christmas period.

'I believe it's not as serious as the club first feared and he could be back in training within a fortnight,' I said.

The Colonel nodded sagely, still fixing me with his gaze.

'Colonel, if I may be permitted a question of my own,' I ventured, 'what exactly do you want with us?'

Still the Colonel's eyes didn't leave me.

'A fair question, Mr Race,' he said. 'Planes, and what they contain, are very useful to our cause – which is why we shoot them down. But this is something we did not foresee. We had no idea, when we opened fire, what your plane would prove to be carrying. It's not every day after all that an English football side passes overhead, here in Beltigua.'

'I imagine not,' I said dryly.

'Incidentally,' he said. 'While I think of it, we found, among your players' personal items, a leg of lamb.'

'Belonging to Paddy Ryan,' I said. 'What about it?'

'It's illegal to carry uncooked meat on a flight originating outside South America without a fully completed customs declaration.'

'Then I apologise,' I said. 'We did so in ignorance of the rules.'

'We have confiscated the leg of lamb,' said the Colonel.

'And the table lamp, by the looks of it,' I said, with just an edge of bitterness, nodding towards the corner.

'Goes well in here, doesn't it?' said the Colonel. 'Although I may end up changing the shade for something . . . quieter.'

I didn't react.

'Here's my proposal for you, Mr Race,' the Colonel said, now sitting forward. 'A game of football.'

'A game of football?'

'Yes. A game of football. My boys versus your boys. A friendly, of course.' At that, he laughed coarsely, suddenly showing a set of badly yellowed teeth. 'A game of football with the great Melchester Rovers.'

'And afterwards?' I asked.

'And afterwards, nothing,' he replied. 'Ninety minutes of football, plus any time added on, and you go free.'

This was a surprise. I was thinking fast.

'We'll need our kit,' I said.

'You'll get your kit,' he replied.

'And a plane to get us out of here. Our plane wasn't looking too good back there for having been shot out of the sky by your men.'

'We can fix your plane,' the Colonel said evenly, sitting back again and bringing his fingertips together.

'OK,' I said. And then, thinking of Dick Stokes, I added, 'And one other thing: we'll want the table lamp back.'

The Colonel didn't move, but the expression on his face abruptly became cold and a steely fury entered his eyes. His voice was still quiet and even, but there was now a level of menace in it that hadn't been there before.

'Mr Race, I urge you not to push your luck.'

Scalded, I allowed a moment to pass.

'Let me talk to my men,' I said.

The Colonel snapped his fingers and the guard reappeared. I was marched back to the cage, where I immediately put the rebels' demands to Ben Galloway and the rest of the lads.

'Well, that doesn't sound too bad, does it?' said Blackie. 'I quite fancy a kick-about.'

'Can the table lamp not be brought back into the negotiations at all?' asked Dick Stokes plaintively.

'My sense, when I talked to the Colonel, was very strongly that the table lamp is now absolutely off the table,' I explained.

'And the lamb?' asked Paddy Ryan.

'The same,' I said.

'Those things apart, it's an attractive enough package,' argued Hughie Griffiths. 'And we could be out of here by nightfall.'

There was a general murmuring of approval at this – but not from Jim Hallett. Jim was a thoughtful man who quite often saw through to the essential moral heart of an issue, and this was one of those occasions.

'You can't negotiate with terrorists,' Jim said firmly. 'You simply can't. It's just wrong.'

'It's only a game of football, Jim,' argued Tubby Morton.

'This time, yes,' said Jim. 'This time it's just a football match they want. Next time, though, it'll be money, weapons, prisoners freed from jails . . . It escalates. Don't get me wrong: I want to be out of this place as much as the next man. But there's a point of democratic principle here. If you negotiate with terrorists, terror wins.'

The cage fell quiet as we all thought about this for a while. Eventually, I spoke.

'I think the key to this is to understand what we, as a football team from England, represent to these remote mountain people of Beltigua,' I said. 'To them, English professional football is a fantasy that they can only read and dream about. And now here we are, in the flesh, moving among them. Now, let's reflect that there were – and, indeed, there remain – other courses of action open to our hosts, other ways in which they could have elected to capitalise on their good fortune in having shot us out of the sky. For example, they could have proposed holding us for ransom, maybe indefinitely. They could have employed us as some kind of bargaining chip, locally or internationally. They could have used our captivity in any number of ways as a means to raise the profile of their cause around the world. The fact is, though, that, even with those other, perhaps more typical options to select from, they instinctively chose to suggest a football match – seizing a valuable, once-in-a-lifetime opportunity to pitch themselves against quality English opposition, observe us up close, and learn from the way we go about things. And, OK, one doesn't instinctively approve of the way our hosts have brought this situation about, nor of the way they are now forcing the issue. At the same time, leaving politics aside, I think, in the circumstances, and all things considered, this is a deal we can strike without bringing dishonour on ourselves. On the contrary, in fact: if we do this, we can think of ourselves, not as collaborators, but as ambassadors – ambassadors for English football, and for English sport in the wider definition. And the other thing, of course, is that, as Hughie says, we'll be out of here by nightfall.'

'That's a fair point, Roy, and well made,' said Jim. 'Let's teach these terrorists a lesson – but in the best possible sense.'

I asked the guard, through the fencing of the cage, if he could convey our assent to the Colonel's proposition. Not long after, the bags containing our kit were pushed through the door and we got changed and began to warm up, as best we could in the space provided. Ben Galloway gave a pre-match team talk in which he stressed the need to concentrate at set pieces and be especially mindful of attempts to catch us on the break. He also urged us to go easy and suggested that once we got two or three goals ahead, we should drop back a bit and let them come on to us. 'Remember: it's about creating goodwill, at the end of the day.'

Some while later, a band of guards led us at gunpoint from the cage, out through the back of the camp where, somewhat counter-intuitively, there was a pitch crudely marked out on a flattened rectangle of ground, with two full-size goals, albeit without nets. Our opponents were already warming up at the far end. None wore shirts. One or two had football boots, but most wore battered old canvas plimsolls, or even shoes, and a couple were, incredibly, barefoot. It couldn't help but prick your conscience to be lining up in full Rovers finery amid this evident poverty.

The pitch, in truth, left a lot to be desired. It sloped significantly at one end, was entirely bereft of grass and was fairly widely covered with small but sharp-looking stones, as well as a scattering of dis-carded shell cases and a number of chunks of metal which turned out, on closer inspection, to be bomb fragments. But it was nothing worse, all in all, than we had faced at lower league grounds in the FA Cup. And at least it was relatively late in the afternoon by now and the sun had dropped low, meaning that, apart from the sharp stones, we would only have the raging humidity to contend with, along with the clouds of insects. We were an extremely well-trained professional unit too, so I knew we would cope, and without complaint. Plus, if those disadvantages helped level the playing field – at least metaphorically speaking – that would be no bad thing.

The entire rebel army seemed to have turned out to watch the game. They were gathered three or four deep beside the touchlines. As I jogged up for the toss, I noticed the Colonel looking on from the halfway line. A chair had been provided for him. I waved across to him and he nonchalantly raised a forefinger from the armrest.

It was the first game any of us had played in which the referee (Mr E.F. Sanchez of Pandiamo) had been armed with a pistol. Even in some of the behind-closed-doors games that my dad had got me involved in, the officials had never carried firearms. Just occasionally they had carried a stick or a bludgeon of some kind, normally for their own safety. But never a gun. It might be a move today's officials could consider! I often find myself pointing out to the youngsters these days that it would certainly reduce incidents of dissent if players knew the ref had the capacity to blow off their kneecaps, or worse!

The match kicked off and, to our surprise, the rebels were immediately on the attack. They were like Flaudermitz of Austria, only much quicker and stronger and with a far greater intensity to their pressing game in the middle third. They were also significantly more comfortable on the ball than teams we were used to playing against, and ready to accept a pass from a team-mate, even if they were under pressure from markers, so confident were they of their ability to control it and move it on as necessary. This was true even of the ones who didn't have any boots. Highly impressive.

We, on the other hand, seemed to have some problems acclimatising. Moreover, we were effectively reduced to ten men from the off by the fact that Ted Barker's hair lacquer seemed to attract the early evening insects in unusually large quantities, to the point that his head was permanently encased in a cloud of fizzing wings, no matter how much he flapped his hands around his ears in an attempt to palm them off. Ted continued to probe and look for spaces as best he could, but his positional play was inevitably hampered, along with his concentration, and as a result we were always light on the right-hand side, coming forward.

Accordingly we quickly went behind, and were 9–0 down at half-time. I managed to pull one back in the second half, going on a mazy, extended run at one point which earned a smattering of applause from the crowd. I thought I had managed a second in the fifty-sixth minute, stabbing home at close range from a Blackie cross, but I was adjudged by Mr E.F. Sanchez of Pandiamo to have been marginally offside. The rebels, meanwhile, continued to boss the midfield and added five more, and we ran out 14–1 losers.

As we left the field, the Colonel was grinning broadly. 'Your boys took one hell of a beating,' he said.

'We did, indeed,' I said. 'I'd need to look at it again before I knew quite what went wrong for us out there. The jet lag and the plane crash might have been a factor – also the altitude and, to a degree, the insects. But I'm not going to use that as an excuse. Quite simply, the better team won today.'

'Thanks, Mr Race,' said the Colonel. 'And if you're ever flying over Beltigua again . . .'

'We'll be sure to drop in!' I said, and we both laughed.

We returned to the cage and got changed back into our club suits, and were then led out of the encampment by the guards and back to the clearing, the noise of the rebels' victory party diminishing gradually behind us through the trees. The lads were in a sombre mood after the defeat, naturally enough; no one really wants a 14–1 drubbing on their record. But as I said to everyone, you discovered a lot about yourself in adversity, and it's all about how you bounce back. 'We'll look at it on the training ground tomorrow, and go again,' I said.

The rebels seemed to have done a decent job of patching up the plane, and Stu once more hauled himself into the pilot's seat and put on his headset. The engines fired, we bumped over the grass and soon, with a deeply sickening sensation, we were sweeping up above the forest canopy and turning towards the magnificently setting sun while the rebel guards waved us a fond farewell from the ground.

We flew on down to San Angino and checked into our hotel soon after midnight. The following afternoon we lost 1–0 in the first round of the International Club Cup and were eliminated. We then took the night flight back up to Dos Pedros, during which, fortunately, we weren't at all shot down, and then we connected with a scheduled flight back to Melchester.

It had been a tiring experience, no question, and slightly disappointing from a strictly football point of view. Nevertheless, I had seen things that, growing up, I had never in my wildest dreams expected to see, such as a parrot, and I had learned lessons that would no doubt prove invaluable in the unlikely event that I were ever again taken hostage by rebel forces in a war-torn South American state. I didn't see how I could ask for much more from my first trip abroad with the club.

One other key thing: it didn't seem to affect our league form. True, by the time we got back – and factoring in the Boxing Day postponement caused by the fire – we were playing catch-up, both with Portdean and the fixture list, and ended up, in April, having to play six matches in nine days, which wasn't ideal. But we won them all and then faced Portdean, away, in a title decider. A tense, nervy affair seemed destined to end goalless, which would have been enough to grant the home side the honours. But then, in the last minute, shaping to shoot, I was chopped down by Keith Blackmore, Portdean's burly, bearded stopper, and the referee had no hesitation in awarding a penalty. Holding my nerve, I stroked the ball low to the keeper's left – and then watched in agony as the minder guessed correctly and got a glove to it.

Not enough of a glove, though! The force of the shot carried the deflected ball behind him and into the net. The referee – Mr. O.P. Dinsmore of Stockton Brook – didn't even have time to restart the game. Rovers were champions!

It was the second league title of my career. They're all special, of course. But, given the circumstances, that one felt extra special!

13

England Duty

People often ask me if I regret the fact that things didn't work out more profitably for me at international level. And I always have to put a hand up and say, 'Yes, to a certain extent, I do.' To have been fortunate enough to achieve so much in club football – to have won everything there is to win, and most of it many, many times over – and yet not to have been given the opportunity to prove yourself on the biggest stage of all . . . well, it would be bound to rankle, with any player, to a degree. If you had asked me at any point (indeed, if you asked me now), I would always have said that there is no greater honour than to be asked to pull on a shirt and go and do a job for your nation. And that's whether you're a soldier, a footballer, a plumber, a greengrocer, or whatever you are. So it wasn't a lack of willingness on my part. If my England career was patchy, it was largely on account of a freakish run of minor injuries at precisely the wrong moments. You can't legislate for that.

I'll always remember the excitement of getting the international nod for the very first time. It was the autumn of 1962 and the Rovers had a midweek home game against Eastoke. Ben Galloway told me in the dressing room before the match that Wilf Hargreaves, the England manager, was in the crowd to watch me and, though I tried to shut the thought out of my mind, attempting to convince myself that Galloway must have got it wrong, and that Hargreaves was there to have a look at someone else, there's no question it affected me. You can be so determined to impress that it backfires on you, and that was certainly the story of my first half against Eastoke that night. I kept over-complicating my game when better, simpler options were available. At one point, for instance, Blackie rolled the ball temptingly towards me along the six-yard line, with only the goalkeeper to beat. And instead of simply side-footing home, I attempted to trap it between both feet, go up into a handstand position, flip the ball aloft and crack it into the net with my left heel. Alas, I got the timing wrong and ended up putting it narrowly over the bar.

That was naïve of me, and I gave myself a good talking to in the dressing room at half-time. After that, fortunately, the second half went a little better. I went back to doing the simple things, where necessary, and attempting to be more ambitious only when it was a genuine option. As a result, I managed to score four and, as Eastoke collapsed into disarray, make two more in a 6–0 mauling.

'Wilf Hargreaves and the England selectors are going to have to pick you now, Roy!' said Blackie as we left the field. I wasn't so sure, though. I was still haunted by memories of that dire first half. I can be my harshest critic and it was a genuine shock, the following Thursday morning, when I returned home from a shoeless forty-mile run carrying in my arms a knapsack filled with house bricks, to find the letter from the FA on the mat: my first England call-up.

We played Caragua, who were ranked 614th in the world – though, as everyone will tell you, there is no such thing as an easy game at international level, and we soon found ourselves soaking up some early pressure. My problem, though, wasn't so much containing Caragua as containing thoughts of Melchester Rovers. In those days, the domestic schedule wasn't routinely suspended while internationals took place. England games and club games frequently ran concurrently and sides with players on international duty simply had to fill the gaps with players off the bench and get on with it. Accordingly, while I was at Wembley with England, Rovers were facing title rivals Wellingbury in a crucial four-pointer at Mel Park. That was a major distraction for me. I couldn't stop wondering how the lads were getting on without me, and, at times, I was straining to see if I could pick up anything about what was going on from conversations in the crowd. Unsurprisingly, my focus wasn't what it should have been and I had a shoddy opening forty-five minutes during which the selectors must have begun to wonder whether they had made a terrible mistake. It was only after half-time, when I had managed to find out that Melchester were comfortably 3–0 ahead, including a brace from new-signing Duncan McElway, that I felt able to relax. I responded by scoring a hat-trick, which is always a nice way to mark the start of your international career.

Everything seemed set fair at that point for a long run in the national side and a few tilts at the World Cup, widely regarded as the game's ultimate prize, although you would have to say, there's a lot of awfully good players who have never won it and that doesn't make them less good. Conversely, there are quite a lot of fairly average players who *have* won it, and it doesn't automatically make them great. Just to put that in the broader perspective.

In any case, it was out of my hands because that run of irritatingly negligible injuries intervened. First of all, I turned an ankle stepping backwards onto the jack in a post-season charity bowls match and missed out on the 1966 World Cup. Obviously, that would have been a nice one to have been involved in, given that it was on home soil and that we won it. However, no one was more pleased than me about the success the England lads had that day, and the lasting joy it brought the nation. I only wished I could have watched the game. Blackie had invited me over to see it on the new black-and-white set his family had just started renting from Rediffusion. I think virtually the whole of Sutton Street must have been wedged in the Grays' tiny front room that day! But unfortunately I had noticed, while out running over at the fields, that there was a pile of old house bricks that someone had dumped and which clearly needed hitting over and over again with a mallet until they were reduced to powder, so I went over there for the afternoon and got on with doing that, prior to coming home for supper and having an early night.

When a groin strain kept me out of the 1970 World Cup in Mexico, family history seemed to be repeating itself. It was a groin strain, you will recall, that put my dad on the sidelines for the duration of World War II. Was he as disappointed about missing that opportunity to serve as I was about missing Mexico '70? I can only imagine he was, although he didn't really talk about it.

England didn't qualify for either the 1974 or 1978 tournaments, so the fact that I sprained a wrist at the start of the summer in '74 and did a metatarsal in May 1978 is, ultimately, irrelevant. However, England did qualify (with some assistance from me along the way) for the 1982 World Cup, so once again I stood on the threshold of a starring part in football's great global festival. On that occasion, though, I was prevented from joining up by an ingrown toenail which, again, was just typical of the niggling misfortune that tended to dog me on the international scene.

The next time the tournament came around, in 1986, I didn't really seem to be featuring in the selectors' thoughts. One theory, much touted in the press, was that I was regarded, among the powers at the FA, as a creative player (possibly even 'a maverick'), and the feeling was that creativity wasn't really what England were about or particularly interested in. In my defence, I would say that, although I was prone to moments of creativity and inclined overall to take a creative approach to the game where possible, I could also be uncreative if the occasion demanded or if called upon to be so, and I would have been more than willing to adapt, if England had asked me to. At that time, I still felt I had plenty to offer my country, whether creatively or uncreatively. But if your face doesn't fit, there's not a lot you can do about it. Even in 1990, in my opinion, I was still capable of competing – even if only coming off the bench late in a game to offer something different. But, again, the people at the FA decided to go in another direction.

Still, I collected forty-two caps over the course of my playing career, which is not a bad haul, even allowing for that career's duration, and scored nine goals. I'm proud, too, to be able to say that I was entrusted with managing my national side – albeit temporarily and just for one match. That was in April 1978, at Wembley, and our opponents were Holland, in a friendly. Over the previous Bank Holiday weekend, the England manager at the time, Don Harvey, had suffered some nasty fairground-related injuries when his mat failed on a Helter-Skelter and he was thrown across the grass and into the path of a passing dodgem. I was honoured to be asked to step in as caretaker manager. The press, as I knew they would, had a bit of a field day with my decision to bring in eight uncapped Melchester Rovers players. I found myself accused of naked favouritism, but as far as I was concerned, I was just picking the players who I thought were the best for the job. I also summoned Mike

Bateson and Nipper Lawrence from Blackport and Johnny Dexter, a player I had long admired and whom I would eventually bring to the Rovers, but who was then plying his trade in Spain with Real Granpala.

My team selection, which included picking myself at centre forward, was thoroughly vindicated on the night when we went out and crushed Holland 5–1 (a hat-trick from me, and further strikes from Lawrence and Dexter, who played out of his skin) in a performance that many still rank as the most fluid and unshackled that they have ever witnessed from an England side. Afterwards there were some calls in the papers for me to be given the job full time, but I can honestly say that, even if I had been offered the role, I would have turned it down. I had far too much unfinished business with the Rovers, and it wasn't the right time for me. In any case, the fact is, I wasn't offered it. The FA went back to Don Harvey just as soon as his bruising went down.

The Dutch skipper Johan Seegrun was very gracious after that match at Wembley, and he and I became penpals. Johan was one of the mercurial masters, an astonishing player to watch and the pioneer of a whole catalogue of skills and moves, the likes of which English football had never seen or figured were worth bothering with. He became famous, above all, for a move known to this day as 'the Seegrun shimmy', where, by somehow swivelling his hips while dropping a shoulder and, at the same time, rotating his neck, he seemed to be running in two different directions at once. It was staggering to witness, and made him very hard to mark at set pieces. I used to spend hours in front of the mirror, squeezing and straining and trying to make myself 'Seegrun', but I never cracked it!

Johan would get his revenge for that international defeat at the end of the 1982–3 season, in the European Cup Final, when Rovers faced Alkhoven and Johan scored twice in a 3–2 victory for the

Dutch side. It was a bitterly disappointing night for everyone in a Rovers shirt, of course, but I couldn't begrudge the silky-skilled Dutchman his moment astride the pinnacle of the club game. He was one of the greats and it was a privilege to have shared a field with him – and, at times, with both of him.

14

Italy Calling

It wasn't just England who expressed an interest in my services in the mid-1960s. I also found myself being tempted from afar – and contemplating the unthinkable: leaving the Rovers for another club.

One morning in early 1964, John Mason asked me if I'd mind putting my head round the door of his office after training. I duly did so, and found the chairman and local supermarket mogul, as ever, sitting at his desk in his large, oxblood leather chair amid a cloud of cigar smoke. He wasted no time in getting down to business.

'We've had an offer come in for you, Roy.'

'Who from, Mr Mason?' I asked. I was expecting it to be Carslake or Wellingford, or possibly Portdean – one of our traditional first division rivals, who were periodically rumoured to be sniffing around.

'Italian side Stadia Batori,' said Mr Mason.

Now, that was a shock. You need to remember that the football transfer market was very different in the Sixties from the fluid international stock-exchange that we are used to these days. It was accepted that, as a footballer, you would ply your trade in the nation of your birth, and sales from country to country were rare. European clubs almost never came in for English players – just as English clubs almost never went in for European players. Bear in mind that it wasn't until 1979 that Rovers signed Paco Diaz from Spanish giants Zaragosa, and were automatically regarded as the pioneers of a whole new 'continental approach' as a result of doing so. (I'll talk about Paco and the exotic flavour he brought to the club later.) On the solitary occasion to this date that a deal had been struck and an English player had ventured abroad, it hadn't worked out well. In 1963, Standard Wasserdram of Belgium had caused a sensation by signing Bobby Hounslow from Elbury Wanderers for the princely sum of £56,000, but the stalwart left-back never settled and came home after three months, claiming that he missed proper sausages.

'If I may ask,' I said to Mr Mason, 'how much is the offer?'

Mr Mason cleared his throat. 'Eighty-five thousand pounds,' he said.

I was gobsmacked and had to sit down. These were the days when £85,000 was a lot of money. Indeed, that sum would have been a record for a transfer fee involving a British player, easily surpassing the £79,000 Everpool had recently paid Shermall Athletic for the mercurial play-maker and guaranteed twenty-goals-a-season man, Alex Wrenn.

'I don't know what to say, Mr Mason,' I said. 'Eighty-five thousand in real terms would be enough to build a hospital or pay the Prime Minister's salary three and a half thousand times over or feed an average family of four and their dog for twenty-two centuries. I don't know what the Italian Serie A side are thinking.'

'It's a lot of money,' said Mr Mason ruefully. 'And I reckon we could probably squeeze them up to eighty-seven thousand, with a bit of haggling.'

A moment of silence ensued while the two of us allowed my shock to subside.

'Look, Roy,' said Mr Mason, 'I'm not going to be anything other than straight with you. You know where I stand. You're the heart and soul of this club – the captain, the talisman, the first name on the team sheet. You're a Melchester boy, born and raised. The fans love you and relate to you on account of that, and on account of what you give them on the field, which is never less than one hundred and fifty percent. On top of that, you're a statesman and an ambassador for the club and the game in general. Your arrival in the first team has ushered in the most sustained period of success, in terms of trophies, that the Rovers have ever known, and, accordingly, whatever Stadia Batori may seem to be implying, you have a value to us that goes way beyond mere money. What kind of message would we be sending out by selling our finest asset abroad – at any price? What would we be saying about Melchester Rovers, as a club, that we would even entertain that notion? Nothing that John Mason would be prepared to endorse – and I mean that as sincerely as anything John Mason has ever said during his years in football.'

'No one player is bigger than the club, Mr Mason,' I replied, 'but I most certainly appreciate your support and gratitude.'

'At the same time,' said Mr Mason, almost as if he hadn't heard me, 'look at the carpet.'

'Sorry?'

'The carpet. Look at it.'

I looked down. The Axminster beneath my feet was thin and largely napless and even, in places, worn down to its backing, especially near the door and where Mr Mason's feet rested under his desk. It also, to the side of that desk, bore a rather unsightly dark red patch – possibly wine – and was dotted with a profusion of what appeared to be cigar burns.

'We haven't been able to afford to replace it for about nine years. The one in the boardroom is even worse. As for the curtains . . .'

Mr Mason's voice was now a little tremulous.

'This club's bleeding me dry, Roy. I can't deny it. The local supermarket business isn't what it was. Lot of competition these days from the nationals: Waitbury's, Sunrose . . . Those b****y b******s with their bulk-buy specials and their three for two offers on toiletries . . .'

At this point, Mr Mason looked away to the window and chewed hard on his lip. I could sense that he was trying not to cry, and only narrowly failing.

'Are you saying you want to sell me, Mr Mason?'

The chairman spun back to face me. His eyes were red but his voice was loud and firm.

'I'm not saying that at all, Roy. Trust me, lad, the day John Mason willingly sells his best player to the Italians is the day that hell freezes over and also, by extension, the day that John Mason does his last piece of business in football. Sell Roy Race? Roy b****y Race? They'd have to drag me to that table at gunpoint, Roy, and make me sign the forms in the blood of my own mother.'

Mr Mason paused for breath. When he resumed, his voice was much quieter.

'I'm just saying that, you know . . . if you did decide you wanted to go and try something a bit different . . . in a warmer climate . . .'

I think I was understanding the chairman's message, as fraught with emotion as it was. The club wasn't prepared to sell me at any price and would indeed move heaven and earth to hold onto me – yet, if I wanted to go, it wouldn't stand in my way. That seemed to be the situation.

'Could I have a couple of days to think things through?'

'Of course, lad,' said Mr Mason. 'Don't leave it too long, though, will you?' he added.

I left Mr Mason's office with my mind in turmoil. To be the subject of the biggest transfer bid in British history – well, that was likely to knock anyone off their stride a bit, independent of all the other factors. There were so many things to weigh up. I had to consider the question of my own development as a player. There was clearly a lot to be said for opening myself up to a different culture and expanding the horizons of my game. At the same time, did I want, at this point in my life, at the age of twenty-six, to leave Mum and Dad and the comforts of home and go and live in Italy?

On top of that, there was the matter of my loyalty to Melchester Rovers. The club was everything to me, and had been so since I was old enough to remember. I could barely imagine pulling on the shirt of any other side without experiencing a deep uneasiness. It would feel like an act of treachery, surely. Yet this too was not straight-forward, because – assuming my understanding of my meeting with the chairman was correct – if I went to Stadia Batori for £85,000 (or £87,000 if Mr Mason managed to squeeze them up a bit), I would be quite plausibly doing the Rovers a favour. I would be enabling the club to receive a vital cash injection which could put new carpets on the floor of Mr Mason's office, refresh both the carpet and the curtains in the boardroom, and still leave money over to build a hospital, pay the Prime Minister, feed a family of four etc.

Frankly, I didn't know which way to turn.

Obviously, the first person I went to see in order to discuss all this was Ben Galloway. Ben had always had my career in mind and I regarded him as an ally in that respect, and, within the club, the soundest judge of what was best for me.

'The question I guess I have to ask myself,' I said, sitting in the manager's office, 'is whether this might be a beneficial move in terms of my own personal growth as a player. I mean, we're talking about Stadia Batori here: big club – massive club, in fact. There isn't a player in the world who wouldn't be flattered by an approach from the Italian champions and three-time European Cup winners.'

'No. Bad idea,' said Galloway firmly. 'You won't like it.'

'Really?' I said. 'But what makes you so sure?'

Galloway looked around his office, almost as if checking that no one else was in the room, listening. He then leaned towards me slightly and his tone was low and conspiratorial.

'Listen, Roy. Between you and me. You've played against enough foreigners to know what they're like. I'm not saying all of them. I'm just saying the vast majority. Diving, feigning injury, biting, squeezing parts of your anatomy, if you get my drift, in the penalty area at corners . . . Squeezing parts of your anatomy is rife in the foreign game, Roy. Fancy that every Saturday afternoon? I don't think you do.'

'But what about the benefits of leaving home, discovering a bit of independence, steeping myself in another culture, even if it was only for a couple of seasons?' I asked. 'I mean, I take your word for it on the anatomy-squeezing, obviously. But, all that apart, don't you think there might be things I could learn over there in Italy which I could bring to bear on my own game, becoming a more complete, more rounded player as a result? And, if I say no, don't you think I might look back at the end of my career and wish that I had seized this opportunity?'

'No,' Galloway said, 'I really don't. Also, that Mediterranean diet, Roy,' he added, wincing. 'Terribly greasy.'

I had hoped to keep the news of Stadia Batori's bid quiet, but nothing stays secret for long in a football club and pretty soon my putative move was the subject of open discussion in the changing room. I was pleased and flattered that none of the lads seemed to be pushing me towards the exit. On the contrary, everybody said they would be very sad to lose me and urged me not to leave. They also had very strong opinions about Italy. Duncan McElway pretty much spoke for everyone when he said, 'Italy? You don't want to go there if you can help it.'

'Have you spent much time over there, Dunc?' I asked.

'No,' said Dunc. 'Like I said, you don't want to go there if you can help it. And so far, fingers crossed, I've always been able to help it.'

Hughie Griffiths, however, spoke highly of the country, certainly as somewhere to visit. 'I've had a couple of very nice walking holidays with Mrs Griffiths in the Cinque Terre region,' Hughie told me as we were getting changed after training. 'I've got some slides which I'll bring in to show you, if you like.'

I thanked him and said he really didn't need to go to the trouble but the next day Hughie brought the slides in anyway, and a projector, which he set up in the laundry room, and we spent three and a half hours that afternoon going through them in some detail. In truth, a lot of the images were rather blurry, and a high proportion of them featured Mrs Griffiths standing beside various rocks and eating various ice creams, but, from Hughie's accompanying lecture, I did begin to get a feel for the place, and certainly for Italian coastal paths, which might well have been helpful to me, even though Batori was 427 miles further south and inland.

Obviously, I talked the whole dilemma over at length with Blackie on our journeys to and from the ground.

'The point is,' I said, 'I don't want to become the footballing embodiment of a certain kind of English insularity – one which instinctively and unthinkingly rejects "abroad" and everything connected with it out of fear or, worse than that, from an increasingly outmoded sense of superiority, rooted in the imperial past.'

'Fair enough,' said Blackie. 'I've always felt the thing about abroad is . . . well, that it's not really here, is it?'

'And then there's the whole economic issue,' I continued. 'Mr Mason made it very clear that things were a bit tricky financially at the moment. The proceeds of my sale to Stadia Batori would sort that out in an instant. It would give the club funds for infrastructure, such as carpeting and curtains, and enable them to invest in some new players and begin again, virtually, on a whole new footing. Maybe, as contradictory as it sounds, my greatest gift to the club could be my willingness to leave it.'

Blackie simply looked at me and shook his head.

'They could buy seven new players, Roy, eight new players . . . heck, they could buy a whole new team,' he said. 'But they wouldn't be able to replace you. You are, quite simply, irreplaceable.'

I was grateful, as ever, for my oldest pal's warm and unwavering support.

I seemed to be getting no nearer to resolving the issue in my own mind, though. Back and forth I went, with the pros and the cons, until I was dizzy. Eventually, on the Thursday afternoon, I did what I always did when I had a pressing problem that I needed to mull over somewhere peaceful, on my own, which wasn't all that often, actually. I left the city behind me and cycled out to Melbury Tor, that never less than surprising geological anomaly which rises out of the earth like a green-swathed thumb beyond Melchester's northernmost outskirts. I abandoned my bike at the bottom and scrambled to the summit, where a bench awaits the breathless climber. From there, you could see all of Melchester spread out below you, and hear only the rush of the wind in your ears. It was an overcast day, but as I sat there alone, thinking – waiting for a sign, almost, it felt like – the sun abruptly broke through the clouds, lending a crisp, gilded edge to the scene: the roofs of the houses, the sinuous form of the River Mel, winding like a silver ribbon through the city's heart, the chimneys of the pickled onion factory, belching their flavoursome smoke into the chilly English sky, and, somehow dominating it all, proud against the horizon, the floodlights of Mel Park. The thought occurred to me, as I looked out across everything in the world that I truly understood and loved, that knowing where you come from is the beginning of knowing who you are. And I realised that Blackie had been right: that whatever Italy could be to me, it could never be here.

I went up that hill a Melchester Rovers player. I came down it a Melchester Rovers player – but even more so.

'That's brilliant news, Roy,' said Mr Mason weakly, continuing to stand at the window of his office, staring out, after I had told him my decision.

'You have my word, Mr Mason, that I am one hundred and fifty percent committed to bringing continued success to Mel Park and, what's more, that I am determined to remain on the books here for the duration of my playing career, however long that should be. So, please convey to the representatives of Stadia Batori my sincere gratitude for their interest – but let that be the end of the matter.'

Mr Mason seemed to sigh and perhaps ever so slightly to whimper.

Still, it was an altogether different Mr Mason that I encountered in the club car park just two days after this.

'You're looking perky this morning, if I may say so,' I said.

'There's a good reason for that, Roy,' said Mr Mason. 'I've just agreed to sell Hughie Griffiths to Shevnik Sparta for sixteen thousand pounds – way over the odds for a player of his age, if you ask me, but I'm hardly going to be complaining, am I? And Hughie couldn't be happier. He says that the Soviet Union is somewhere he and Mrs Griffiths haven't been and are very much looking forward to seeing. So the club is stabilised, financially, and things are looking rosy again, Roy.'

'That's excellent news, Mr Mason,' I replied. 'Come on, the Rovers!'

A couple of days after this a van turned up from E.F. Merchant & Sons, the carpet fitters.

15

Champions of Europe

So, I didn't go to Italy and experience the continent that way. Yet, conveniently, almost immediately after I had turned down the offer from Stadia Batori, Melchester Rovers began having adventures of their own on the continent. In the 1964–5 season, we were entered for the first time in the European Cup, the elite competition for reigning club champions across Europe. It was the start of a long and fruitful love affair for me with that famous pot, one which I would know the rare privilege of lifting five times – each of them, it goes without saying, special.

Anticipating the increased demands that would arise from adding a European contest to our three domestic campaigns (league, League Cup and FA Cup), Ben Galloway sought to bolster the squad, signing Chris Ryan on a free from Salton United, promoting Terry West and Geoff Giles from the youth team, and bringing in a player who would go on to enjoy legendary status at the Rovers – Jumbo Trudgeon, who immediately converted the fans by scoring a hat-trick against Sandford on his first-team league debut.

Jumbo was one of the most distinguished inside lefts that I had the privilege to line up alongside, and certainly the poshest. His full name was Lord D'arcy Plantaganet Trudgeon-Marclay, although the lads immediately dubbed him 'Lordy.' He made an impression on everyone right from the moment he turned up, carrying his kit, not in a holdall like the rest of us, but in a brown leather trunk with his initials on it. We were also quick to note his cravat and velvet smoking jacket, the monogrammed slippers into which he changed after showering, his immaculate ivory shaving bowl and razor blade, his set of silver hairbrushes with tortoiseshell backs and his occasional references to weekend shooting parties in the country with friends called things like Binky, Araminta and Poo. Jumbo was, as everyone at the club immediately agreed, 'different class'.

I never quite got to the bottom of how this aristocratic, Hartwell-educated public schoolboy had ended up in football, which was almost exclusively a working-class preserve in those days (unlike nowadays, of course, when it's almost exclusively middle class). Jumbo once muttered something to me about how 'a little flutter in the City' with a friend of his named Hugo had gone 'slightly squiffy' and left him 'back on the old uppers', but otherwise his path into professional football was a mystery.

'Did they even play football at Hartwell?' I asked him once.

'Heavens, my dear chap – no!' Jumbo replied. 'Perish the thought! Barbarians at the gate! Hartwell was a rugger school. Rugger and cold showers. Absolutely hated the place, with a vengeance. Character-forming, though.'

The thing was, despite the obvious differences in background and upbringing between Jumbo and the rest of the lads, and the fact that he was much given to quoting mottos and phrases in Latin

('Nil desperandum, Roy!' he would cry, drifting in from behind to latch onto a cross that had evaded me), he entirely fitted in. Football dressing rooms tend to be down-to-earth places which instinctively react against flashiness, or any sign that a person is trying to get above himself. But it helped in this respect, I think, that Jumbo wasn't someone who flashed his wealth around. Indeed, he never seemed to have any money on him at all. Many were the times that Jumbo sidled up to me in the dressing room after games and muttered, with the mildest trace of embarrassment, 'I say, Roy, me old chum. You couldn't slip a fellow a couple of bob, could you? Little contretemps with the chaps at the bank . . .' It's a measure of Jumbo's charm that I always did so, and never expected to see the money again, which I didn't.

I only had one run-in with Jumbo in the five years that we played together, and that was over bringing a shotgun into the dressing room. Jumbo had just returned from a grouse shoot on moorland belonging to his friend the Earl of Tuckingham and was demonstrating, to much amusement among the lads, how he had bagged what he believed at the time to be the biggest grouse ever shot, only to discover, when the dogs retrieved it, that it was, in fact, one of the beaters.

'That gun isn't loaded, is it, Jumbo?' I asked, as Jumbo expressively waved its twin barrels aloft to emphasise a point.

'Safety catch on, m'boy,' said Jumbo. 'Worry not! So, anyway, this thing gets up out of the grass, and I'm a little squiffy after a medicinal tot too many from good old Bunty's magic flask, and I thinks to meself, "Pon my soul, I'm having that blighter." So I shoulder it up, like this, and I bring the barrel round, thusly, and . . .'

There was a deafening crump, loud enough to cause your ears to ring, followed by a stunned silence, not least from Jumbo, suddenly wide-eyed and open-mouthed behind the sights. A cloud of gun smoke drifted slowly across the dressing room to the window and embarrassedly made its exit.

Fortunately the double-barrelled blast only hit one of the apprentices, who was bending over to clean the floor in the showers, and whom the club was on the verge of releasing anyway. Still, with pretty much the whole of the first team in attendance, it was obvious to me that we had come within a whisker of an accident that could have had repercussions for the rest of our season, and from that moment on, loaded and cocked firearms were entirely banned from the dressing room, unless by express permission of the chairman.

But then Jumbo was one of those people around whom remarkable things seem to happen, almost irrespective of themselves. It was he, I recall, who was the first to intuit the onset of what history now knows as the Great Mel Park Earthquake of 1965. We were at home to Silford in a league game one Saturday afternoon in February, and Jumbo had just taken possession of the ball on the edge of the centre circle when suddenly, beneath his feet, and to his evident astonishment, that centre circle began to widen.

''Pon my word,' said Jumbo as the ball disappeared into a freshly opened chasm, 'the pitch is breaking up.'

He was right. At once there was a shaking and a deep rumbling, and jagged cracks began to appear and spread all over the playing surface – an earth tremor, no less, one of two to affect the ground during my career. (The second was in the first match of the troubled 1988–9 season, against Blackport, and obliged us to relocate to Wembley Stadium for six months while the repairs took place – extremely disruptive, but we coped OK, eventually winning the league that year.) Some geologists argued that the stadium had been built on a largely dormant fault line, but the science seemed doubtful because nothing else in the town, beyond the boundaries of the pitch, seemed to be affected, and could you have a fault line, dormant or otherwise, as short as that? Other people blamed a delayed aftershock from the necessarily deep and punishing excavation work for the Melchester Metro system, recently completed, but that theory, too, was never definitively proven. In the end, you just had to write it off as one of those things. Or rather, as of August 1988, two of those things.

Obviously the match against Silford, in 1965, had to be abandoned and rescheduled and it was fully five days before the ground staff, working overtime, returned the surface to a playable condition. No one had been hurt, luckily, but I was concerned about the long-term psychological impact on the players of this minor but at the same time, in its own way, quite terrifying natural disaster – whether they would be nervous stepping out onto the Mel Park pitch from that point onwards, and worried that the earth might be about to open up and swallow them, which isn't something that any footballer would ever wish upon themselves.

I needn't have worried, though. The team had a real mental strength to it, no doubt on account of having been through so much in such a short space of time. Accordingly, there were no debilitating repercussions, our league form held more or less steady, and, best of all, our debut European Cup campaign positively flourished. We came through tough ties against Schonved of Hungary and Spain's Real Santana and, in the semi-finals, managed to see off West German side Stalzburg, with me scoring twice at Mel Park to turn over a one-goal deficit from the first leg. That left us facing Nettruno of Italy in the showcase final in Paris.

That Nettruno side, I probably won't need to tell you, boasted some big stars of the world game – Fabio Ponzi and Gianluca LaPerla, to name but two – and there's no question that we were overawed by them in the game's opening exchanges. They went 1–0 ahead in the twenty-fourth minute when Roberto Morissetti linked up devastatingly with Paulo Zappata on the edge of our box, and then they added a second right on half-time, Gianfranco Alanis netting from close range. Our chances of triumphing in Europe at the first time of asking were looking vanishingly slim.

'*Iacta alea est*, Roy,' said Jumbo, shaking his head miserably as we came off at half-time. I had no idea what he was talking about, but it didn't sound good.

I knew I would have to choose my words extremely carefully in my half-time captain's address in the dressing room and find something inspiring enough to bring the team back from the brink. But often it's the simplest things that work the best. I urged the lads to consider what we had come through together, in just a handful of recent years, as a club: two kidnappings, a plane crash, an earthquake and a stadium fire. Those kinds of things are always going to cement a side together, produce an inner steel that can't easily be bent. In the context of those other travails – travails, I pointed out, which had been magnificently overcome – a 2–0 deficit in a European final, with forty-five minutes still to play, was surely the most minor of setbacks, even against a top Italian side containing Fabio Ponzi, Gianluca LaPerla, etc.

'So I'm not asking for anything special out there,' I concluded. 'I'm not asking for anything extra. I'm simply asking that we go out there and be who we already are: Melchester Rovers.'

Whether it was my words that had an effect or not, we were a side transformed in the second half. Blackie struck home a sweet twenty-five-yard volley after fifty-four minutes and then, only three minutes later, I pulled off a scissor kick from near the penalty spot to tie the game at 2–2. With both sides taking turns to probe and press, the game was on a knife edge, and extra time seemed the most likely outcome when Jumbo Trudgeon lost his marker at a corner, and, with a shout of '*Sine labore nihil*, my Italian friends,' back-heeled the ball into the net for 3–2.

The referee didn't even have time to blow for the restart. Rovers had won the European Cup.

It was a fantastic achievement – without question, the most significant in the club's history to that point – but there was very little time to dwell on it. The very next day we were obliged to depart on a lucrative post-season trip to the republic of Malagos in South America, where we were scheduled to meet local champions Bagota. Our flight touched down at dawn and, following a lavish breakfast reception at the Shilton Hotel in Bagota City in which the president of the country, no less, hailed us as 'the champions of all Europe', we boarded a rackety coach to make the journey to our training base in the hills.

Our driver was a squat, smiley, middle-aged man who introduced himself as Beppo and was all over me as I boarded the bus.

'Roy Race!' he exclaimed. 'Melchester Rovers!'

'You Rovers fan are?' I asked.

'Yes, I Rovers fan, I big Rovers fan,' said Beppo, smiling fit to burst. And without any further preamble, he undid some of the buttons on his shirt and wrenched it wide apart.

'You sign for me! Autograph please!' said Beppo, still beaming.

I was completely thrown. 'You want me to sign your chest?' I said uncertainly.

'Yes! You autograph for me!'

It seemed an odd request, but it would have been rude and possibly even undiplomatic to refuse, and there didn't seem to be any harm in it. Getting my signature onto the busman's exposed flesh proved a little difficult on account of the fact that Beppo's chest was quite hairy and fairly slick with sweat, and also because the only pen any of us could come up with was a biro that seemed to have been at the bottom of Terry West's jacket pocket for some time.

Still, I complied as best I could and Beppo seemed extremely proud and happy as he rebuttoned his shirt. I was struck once again by the astonishing popularity of English football and the way it radiates right around the world, becoming a kind of global language, capable of breaking down all manner of international barriers.

Our coach journey into the mountains seemed to go on an awfully long time. I was seated at the front and I remember growing slightly hypnotised by the swinging of the beaded rosary hanging from the rear-view mirror, and listening distractedly to Beppo, singing and whistling along loudly with the bright trumpet music coming from the radio as he wrestled the bus round the hairpin bends.

Up and up we went, and on and on, the roads growing ever narrower and more gravelly, our location becoming more and more remote. Overhanging foliage beat repeatedly against the coach roof and windows as we passed along what were little more than lanes. Back at the reception they had told us our training camp was a short drive away. This was not a short drive. This was the opposite of a short drive.

Sometimes when something is not quite right you get a premonition in the form of a creeping sensation across your skin. I had that sensation sometimes when I came home in the evenings and found Mum, Dad and Mr Sexton from next door sitting together in the kitchen in a silence that I couldn't quite read. And I had that sensation again now – even as Beppo brought the coach to an abrupt halt and switched off the engine.

Ahead of us, strung across the road, perhaps as many as twenty strong, was a band of men with guns. They wore dusty khaki outfits in poor repair. Some had belts of ammunition draped from their shoulders like sashes. The guns were pointed directly at the windscreen of the coach.

''Pon my sainted aunt,' said Jumbo. 'Brigands!'

'Not a-bloody-gain,' said Jim Hallett.

'Ingleesh! Off!' shouted one of the brigands.

One by one, we descended warily from the coach, our hands aloft. I noticed Beppo walk casually away with his hands in his pockets and stand chatting with some of the brigands. He opened his shirt and excitedly showed them his chest. They drew closer to look, curious and obviously impressed. Beppo! Beppo was in on this. Rovers fan, autograph hunter . . . and traitor.

We were prodded into a line and then made to march, in our club suits, about half a mile through hot, scrubby woodland to an encampment in a clearing, perfectly concealed in the folds of the hills. Smoke rose from fires, and brigands lay or sat around, raising their heads curiously at our arrival. We were taken to an open area, off to one side of the camp, and made to kneel on the ground with our hands behind our backs.

We had been in this position for about half an hour when a brigand with a gun approached and shouted, 'You! Captain! Come with me.'

'Where are you taking me?' I said, standing stiffly.

'To the Colonel,' he said.

I was led at gunpoint to a tent at the centre of the encampment, in the shade of a broad tree. The brigand lifted the flap and pushed me through. It took my eyes a while to adjust. The air smelt spicy and the floor underfoot was carpeted. The room was dark except for the faltering yellow glow coming from something in the corner that looked like Dick Stokes's table lamp but couldn't possibly have been because we were hundreds of miles away from San Angino. The light was enough to make out a chair, and in that chair I could gradually discern the Colonel's broad, thickly bearded face and his narrowed but unwavering eyes which fastened on me appraisingly and didn't move.

I was beginning to notice a pattern emerging from our South American kidnapping experiences. Once again, the Colonel stared at me in silence for a while, and then asked me if there was any truth in the rumour that Portdean were readying a bid for Shermall Athletic's England U21 international left back, Bobby Prosser. (I said that I wasn't privy to any inside information but I could see why Portdean would consider a summer move for the Halton-born player to bolster a defence which had shipped a disappointing twelve goals in the last five games of the term just ended.) The Colonel then proposed that our freedom could be gained in exchange for a game of football against his men.

'Usual deal,' I said, when I reported back to the others. 'We play them over ninety minutes, plus anything added on at the referee's discretion for injuries, et cetera, and after that we go free.'

'Sounds fair enough to me,' said Dick Stokes.

'One piece of good news, Dick,' I said. 'This time I managed to barter successfully for the release of a table lamp. It's not yours, but it looks quite a lot like it, and it's the best I could do in the circumstances.'

'Thanks a lot, Racey,' said Dick. 'I really appreciate it.'

'Let's hope we don't get pasted this time,' said Jim Hallett.

'Let's use that experience, Jim,' I said, as the kitbags were brought off the coach and delivered to us. 'This is the perfect opportunity to right the record and exorcise the demons of that 14–1 reversal at the hands of the rebels in San Angino. Let's seize it.'

Once everyone was in their kit, we jogged out to the crude pitch on the far side of the encampment where the Brigands XI were already warming up. The early signs, after kick-off, were encouraging and it was immediately clear to me that the still haunting humiliation of San Angino would not be revisited upon us on this occasion. For one thing, the brigands were clearly a less attacking outfit than the rebels. Also we had far less trouble acclimatising to the altitude and adapted fairly quickly to the entirely grassless, extremely uneven and liberally stony surface. Nevertheless, the brigands flooded the midfield and, outnumbered in the centre of the pitch, we simply didn't have the requisite answers to the questions they were repeatedly able to pose from deep. Accordingly, despite a hat-trick from me, we ran off 3–4 losers.

With the exception of Dick Stokes, now clutching the Colonel's table lamp, it was a disconsolate side that climbed back on the coach, ready to head down to Bagota City. However, Beppo eventually got a bit of a sing-song going and the mood had almost completely lightened by the time we arrived at the Bagota Stadium, right on cue to face our hosts in the scheduled evening showcase.

There were some perhaps inevitable signs of tiredness in the first half that night and we found ourselves 2–0 down at the interval. However, we were a galvanised force in the second half, with Blackie scoring one and me adding an equaliser. Scorer of the winner in the dying seconds? Rovers legend Jumbo Trudgeon.

'*Per aspera ad astra*, Roy,' said Jumbo, clapping me on the shoulder as we left the field to tumultuous applause.

Indeed.

The Sixties were, of course, a period of massive upheaval and change. Youth found a voice and rose up against the conservative norms that had dominated in the previous decade, the availability of the contraceptive pill radically altered sexual mores all around the world, including Melchester, and, from 1966, substitutes were allowed in English league football – just one at this stage, a twelfth man who could be brought on in the event of an injury, but for no other reasons, and certainly not tactically.

Ben Galloway was not, I'm sure, the only manager to spy a

loophole in this new legislation straight away. 'If you're having a shocker,' he told us in the dressing room on the first day of the season, 'start limping and give me the option.'

Personally, I didn't think that sort of conduct was in the spirit of the game, but clearly the law was virtually unenforceable as it was written and, sensibly, just two years later, in 1967, it was adapted to allow for tactical replacements, removing the moral quandary.

We were certainly grateful to be able to call a spare man off the bench in the 1969 European Cup final. That year we found ourselves once more in Paris, on a wonderful, warm May evening, contending for the trophy against Santova Rapid of Portugal. I've said all along that you can't beat Paris in the springtime – especially as the host city for a major club competition final – and I'd stand by those words today.

On the way into the ground, two hours before kick-off, with the lowering sun casting lovely long shadows across the concourse, Blackie paused briefly between the team bus and the players' entrance to pet a police horse, which he often enjoyed doing – but this time with disastrous consequences. The horse, perhaps not quite having enough time to pick Blackie out in those long shadows, reared up at the touch of his hand and delivered the trusting inside right a ferocious blow to the side of the head with its prodigious right hoof.

The kick dropped Blackie to his knees, but even as we turned and rushed to help him in our panic and concern, he was already clambering back to his feet.

'I'm absolutely fine,' he said. 'No problems whatsoever. Really.'

Blackie did seem to be entirely unaffected by the incident, changing and warming up exactly as normal. But I don't think it helped when, five minutes into the match, my oldest pal was then involved in the most almighty clash of heads with Santova Rapid's uncompromising stopper, José Dos Passos.

I can still hear the terrible 'thunk' as, diving towards a waist-high ball in the box, the in-rushing Blackie met the out-rushing Dos Passos in a rare forehead-to-forehead collision. Again, though, Blackie was almost immediately off his knees and up again, waving away Taff Morgan, who had come directly to the touchline with his bucket and sponge.

'Not a problem, everyone,' Blackie insisted. 'I'm totally OK.'

Alas, it was only twenty minutes after this when, stooping to clear a vicious in-swinging corner, Blackie managed to get his head to the ball, only for Dani Cristiano, Santova Rapid's gifted but careless international striker, to get his flying boot to Blackie's temple. How Blackie's head wasn't lifted clean off his neck by the blow, I still have no idea. Once again, Blackie was on his knees, but once again he picked himself off the ground.

'Perfectly fine,' said Blackie, as Taff now bound his head tightly in a turban-style bandage to at least partly stem the profuse bleeding. 'Just one of those things.'

And maybe he would, indeed, have been perfectly fine if, right on the verge of half-time, a desperate chase out wide to prevent a throw-in hadn't caused Blackie to fly off the edge of the pitch, trip on the surrounding cinder track and crack his head against the advertising hoarding.

'Right as rain, everyone,' Blackie said, springing up – only to clang his head yet again, this time hard against the underside of a fixed-position television camera, and go down again.

'All good,' he added, climbing up again and pausing only to tuck in a loose strand of the bandage before rejoining play.

Naturally, I kept a close eye on Blackie during the interval, but he was showing no untoward signs whatsoever – not even of mild dizziness. He drank his tea and sucked on his quartered orange perfectly normally, collaborated straightforwardly when Taff Morgan changed his sopping bandage, and appeared to pay close attention, as ever, to Ben Galloway's half-time team talk and said 'Yes, boss' when asked to track back more tightly over the next forty-five minutes. His eyes were bright, and he seemed entirely alert.

A minor alarm bell sounded, however, on the way out for the second half, when Blackie stopped me by the dressing room door.

'Merry Christmas, Roy,' he said, taking hold of my hand and shaking it firmly. 'And a happy new year to you and the family.'

And, with that, he set off up the tunnel.

That puzzled me slightly. Christmas was still seven months off, after all, and Blackie and I and our families would, I felt sure, be seeing each other on the day to exchange seasonal greetings, as we always did, every year.

However, Blackie's bafflingly untimely words didn't puzzle me nearly as much as what happened six minutes into the second half. Accepting my pass out wide near the halfway line, Blackie spun, jinked his way down the wing, cut inside, left three defenders standing in amazement, and side-footed home . . . into his own net.

Fifty-one minutes into a European Cup Final, in front of 74,590 fans and hundreds of thousands more watching on live, mostly black-and-white, television, Blackie Gray of Melchester Rovers had just run half the length of the pitch to put Santova Rapid 1–0 ahead.

Blackie's goal celebration took him on a long and necessarily solo gallop out to the touchline, where he then dropped to his knees in exultation – bloodied bandages flapping, chin tipped back, arms aloft – and finally passed out.

Ben Galloway already had Chris Ryan, our appointed number twelve, warming up. Blackie was stretchered off to a warm round of applause, especially from the Portuguese end of the ground, Chris came on, and we set about reducing the deficit.

Santova, though – as continental sides so often are – were

content to sit back, get men behind the ball and play on the break. Time and again, we probed, and time and again we came up against an unbreachable defensive wall. The breakthrough came in the eighty-eighth minute when I earned a free kick on the right-hand side of the penalty area and hung it up at the back stick. '*A pedibus usque ad caput*, Roy, m'boy,' shouted Jumbo Trudgeon, rising triumphantly to nod home.

Then, incredibly, with the referee already looking at his watch, and extra time seeming almost a certainty, I intercepted a loose pass just inside the opposition's half, beat three and crashed a speculative twenty-five-yarder in off the crossbar for 2–1.

The referee didn't even have time to restart the match. Rovers were champions of Europe, again.

It was fun breaking the news to Blackie when he finally came round the next day. He had been flown back overnight on the team plane, still unconscious, and then transferred to Melchester General Hospital, and a bunch of us went in that afternoon with some bags of grapes.

'Guess what, Blackie?' I said, laying his medal gently on the bed as my greatest friend blinked thickly from the pillow and tried to find a point of focus on the ceiling. 'We won the European Cup.'

'That's fantastic,' said Blackie.

'And you scored a world-class goal,' said Andy Croydon.

'Obviously, I'm pleased with that on a personal level,' said Blackie, wincing, 'but it's about how the team gets on, at the end of the day.'

'Except you scored it for them!' said Duncan McElway.

'You're kidding,' said Blackie faintly.

'No. An absolute peach – at the wrong end of the ground. Beat about five, rounded the keeper, slotted it home – world class!' shouted Terry West.

'Ah, well. They all count,' said Blackie. 'There's not many people who can say they scored a world-class goal in a European Cup final.'

'And there's even fewer who can say they scored it for the other side,' Terry added, perhaps slightly labouring the joke.

Looking back at it now, this whole incident, in many ways, told you all that you needed to know about Blackie Gray. Yes, the own goal had been a bit of a setback, and there were clearly questions to ask about our man-management with regard to the player that night – whether he should have been on the pitch at that point, or whether we should have withdrawn him after the third of his five head injuries, or possibly even earlier, after the second. But you had to respect the commitment of the man and the readiness to give everything to the cause, even when not, conventionally speaking, conscious. That was the kind of player Blackie was, and the kind of player England bred in those days, and (without wishing to take anything away from the current generation) breeds all too rarely now.

That 1969 European Cup victory was duly marked with an open-top bus parade through the streets of Melchester, followed by a reception at the Town Hall. I reckon the whole population must have turned out to see the trophy that day. The streets were stacked twelve deep and more, in places, with people cheering and waving up to us, twirling scarves and flapping banners, and the crowd was so thick outside the Town Hall that we had to make a special appearance out on the balcony to satisfy their demand. We felt like royalty. It was amazing and somehow humbling to see how much it meant to the people of Melchester.

And I was especially pleased, in the circumstances, that Blackie could be a part of it. The doctors weren't keen for him to be up and about so quickly, but we got around the problem by arranging for his hospital bed to be transferred onto the upper deck of the open-top bus for the afternoon, which meant that he could lie there as we drove around and soak up the atmosphere. The arrangement was that, after it had dropped us at the Town Hall, the bus would take Blackie back to the hospital where his bed would be craned-off and returned to the ward, with Blackie still in it. Unfortunately, caught up, I'm sure, in the excitement of the day, the driver forgot to make the detour, meaning that Blackie spent that night alone on the top deck, locked up in the dark in the Windsley Street Bus Depot and unable to rouse anyone with his shouting, which was, for obvious reasons, quite weak. Ah well. At least he had his bed. And he wouldn't have wanted to miss it. None of us would.

After the Town Hall dinner (prawn cocktail, beef Wellington, 'spotted dick' and custard) and an extremely flattering and moving speech by Alderman Cecil Warbhoys about the pride that our community took in us, some of the lads proposed going on to White Lace, one of the new-style discotheque/nightclubs that had begun opening in the centre of town, where, at the weekends, the bar stayed open until three a.m. and where a young and frequently miniskirted clientele could normally be found, happily dancing the night away to contemporary sounds by the likes of Mervyn Jay & The Jay-Notes, Diana Eden Plus Four, and The Pippins.

'You know what they say,' a well-refreshed Ken Cooper was heard to tell Alderman Warbhoys as they spilled out onto the street at the end of the evening. 'If you can't pull at White Lace, there's something up with your puller!'

I wanted to get an early night, though, so I didn't join them.

16

Penny (and Tony)

As the progressive, so-called 'swinging' Sixties gave way to the more troubled and politically complex Seventies, I could look back over a sixteen-year professional playing career in which I had won four league titles, two European Cups and four FA Cups. But looking back was not something I was temperamentally inclined to do. I preferred to look forward. I was thirty-two, on the books of the biggest club in the world, as hungry for success as I ever had been, and convinced that my best years were still to come.

I wasn't wrong.

In 1970, Melchester Rovers again put the FA Cup in the trophy cabinet and then went on, in 1971, to win the European Cup Winners Cup, defeating Standard Wasserdram of Belgium in a tight final at the Meltzburg Stadium in West Germany.

It was following this that Ben Galloway made two appointments which, in their very different ways, would shape the course of the rest of my life. First, to the surprise of a number of us, he brought in Tony Storme to act as assistant manager. Tony had had a brief spell at Rovers as a player, and had provided some valuable service from midfield when called upon, but he had never given any indication of being future management material. Indeed, Tony was mostly famous for his interest, bordering on an obsession, in magic – sleight of hand, card tricks, etc. He was forever pulling coins or rolled up pound notes from people's ears and shouting 'Ta-da!', in a way that, with constant repetition, seemed to irritate some of the lads. He had also not been averse to practising his magic at clearly inappropriate moments, such as during half-time team talks or, most famously, seventy-four minutes into a League Cup tie away at Stormont when he produced a pigeon from the referee's shorts and got sent off.

'It's just a bit of magic, ref,' Tony protested bitterly as the official, Mr J.D. Bandiman of Exerton, wrote his name into the notebook.

'Just leave it and go, Tony,' I said. 'The referee's decision is final. And you'd better take the pigeon with you. And the wand.'

Down to ten men, we struggled badly that afternoon, and it took a last-minute goal from me to spare Rovers the embarrassment of a major cup upset. With these memories still fresh, Ben's trust in Tony seemed unaccountable. It was hard not to worry how this might pan out for the club in the imminent future.

Secondly, Ben appointed a new secretary.

'Roy, meet Penny,' said Ben.

I confess that, up until this point of my life, I hadn't given affairs of the heart much thought. I had been concentrating on my game, living at home, cycling in and out of Mel Park most days, getting a lot of early nights. Finding someone to marry and settle down with simply wasn't something that preoccupied me, the way it clearly preoccupied some of the other lads – not least Lofty Peak, our recently signed formidably tall centre back, who seemed to be finding people to settle down with all the time. Duncan McKay, the tough, battling Scot who was also a new signing: he was another big finder of people to settle down with. And I lost count of the number of people Terry West found to settle down with – in Melchester town centre, at White Lace, in the hotels that we stayed in for away games, on pre-season tours, you name it! But this wasn't a project that detained me in the slightest. I was in no hurry. I figured that when the right person to settle down with came along, I would know.

I wasn't wrong about that, either.

The woman who looked across from the open filing cabinet that auspiciously sunny morning in the late summer of 1971 and gave a smile and a wave of greeting, had thick, shoulder-length black hair. She wore a pale tan cotton blouse, an orange patterned miniskirt and knee-length brown leather boots with a fashionably chunky heel. But these were not the things that connected with me straight away. What drew me to her immediately, inexorably, with a jolt of recognition that shot the length of my body, was her eyes. Dark, engaged, humorously inquisitive, immediately warm, they were eyes that seemed to understand; seemed to understand me, seemed to understand the world around us, seemed to understand everything.

It was like a light going on. In a flash I realised, as certainly as I had ever realised anything, that I had met the woman with whom I would eventually want to spend the rest of my life and that, in five years' time, I would finally marry her.

Penny said it was a slightly more gradual thing for her. At first she wasn't sure whether she fancied me or not. She said she felt some stirrings of attraction for my blond hair and firm jawline and she liked the way I behaved around people – 'kind of deferential, but at the same time solid,' was how she put it. But she was wary of the fact that I was a footballer. She hadn't dated a sportsperson before – unless you count bullfighting as a sport, which I personally don't, and neither did Penny. (For four months, Penny went out with a matador whom she had met while on a holiday in the newly developed Spanish resort of Malatorinos; she didn't talk a lot about that period with me, but she did say that she found this matador both exhausting and evasive.) Her previous boyfriends, so far as I could gather, had been archaeologists, marine scientists and Danish independent film makers. I got the impression that, in all of these cases, it had been Penny who ended it.

I tried for ages to summon the courage to ask her out. My half-baked plan was to try and 'bump into' her in the vicinity of Ben Galloway's office after training, when no one else was around, and ask her if she fancied lunch at the Shepherd's Market Café. I must have run through this scenario in my head a thousand times and rehearsed my part in it at home, in front of the bathroom mirror, a thousand more. It was quite a relief, then, when she saved me the bother.

'I've got an invitation to a private view thing tonight,' said Penny one morning, perfectly casually, passing me in the corridor. 'It's a plus-one. Do you fancy going? Might be quite interesting.'

'Yes!' I blurted. 'Fantastic!'

To be honest, I had no idea what she was talking about. A private view? A private view of what? Why private? What view?

'Great!' said Penny. 'It's at Mowbrays Gallery in Dorrick Street. I'll meet you outside at, what, seven-thirty?'

I was there at 6.43 and spent the ensuing forty-two minutes walking up and down the street, occasionally checking the state of my hair and my club suit in the reflection of the shop windows. I had plenty of time to wonder whether she wouldn't show up but, finally, there she was, coming round the corner in a brown striped midi-dress with a denim jacket over it and a pair of white clogs.

'Hey, you came!' she said, fixing me with those eyes of hers, so that I nearly melted on the pavement. 'I wasn't sure you would.'

'Ah, you know me,' I said. 'I never miss a viewing . . . in private . . . sort of thing.'

'Shall we?' said Penny, and we stepped into the gallery.

Just inside the door, a man in a black shirt offered a tray of drinks. Penny took a tall glass of white wine and I took an orange juice and we moved into the brightly lit and not especially crowded room.

Inside was an art exhibition. The work on display was by an artist from Denmark called Anders Jank and, according to the printed labels beside each piece, had puzzling and seemingly unrelated names like 'Spectrum IV' and 'Spectrum V'. It mostly seemed to be piles of builders' cement, left in the middle of the floor, with coloured pipe cleaners sticking out of them.

'What do you think, Roy?' said Penny.

I had no idea what I thought, or even why I should be thinking anything at all.

'Well . . .' I began.

'I think it's pretentious,' said Penny. 'Let's go.'

So we did, just like that – to Grantham's Wine Bar, where Penny ordered a mojito and I had a glass of water and we sat at a table lit by a candle stuck in a wine bottle and talked to each other – about football and secretarial work and marine science and bullfighting and pretty much anything that came to our minds.

And then, still talking, we walked a bit through Melchester where it was now lightly raining, as it often is – not that we cared or even really noticed – until Penny suddenly stopped and said, 'I live over that way.'

'OK,' I said. 'Well, my bike's still over by the gallery.'

We looked at each other for a moment, and Penny, her face slightly damp and glistening with the rain, smiled.

'Goodnight, Roy,' she said.

And then she leaned in and kissed me on the cheek and walked away.

That was it. We began dating regularly after that, going for dinners or drinks – not in a hasty way, taking it slowly, feeling each other out; once a week at first, for a year or so, and then twice a week, fixtures allowing, for another year, and eventually, after a third year, spending most Sundays together. And it was absolutely brilliant. I felt I was in a whole new world.

I learned so much from Penny. She was seven years younger than me, yet clearly far more mature than I was, in a worldly sense, and she awoke me to so many things.

Fondu, for instance. She couldn't believe it when I quietly admitted to her that I had never had fondu.

'You're a thirty-five-year-old man and you've never had fondu?' she said, aghast. 'For goodness sake! It's 1973! Maybe even 1974 at this point! Which would make you thirty-six!'

I shrugged and smiled sheepishly.

'Well, we're just going to have to do something about that, aren't we?' said Penny.

So, one night, we did. And, of course, the first time I was hopeless! I went at it in a ridiculous hurry, nervous as a kitten, prodding blindly, as you do, and only ending up with the stuff all over myself – and all over Penny and the surrounding linen! It was finished in seconds, and I don't suppose either of us felt remotely satisfied. I know I didn't! I could only apologise and try to cover my mortification, although, deep down, as both of us wiped ourselves off with napkins, I wondered whether I would ever in my life manage to have fondu properly.

But Penny (and this was definitely one of her key attributes, certainly in the early stages of our relationship) was wonderfully forgiving and patient. Later, we did it again and this time she showed me what to do – how to fork, how to go at it slowly, allow the burners underneath to do their work, get a nice, gentle but insistent rhythm going between the two of you and make it last for an evening. These were lessons I never forgot.

There were so many other lessons too. She had her own flat – a one-bedroomed place above a hairdresser's in South Woking Street. I was so impressed by that. It seemed so incredibly grown up – so responsible. The place was tiny, with a little galley kitchen, but always immaculately tidy, give or take the odd pile of books or records, and had fresh flowers in vases and ornaments on the mantelpiece. She took me to art galleries to look at paintings and sculptures. She took me to the cinema to see films which were French and had subtitles. She played me records on her little all-in-one hi-fi system – Sixties stuff, mostly: Mervyn Haye, Lotus Hedding, Stevie Wyman & The Heartaches. She persuaded me to learn to drive. ('You can't really take me out on your bike, Roy!') She bought me a book of love poems by the seventeenth-century metaphysical poet Henry Cunnycliffe, whom she said she loved, and read some of them to me while we lay on her sofa one evening after a fondu. I can confidently say that – speaking personally, as distinct from professionally – I had never been happier.

In due course, after a couple of years, I took her home to meet my mum – a sure sign that we were getting serious! Mum, of course, loved her (as did Mr Sexton from next door, who happened to be there) and made a ridiculous fuss, producing an enormous coffee and walnut sponge and plates of cucumber sandwiches and a tray of chocolate-coated flapjacks, as well as a home-made Battenberg and some almond slices. I kept saying, 'Mum – it's nine in the morning!' But it didn't make any difference; out came the macaroons and the scones with clotted cream and jam, regardless!

I did wonder whether part of Mum might be upset at the prospect, now so clearly raised by Penny's arrival on the scene, of her only son leaving home – a premonition of the 'empty nest' syndrome, as it were. But if the thought entered Mum's mind at all, she certainly didn't show it – and, of course, she had the company of Mr Sexton, who seemed to be around nearly all the time now. Dad, by this time, had long since fled to Spain with the eldest Sexton girl, Bethany – for the sun, mostly. He was finding the cold and damp of an English winter increasingly hard on his chest, Mum had said, so I'm sure he found some relief in the warmth there. We never heard from him, though. Which might sound odd, but you've got to remember that Spain, and indeed all of the continent, felt a lot further away in those days – not like today, with Easyplane and the internet making it that much easier for people to stay in touch.

Penny, of course, for her own part, was charming at that first meeting, and ate as much of Mum's baked goods as she could get down, given the time of day and that she had only recently finished a bowl of muesli and a pot of yoghurt back at her flat. She certainly passed the audition! Afterwards, Mum described her as 'a really nice girl' – and, in Mum's lexicon, there genuinely was no higher term of praise. I knew Penny had the all-important seal of approval.

If only the same could have been said for Tony Storme . . .

I don't think any of us begrudged Ben Galloway his decision, at the beginning of the 1975–6 season, to go upstairs. Ben had been manager of Melchester Rovers for an incredible forty-six years. He had joined the club at a relatively low point in its history and had steered it through its most successful period, transforming it from an outfit in the doldrums into an unparalleled force in world football. Most recently, in the 1972–3 season, he had helped us to a League and Cup double – a first for the club – and then managed us to a third European Cup victory the following year. In football, of course, there is no such thing as having seen and done it all; but there could be no denying that Ben had seen an awful lot of it, and no contesting his right to believe that he had, possibly, taken the club as far as he, personally, could. His desire, and indeed his right, to step back, remove himself from the firing line and accept a more administrative role as general manager and, within that, have more time to spend with his wife Bunty and their two wonderful children, who had by now grown up and left home, was regretfully but entirely accepted by everyone.

That move, of course, left a vacancy at the club for a manager. I talked to Penny about it over dinner one night.

'Why don't you put yourself forward?' she said. 'You're clearly player-manager material.'

I laughed.

'Oh, Penny. They'll be looking for someone with a deep and proven experience of the game at the highest levels, a genuine figurehead who can inspire respect and who was perhaps once the recipient of a school report stating that he had a steadying influence on his fellow pupils.'

'That's exactly what I'm talking about, Roy Race!' smiled Penny.

I also talked to Blackie about the conversation I had had with Penny. Blackie was silent for quite a long time.

'What's the matter, Blackie?' I asked.

'Nothing, really, Roy,' he said, sighing and scuffing lightly at the ground in front of him with the toe of his shoe. 'It's just that, in the past, before you had Penny in your life, that was the kind of conversation you would have had with me – and only me.'

I was sad to see my oldest friend clearly laid low by my apparent desertion of him for another. However, soon after this, Blackie met, immediately fell in love with and very quickly married Celia

Upton, then the reigning Miss Melchester, later a renowned catalogue model, and the subject of the intimacy that the two of us no
longer shared never came up again.

The fact was, it didn't matter whom I talked to about it – the
choice of our next manager was going to be Ben Galloway's and
Ben Galloway's alone. I can see that there's a general argument to
be had about whether an outgoing manager should be allowed to
choose his successor. But given Ben's standing within the club, it
wasn't even a matter for debate. The week before the season started,
Ben Galloway called me into his office.

'It's about the manager's role,' he said.

'Can I just say, boss,' I interjected, 'that you've absolutely earned
the right to make this choice, and whoever you eventually decide to
hand the role on to, they, and you, can be sure of my continued and
unstinting support.'

Ben smiled, and looked genuinely touched. 'Thanks, Roy,' he
said.

And then he told me that he had decided to promote his assistant, Tony Storme.

'Sense of thwarted ambitions, Roy?' asked the always pertinent
Bob Dickens of the *Melchester Evening Chronicle*, a beat reporter
who was newly arrived on the scene, for whom I would always
have the utmost respect and whom (as you may remember from
way back at the beginning of this book) I would eventually appoint
to help me put this story of mine in order. We were speaking at a
pre-season press conference, or 'presser', as we always referred to
them.

'The only ambitions I have right now, Bob,' I replied, 'are to help
Tony Storme turn Melchester Rovers into a league-winning force
this season.'

'But you must have been gutted not to have been asked,' pursued

Bob Dickens, who would always probe that little bit further than the average reporter and whose prose style put him a cut above the rest.

'I'll be gutted if we don't beat Portdean on Saturday afternoon,' I replied.

Bob Dickens narrowed his eyes in a way that was both piercingly intelligent and ineffably handsome, and closed his notebook.

I guess one or two quiet warning bells sounded in my mind about Tony Storme when he wore a top hat for the start-of-season team photo. I can't say his team talk for that opening day game against Portdean was entirely convincing, either: it basically involved him using the treatment table to do a long and elaborate cup-and-ball trick, at the end of which he simply said, 'Now, go out there and win, me duckies.' Nevertheless, as we took to the pitch in front of a crowd of 79,453, I looked up to see that the fans at Mel Park had hung a banner over the advertising hoarding in the middle tier of the West Stand, reading: 'Tony Storme: The Chosen One'. If the fans could get behind him, I reasoned, so could the captain.

Sadly, we were chaotically disorganised that afternoon against Portdean and lost 3–0 – our worst ever opening day result and the start of a disappointing run of form that would last all the way up to Christmas. Those initial warning bells about Tony only grew when he started sitting in the dugout in a floor-length black cape, decorated with silver stars of various sizes, and conducting his business from the touchlines with a white-tipped wand. When he wanted a player to come off, for instance, he would leap forward, dramatically flourishing the wand, and shout 'Shazoooma!' He also began signing off his press interviews with a big thumbs-up and the phrase, 'That's magic!'

The press lapped all this up, of course. For them, Tony was an uncompromising maverick and a breath of fresh air – and great copy. Behind the scenes, though, there were worrying signs that he might be losing the dressing room. I walked in there one day to hear Duncan McKay saying, 'If that w***er produces those bloody steel rings one more time . . .' Duncan saw me and immediately stopped what he was saying, and the group of players who were around him rather embarrassedly broke up. But it was too late; I had taken note of the rising antipathy towards the new and, as yet, entirely unconvincing manager.

The watershed moment came early in January. Jumbo Trudgeon was out for three weeks, having been hit in the eye by a champagne cork at a New Year's Eve party thrown by the Marquis of Hanningdale. It seemed to me that the obvious solution was to bring in Gary Spennymuir from the youth development squad, who had trained with the first team on a number of occasions and had always looked the part. Tony Storme, however, had different ideas.

'Roy, I want you to meet the legendary Sammy Spangler,' said Tony. In front of me stood a tall, slight figure with immaculately coiffed blond hair, and wearing a black singlet and Capri pants.

'So spesh to meet you,' said Sammy Spangler, smiling with a set of unusually white and uncommonly straight teeth for the 1970s in Britain, and offering a hand. His shake was weak and a little clammy, although there's nothing whatsoever wrong with that and I tried not to judge him in any way on the basis of it.

'I want Sammy to replace Jumbo Trudgeon in the inside left role,' said Tony Storme. 'Show him around, would you?'

I took Sammy Spangler down to the changing rooms and helped him find an empty locker. Along the way, I asked him about his career.

'Well, I was taught to juggle in France by the great André Flambert,' said Sammy Spangler. 'I did circus work for a couple of years around Europe, and a bit of vaudeville, then came back to

Britain where I got a break on the television show, *New Talents*. The work's been coming pretty much non-stop since!'

'And, er, football?' I asked.

'Love it,' said Sammy Spangler. 'Absolutely love it. Haven't played all that much, to be honest. But, you know – looking forward to the challenge.'

I left Sammy to get changed and went out to the pitch feeling more than a little troubled. However, when he duly emerged, and with the introductions accomplished, all seemed more or less OK for the first section of Taff Morgan's session. Taff had us, as usual, doing light running and stamina work and Sammy looked fine – possibly in slightly better shape than some of the lads, if I'm being frank.

But then the balls came out and immediately it became apparent that we had a serious problem. Sammy appeared to have no natural talent for the game at all. The ball would go under his feet, or past him, and he would turn and chase after it, talking and shouting, 'Dammit! Dammit!'

I went back to see Tony Storme at the end of the session.

'Tony,' I said, 'I'm not questioning your managerial acumen here, in any sense. But some of the lads are muttering a bit about Sammy Spangler and what you think he can bring to the table, and it would just be useful for me to hear it from you, so I can convey it back to them and put their minds at rest.'

'The lad Spangler's a genius, Roy,' said Storme, with a glazed, almost evangelical look in his eye. 'An absolute genius. I first saw him juggle during a summer season variety show at Butley Tower last year, where he did some utterly wonderful stuff with some lit torches. Caught one in his teeth, at one point, Roy! The thing's alight! Amazing bit of business.'

'And the application of this to football?' I asked, as mildly as I could.

'Open your imagination, Roy. Agility, courage, poise, a total unflappability under pressure, innovative and well-crafted bits of business . . . what team wouldn't want some of that in the mix? Plus, football is show business, Roy. If the Seventies thus far have shown us one thing, it's this. And in the magical illusions of show business we glimpse beyond the limits of the possible and lose ourselves completely, don't you agree?'

'Fair enough,' I said. 'I take all that on board, and I will relay it. But could you at least talk to him about wearing the sparkly tights at training? I think some of the lads are finding it a bit hard to see past the tights.'

'Once a showman . . .' said Storme, and he winked and tipped his top hat at me. And, as he tipped it, a dove appeared in his right hand.

'That's actually quite impressive, Tony,' I said.

Fortunately fate decreed that Sammy Spangler would make his debut at the beginning of January in a third-round FA Cup tie at home to non-league Sleeford Town. In prospect, matches don't come much easier than that, especially if you are looking to blood a juggler with no prior first team experience – no offence to Sleeford, obviously, whom we would treat with the utmost respect, come the day. But essentially, although you can never entirely write off the possibility of a banana skin, this was a giant mismatch in which we would most likely bang in a hatful, Sleeford would get a large lump of the gate money, which could make the difference between extinction and survival for a club at that level, and everyone would go home happy – even, with a bit of luck, Sammy Spangler.

Alas, Spangler was immediately out of his depth, even against non-league opposition, and I'm afraid that, after about five minutes and a similar number of basic errors on his part, we simply stopped passing to him. Entirely against the run of play, the visitors took the lead in the thirty-third minute with a heavily deflected shot which was probably heading for the corner flag before it struck the cowering Spangler on the shoulder blade and rocketed into the top corner. The opposition then spent the remainder of the game getting men behind the ball – as is entirely their right – and, because we were playing in effect with ten men, we were powerless to make the breakthrough. When the referee blew the final whistle, Sleeford had nicked the tie and a lucrative berth in the Fourth Round. It was the most humiliating result in the history of the Rovers. Our fans left the ground in a state of shock, the riotous jeering of the away supporters blowing them up the road as they returned to their coaches.

Sammy Spangler was a shell of a man in the dressing room afterwards, mortified by his failure to perform and by the howling opprobrium that had rained down on him from the stands. 'They were never like this at Butley Tower,' he kept saying, close to tears. I did my best to console him, suggesting that it wasn't his fault at all, that he had been promoted beyond his ability to cope and that he shouldn't worry about it. I also pointed out that he still had juggling, and that, moreover, he would always have juggling, and that not many of us could say the same. He seemed a little consoled by that.

I was expecting Tony Storme to come in and accept his share of the responsibility at this dark moment in the club's history, but he didn't show up. Neither did he wait around after the match to attend the press conference and offer the room a hearty 'That's magic!'. Indeed, that evening, Tony Storme did what magicians have been doing since time immemorial: he disappeared.

On the Monday morning I was summoned to a meeting in the chairman's office with John Mason and a slightly sheepish Ben Galloway.

'Well, the good news,' said John Mason, 'is that Tony Storme has contacted his sister. He's in a B&B in Belgium, apparently, trying to get his head back in the right place.'

'Why Belgium?' I asked.

'Because that's where you go,' said Mason.

'Some kind of mental breakdown, do you suppose?' I asked. 'Should we be reaching out to him in some way?'

Mason shook his head. 'In years to come, people may arrive at a more understanding stance on mental health issues within the sporting workplace, but right now, as far as I'm concerned, Storme is fired and off our hands. We need to draw a line, as a club, appoint a new manager and move on.'

'Any idea who that new manager should be?' I asked.

Ben Galloway said, 'We're looking for someone with a deep and proven experience of the game at the highest levels, a genuine figurehead who can inspire respect and who perhaps was once the recipient of a school report stating that he had a steadying influence on his fellow pupils.'

There was a silence. Both Mason and Galloway were staring at me. I felt my heart quicken.

'Are you . . . offering me the player-managership of Melchester Rovers,' I asked hesitantly. 'With immediate effect, subject to salary negotiations?' I added.

'You're the right man at the right time,' said Ben Galloway.

'And you always were,' said John Mason.

And just like that, I was in charge of the Rovers.

Penny and I were married in the summer of 1976, at the end of my first half-season in player management – a period in which I had managed to right the rocking boat a bit, bring some much-needed stability and take us back up the table, albeit that the damage had already been done during Tony Storme's spell in charge, and there was no hope of contesting the title, even after the sixteen-game unbeaten run with which the club marked my arrival. I also made some amends for the FA Cup disappointment by taking us through to the League Cup final, although sadly we lost on the day to Horndean, courtesy of a hotly disputed goal. (With the score at 1–1, a late shot from Horndean stalwart Dave Cassock hit the crossbar, bounced down and came out, but the ball was adjudged to have crossed the line by the linesman with the red flag, Mr D.H. Tilson from Market Darborough.)

Still, the wedding was potentially a good way to lift the spirits after that Wembley setback, get at least something out of the year, and, with a bit of luck, begin to put those 1975–6 blues behind us. Penny and her mum Shirley (whom I haven't mentioned and whom I really must!) spent ages planning everything – the church, the hymns, the vicar, the bridesmaids, the dress, the flowers, the food, the table arrangements, the place cards, the music, the cake and on and on and on and on and on and on it went! You could tell how much it meant to them.

Come the big day, Blackie was my best man, a role which caused him some anxiety in the run-up. He came to see me about it one night.

'I'm worried about the speech, Roy,' said Blackie.

'Honestly, Blackie – just say what you like,' I said. 'No one's going to worry if you step over the mark. That's what a best man's speech is!'

'Yeah, but, you see, that's my problem,' said Blackie. 'Normally, in a best man's speech, you'd tell a few stories that showed the groom in a comically bad light – talk about the embarrassing things he'd got up to down the years, the occasions when he'd got drunk, said stupid things, made a complete berk of himself. And, in your case, there aren't any.'

'Oh, come off it, Blackie,' I said. 'There must be! There always are!'

I thought about it for a while. And I had to concede, after a few minutes of racking my brains, that it wasn't easy to come up with something.

'I know!' I said eventually. 'What about that time I missed a penalty against second-division Actringham in the third round of the FA Cup! That was embarrassing – no disrespect to Actringham. Their goalkeeper guessed correctly and palmed it out.'

'I'm not sure that's really going to do it,' said Blackie. 'Plus you netted the rebound. And we were already four–nil up.'

I thought again.

'Hmm,' I said, after a few more minutes. 'You may have a point here.'

So, we reached a compromise where, on the day, Blackie stood up and said some lovely words about Penny, told a joke about a greengrocer's wife, a courgette and a coal scuttle, and then read out a full list of my honours as a Melchester Rovers player. It seemed to go down well.

Before the reception, the lads had lined up in their Melchester Rovers strips to form a guard of honour outside the church. Confetti flew, Penny threw her bouquet to the bridesmaids and I punted out a couple of signed footballs to the crowd that had gathered on the opposite pavement, making a good connection in both cases and managing to get it up and down in a short space, which is often quite tricky. Then we had the wedding breakfast and the speeches, in the chairman's dining suite at Mel Park. And then, breathless and actually rather skittish with the joy of it all, Penny and I were driven in a cream-coloured limo to the Copwick Grange Hotel near Beston for our first night together as man and wife.

Ripple, dissolve, fade!

And on the Sunday morning we flew to Stygikos in Crete for our honeymoon in a beautiful five-star resort, sorted out for us by John Mason, the club chairman, with our own private chalet and plunge pool and a good range of fitness equipment in the hotel gym facility, although perhaps a broader range of dumb-bells on the weight-rack might have not gone amiss.

It was an utterly blissful experience – just the two of us, completely away from it all, lying in the sun, playing in the warm Mediterranean water, eating wonderful food, utterly focussed on each other and talking together about every subject on earth for a whole week, albeit that on the Wednesday I had to leave and fly on to Turkey to appear for a Pan-European XI in a fundraiser for the cash-strapped Turkish side Kyriktas, whose ground had been hit by a landslide. But I was back by Saturday evening and the bliss resumed until the following day when we flew home.

I was earning decent money now – not the kind of sums that today's top players earn, obviously, with the money that has come in from television, but, comparatively speaking, an extremely comfortable wage. Plus I had been able to salt a fair bit away while living at Mum's all those years. So we were able to buy a lovely five-bedroom new-build detached house in leafy Hinton Wood in west Melchester, with an en suite bathroom and a double garage and a terrace beyond the French windows, and a sweep of lawn beyond the terrace. And Penny picked out the carpets and the curtains and a wonderful brown leather three-piece suite and within a matter of moments, it seemed to me, our house was a home.

We didn't have security gates, or even tall hedges. We came and went as we pleased and just got on with our lives perfectly happily. Everyone knew this was where Mr and Mrs Roy Race lived, and nobody seemed to make a big thing about it.

Yes, boys from the nearby estate often gathered in clusters outside the house on their bikes – but they were no trouble. Sometimes they might want an autograph, but most of the time they just wanted to say hello or ask, 'How's the game going to go tomorrow, Roy?' But these were more innocent times in which to be a so-called 'celebrity', when the cry of 'There's someone in the garden with a Chopper' caused none of the unease that it would be likely to induce today.

Day sped after day in a cavalcade of pleasure and new-found married contentment. It wasn't long before Penny was saying to me, 'I think it's time for us to take the next step, don't you, Roy?'

'What, get a barbecue?' I said.

'That's not what I mean at all, Roy,' said Penny softly, running her forefinger around the rim of my ear.

Supper that night was fondu and very shortly after that Penny was pregnant.

17

New Arrivals

That mid-to-late 1970s Melchester Rovers side – the team that I partly inherited from the Ben Galloway era and partly constructed within my new role as player-manager – holds a special place in the hearts of Melchester Rovers fans, and always will. It contained a number of players who earned a permanent and prominent position in the pantheon of Rovers legends.

For instance, there was Charlie 'The Cat' Carter, the goalkeeper whom I brought into the side on the back of some stunningly agile performances for the reserves. (Tubby Morton couldn't have been more reasonable about making way and going back to the bench, incidentally. He was up to forty-three stone by this time and I think he quite liked having the opportunity to sit down.) And in front of Charlie we had Duncan 'Big Dunc' McKay and Lofty Peak shoring it up at the back, and Merv Wallace alongside me up front and Geoff Giles who would run all day, and, on his days off, sometimes did. (One of my big regrets as a manager is letting Geoff go to newly promoted Melboro, where he returned to haunt us on a couple of occasions. But if a player wants away, I don't believe a club should stand in his path.)

There was a lot of character in that side – and a lot of characters. There was Noel Baxter – the clown of the team, always ready with a whoopee cushion or a boiled sweet that turned out to contain mustard or some other prank to lighten the tone and keep us all sane when the pressure was at its most intense. The lads loved Noel – and frequently gave him as good as they got, locking the continuously grinning redhead in a lavatory for a whole weekend, encouraging the coach to drive off and leave him behind after any number of away games, and booking him into another hotel entirely on so many occasions that I lost count! Every club, to my mind, needs a Noel Baxter figure.

Then there were the hard men – and none harder than Big Dunc McKay. Big Dunc was famous for having started a fight in an empty house. The empty house in question was the one he had just moved into, over at Rollerton Grove, and he was waiting in for the removal men to arrive with his furniture when he looked out and saw some blokes on the other side of the pavement whom, for some reason, Big Dunc didn't like the look of. Big Dunc threw up the sash and shouted, 'Oi, you lot: want some?' And, just like that, it was on. (These were the Seventies, don't forget, the time of industrial unrest, Glam Rock and permanently available street violence.) Apparently the ensuing scrap lasted for about four hours, with numbers swelled by the removal men, who arrived, saw what was happening, put Big Dunc's reproduction rosewood sideboard down in the front garden and joined in. The altercation only stopped when everyone was exhausted and agreed to go to the pub instead – where, having taken some to time recover and get their breath back, they resumed in the car park. I'm not really sure how the scoring works on those occasions but, in Big Dunc's version of the story, he won. He normally did, though!

Merv Wallace, too, with his trademark dark moustache and long, unkempt hair, had quite a temper on him. I once saw him pull three lockers off the wall and crush the treatment table with his knee after having become enraged while trying to untie a knot in his bootlace. He was also not above disputing refereeing decisions and getting in the face of the officials in an intimidating manner – which I did not in any way condone and did my best to discourage. The way I saw it, referees had a hard enough job as it was without having Merv Wallace threatening to pour petrol in their garden ponds and set light to it, or let off a fire extinguisher down their throats. At the same time, it was clear to me that, if you took that side of Merv away completely, you risked losing the player. So it was about handling these people, trying to direct their aggression positively, putting an arm round them from time to time, and calling the police only when strictly necessary.

Merv was very much at the heart of things during the remarkable 1976–7 season – an extraordinary term in the history of the club by any standards. After a pre-season tour in the war-riven African nation of M'zele, including a relatively uncomplicated kidnapping (Wutu Rebel Forces 2, Melchester Rovers 7), we returned to England to learn that Meadways Supermarkets had announced a prize of £30,000 for the first player to net fifty league and cup goals in the ensuing campaign. These were the days when £30,000 was a lot of money, and, as a consequence, there was quite a bit of excited chatter about it among the lads – and, of course, in the media, which is presumably what Meadways were after.

Let me make my feelings about this absolutely clear: I was entirely against the Meadways 'Goal Rush', as they wittily dubbed it. You didn't need to be a genius to work out how it was going to dominate, and potentially even warp, the narrative of the season and I couldn't see how it would be anything but an unhelpful distraction. The thought of players ball-hogging and greedily going for goal in order to increase their tallies, rather than taking a view on the best available option in each developing in-game scenario, horrified me. Indeed, on a moral level, the bonus culture which was now creeping into the game (for scoring, for winning trophies, for appearing, whatever) was anathema to me and totally outside the spirit of the game as I saw it. I appreciate that people have families to care for and futures to tend to, but even so, it has always been my firm belief that if you need a cash incentive in order to get up in the morning and be inspired to give the best of yourself on a football field, then you are in the wrong sport and probably ought to have become a professional golfer.

Sure enough the 'Goal Rush', and the question of who was likely to clinch the money, was pretty much all that the fans and the press could talk about in the early weeks of that season. I found myself tipped hotly, along with Merv Wallace, and also Eddie Hamilton of free-scoring Gatesfield. In order to take some of the personal sting out of the issue, I immediately announced that, in the event of me winning the £30,000, I would donate it to a worthwhile sports-based charity in the local community. But that little ploy backfired when I was immediately besieged by local charity workers, all desperate to convince me that their project should be the beneficiary. That was a real lesson to me about the disadvantages of using the press to counter the press: wishing to douse a media fire, I had merely succeeded in creating a bigger one.

Meanwhile, the goals kept going in, regardless. I was bagging a hatful that season, and so was Merv Wallace. (Eddie Hamilton wasn't far behind but, in his determination to get in the way of a team-mate's shot and be credited with a crucial deflection, he ruptured a testicle which put him on the sidelines for a week and effectively took him out of the running.) The only consolation, from my point of view, was that, on the back of all those goals, the Rovers were creating an ongoing football story to rival the running Meadways story. Starting just after Christmas, we went on a massive unbeaten league run that looked set to eclipse the club's previous record of nineteen games undefeated.

We equalled the record away at Sandford in an extraordinary, error-strewn 4–4 draw, despite an injury crisis which had forced me to make five changes to the side, including bringing in Tubby Morton for Charlie 'The Cat' Carter, who had picked up a niggle. In truth, Tubby had never been in worse shape, and I probably would have risked young Terry Venner from the youth side if he hadn't been involved in an unfortunate career-ending lawnmower accident on the eve of the match. (Terry was lying on the ground doing some stretches after staying behind to complete some extra training on his own – which tells you a lot about the kind of player Terry was. In fairness to the groundsman, he wouldn't have seen him.) But, as ever, Tubby dug deep on the day and pulled off a stunning save in the dying seconds to keep the undefeated run going. We tried to chair him off afterwards, but failed.

The team was back to full strength for the next game, at home to struggling Everpool, and with in excess of 74,572 eager supporters packing the stands, all the signs indicated that a new record was in the offing. However, it turned out to be one of those afternoons. The ball simply wouldn't go in the net. We had thirty-four shots on target, hit the post nine times and the bar fourteen times. We also had 106 corners, which was a new league record. Alas, that was the only record to be broken that day. Everpool went up the other end in the ninetieth minute and scored with an in-swinging corner of their own (the only one they had) that caught the inside of the far post and dropped over the line.

When we followed that disappointment with a Tuesday night defeat at Barmouth, I was beginning to worry for our title chances. However, a 3–1 win at Walford settled a few nerves and it was all set up for the final game of the season, at home to struggling Tynecaster, where a win would see us crowned champions.

But, of course, there was one other matter to be resolved as well. My goal at Walford, which saw me combining nicely with Gerry Holloway and Roger 'Super Sub' Dixon, had taken my personal tally to forty-nine for the season – one shy of the £30,000 'Goal Rush' prize. Merv Wallace was just behind me on forty-seven. Saturday's game was clearly going to be a decider in more ways than one.

Anticipation was, inevitably, high among the supporters, and the gates to the ground had to be closed an hour before kick-off, leaving thousands more out in the street, straining for news. Once again, as we ran out, I had cause to marvel at the sheer electricity generated by a packed-to-bursting Mel Park. How much of what I achieved in my career do I owe to the energy generated by those fans? It's a cliché, I know, but the thing about clichés is, they tend to be true: it was like having a twelfth man on your side, a whole extra player, another heart.

Merv Wallace struck early to disperse the tension. He then added another from my cross – bringing us level for the season, with forty-nine goals apiece, and both just one short of the Meadways money, not that I was concerned with that. Late in the game Jimmy Slade came off the bench to make it 3–0, putting the day's real issue – the destination of the title – beyond doubt.

Time was clearly running out, though, and, to the despair of the crowd, neither Merv nor my yet-to-be-nominated local sports-based charity were looking likely to be the beneficiary of a significant cash boost.

There must have been just seconds remaining when I found myself on the edge of the opposition's penalty area. Looking up, I noticed, as so often, Merv and his lank hair ghosting in on the right-hand side, entirely unmarked. I leaned back and dinked a nicely weighted pass into my fellow forward's path, where Merv had time to take a touch and then, from the edge of the six-yard box, chip the rapidly advancing goalkeeper.

Goal, surely. Goal number fifty for Merv! Goal Rush decider!

Or was it?

Merv's chip rose over the keeper – but agonisingly slowly. The keeper turned and hared back towards his line as the ball fell goalwards. I, meanwhile, had continued my run into the box, in case of a rebound. (Youngsters take note: it's always good to follow in because you never know how the ball might break. Having passed, don't stand and admire your handiwork: continue your run.) I realised that there was a decent chance that the keeper would get there in time to palm the ball away. I had to make sure.

With the ball still falling, I flung myself forwards. The keeper flung himself too, and the pair of us came together in a tangle of limbs on the goal-line. But I was, by the narrowest of margins, ahead of him. I stretched my neck, felt the oh-so-familiar and oh-so-satisfying smack of the ball against my forehead, watched the net bulge ahead of me and heard the ground explode with noise.

The referee (Mr D.T. Hobsbawn of Billyhampton) didn't even have time to restart the match. Rovers had won the title, and the Goal Rush prize had found a home.

Blackie was the first team-mate to reach me. 'You've only gone and had away the Meadways booty, Roy!' he shouted.

Merv Wallace – all credit to him – was next to arrive. 'What a way to wind up the season!' he bellowed. 'What are you going to spend it on, Racey?'

'No, but you don't get it,' I said. 'Didn't you see what happened just then?'

But there was too much noise. The crowd was going nuts, the team was bouncing around. I couldn't make my team-mates understand – let alone the crowd, who were chanting my name in selflessly euphoric delight at my new-found fortune. I realised that I needed to get on the tannoy and put everyone in the picture.

I left the pitch and dashed up the steps to the PA platform above the tunnel, took the microphone and held out my arms. A hush fell over the ground.

'First of all,' I said, when the whining of the feedback had died away, 'I want to thank the greatest fans in the world for helping us bring the title back to Melchester. Couldn't have done it without you!'

There was a huge cheer at this, and then the ground fell quiet again.

'But as far as the Goal Rush is concerned,' I went on, 'you're cheering the wrong man if you think it's me.'

'What?' said a conveniently audible voice in the crowd. 'But you were the only one in the running, Roy.'

'You're forgetting Merv Wallace,' I said. 'Merv needed a hat-trick today – and Merv, in fact, got a hat-trick, including a goal in the very last minute of the match.'

'What?' said that convenient voice again. 'But it was you who scored in that scramble in the dying seconds, Roy.'

'No,' I said. 'It wasn't. Go home and watch *The Big Match of the Week* presented by Billy Dill on your televisions tonight. There I am sure you will see it conclusively demonstrated by the cameras that the ball had crossed the line from Merv's lob *before* I made contact with it. The goal is Merv's – and so is the prize!'

There was a murmur which gradually grew in volume and was

eventually swelled by applause and then cheering and, over the top of that, a chant: 'Mer-vyn! Mer-vyn! Mer-vyn!'

Up on the gantry, Merv looked me deep in the eyes.

'Roy, I don't know what to say . . .'

I was about to put my arms around him in congratulation when I felt someone urgently tugging at my shirtsleeve. I turned to see Ben Galloway. He looked as pale and as grave as I had ever seen him.

'I've just had a phone call from the hospital,' he said. 'You'd better get over there.'

Anxiety immediately flooded through me.

Penny!

My pregnant Penny!

I didn't even bother to get changed. I pushed my way past everyone on the platform, dashed out of the back door of the stand, jumped into my car and drove – drove wildly, almost blindly, like an automaton through the blessedly deserted streets to Melchester General.

And then I was running along corridors and up stairs, the clacking of my studs causing people to turn and stare as I swept past them, until I was on the third floor and banging through the swing doors onto the maternity ward, only half-aware of the matron stepping towards me, concern on her face, and saying, 'Oh, Mr Race – I'm sorry but you're too late' and almost pushing her aside and continuing my run down the ward, looking from side to side, looking from bed to bed, looking in panic, looking for . . .

Penny! There on the bed in the furthest corner propped up on pillows and smiling and holding something, something small and swaddled, and saying, 'Your son, Roy!' . . .

My son!

. . . 'And also your daughter!' – pointing to a plastic crib beside the bed containing something else small and swaddled . . .

And also my daughter!

Twins!

'One of each,' said Penny. 'Aren't I clever?'

'Maybe we could have done with that thirty thousand after all,' I said, not meaning it, just saying it dumbly, as a joke, for something to say, and then I broke down and wept with joy as a father for the first time because the arrival of two children *and* a league title on the same day – well, surely nobody on earth has the right to be this lucky.

18

Temptation and Despair

It's the most difficult job in the world. Nothing prepares you for it. It will drive you to the brink, at times, and yet it will also be the most rewarding thing that you ever embark upon. Everyone tells you this beforehand, and you listen and nod and perhaps think, deep down, that they're probably exaggerating. And then it happens to you and you realise that, if anything, they underplayed it!

But managing a leading top-flight football club was really only half of my problems as the 1970s gave way to the 1980s, because I was also having to accustom myself to the trials and tribulations of being a new parent. Twins, I probably don't need to tell you, are quite a handful! The nappies, the sleepless nights, the crying, the washing – it's everything-times-two for whoever ends up doing it! And Penny and I certainly didn't make the workload any easier for her in 1980, when, with Roy Junior and Melinda by then highly active and extremely demanding three-and-a-half-year-olds, we produced our second beautiful daughter, Diana.

It helped, of course, that we were blissfully happy. But, looking back, I only wish I could have been around more to help out domestically. You miss so much just by not being there. Had I simply been a player at this stage of my career, of course, things could have been different. Players tend to train in the mornings and then go home at lunchtime and, although they are often on the road, they get to spend a fair amount of time around the house, comparatively speaking. Indeed, I always think of something that Blackie said to me, a couple of years after he and his wife Celia had devoted themselves to raising their lovely sons, Dwayne (now head of youth development at Blakelock Athletic) and Marlon (a big figure on the Melchester cage-fighting scene): 'You know what I'll always regret, Roy?' said Blackie mournfully. 'Seeing quite so much of my children while they were growing up.'

But that certainly wasn't my problem. My days were packed. I was going into the club very early in the morning, and then training with the team, and then, after lunch, I would have several more hours of managerial office-work to do, prior to my own personal afternoon session in the gym and a five-mile run. And sometimes in the evening, even if the Rovers weren't playing, I would head off with Ben Galloway to watch a match, maybe to look at a player we were interested in or to run my eye over an upcoming opponent. It was around this time that I began to learn how to pilot a helicopter – not just because the challenge fascinated me, but also to make the travelling I was doing up and down the country that much easier. Even then, there were many nights when, by the time I got home, Penny and the kids would frequently be asleep, and they would often still be asleep when I crept out as softly as I possibly could in the morning.

Still, this was the routine of our lives at this time, and we were hardly going to complain about it. Or I wasn't, anyway. We were exceptionally lucky people and we knew it.

However, a huge change in that routine seemed to be in the off-ing shortly after Diana's birth in 1980, when I was offered a million pounds a year by Sheik Ibn Hassan to coach the national side of the Arab Emirate state, Basran. This was in the days when a million pounds a year was a lot of money.

'Do we really want to live in the desert?' said Penny, as we enjoyed a rare late-night supper together in the kitchen.

'I expect we don't,' I replied. 'But it's such an enormous and generous offer that I think we at least owe them the honour of going out and having a look.'

Which is how Penny, myself and the kids found ourselves aboard a private plane belonging to Sheik Ibn Hassan and winging our way in leather-seated luxury towards the Gulf and the astonishing, newly built, sun-baked skyscrapers of oil-rich Basran City. An air-condi-tioned limousine collected us from the airport and sped us on fresh tarmac all the way to the six-star Burg Al Wazan Hotel, where we were given a suite on the 497th floor. Needless to say, we had never stayed anywhere quite so breathtakingly opulent. We were aghast.

'Have you seen these taps?' gasped Penny from the bathroom. 'They're shaped like swans.'

They were indeed. Life-sized swans.

While Penny and the kids settled into the suite, a car came to take me to the National Football Academy of Basran where I had my first meeting with Sheik Ibn Hassan himself.

'It's a very fine facility you have here, Sheik Hassan,' I said.

'Ah,' said the Sheik. 'Facilities, we can do. Footballers, less so. What do you think of our fine national squad, Mr Race?'

The Sheik gestured to the air-conditioned AstroTurf pitch where a training match was in progress. It was hard to form a detailed impression, but what was going on there didn't exactly look first class.

'Well,' I said, trying to be as diplomatic as possible, 'it seems you've got a promising little unit there.'

'Mr Race,' said the Sheik, 'please don't trouble to be polite. The players you see in front of you could not – what's the phrase you use in English? Kick their way out of a paper bag. Is that right?'

The Sheik let out a booming laugh.

'Which is where you come in, Mr Race,' he went on. 'With your tactical brilliance, your galvanising presence, your iconic standing within the world game and your supreme English training methods, in no time at all you will convert these players into the finest footballing power in the Middle East.'

'And if I don't?' I asked.

'Let's face it, Mr Race,' said the Sheik. 'They're hardly going to get any worse, are they?' And with that he let out the booming laugh again.

'Now,' said the Sheik, 'my assistant, Tewfik, will show you where you will live if you accept our offer. Or perhaps I should say, when you accept it!'

I shook his hand and smiled as non-committally as I could.

'I shall look forward to seeing you tonight for dinner, Mr Race, when we can continue our discussions,' said the Sheik.

Tewfik drove the limo via the hotel to pick up Penny and then we headed out west of the city, parallel to the sea, before turning inland and passing through the gates of what was clearly some kind of private community. Behind further gates and tall hedges, we caught tantalising glimpses of fabulously imposing houses in every kind of style. Sprinklers played on lawns and white-frocked gardeners moved quietly among beds of exotic flowers. Eventually a set of electric gates opened and we passed along a brick drive and pulled up in front of a beautiful white, three-storey, Spanish-inflected house with a fountain splashing on the forecourt. Tewfik led us up the broad steps and through the tall double doors. The tiled hallway was beautifully cool, dotted with plants and statues, and gave onto a wide sweeping marble staircase. There was a huge kitchen with a breakfast bar and an American-style fridge which was almost the size of a garage, and a wonderfully comfortable sitting room fitted with white linen-covered sofas and elaborately patterned kilims hanging from the walls and a huge television set in a wooden cabinet. Upstairs there were seven bedrooms of various sizes, none of them small, and all with en suite bathrooms where the fittings were silver and marble. Penny and I descended the stairs after our tour feeling quite dizzied by the opulence of it all.

'So, this is where your servants will be quartered,' said Tewfik. 'Now let's go up to the main house.'

Now almost entirely disoriented, Penny and I followed Tewfik back to the car and he drove us up the brick drive for several more minutes, past more beautifully sculpted trees and shrubs, until we rounded a corner and almost lost our breaths at the sight of a magnificent palace, whose forecourt looked out through palm fronds across the city to the winking blue sea beyond. We walked in an open-mouthed trance from room to room, drifting eventually up the stairs to the master bedroom with its hot tub and its Jacuzzi and its huge balcony and its outdoor shower and its indoor shower and its enormous bed, wrapped in cottons and silks and sprinkled with rose petals. Outside on the terrace there was a vast kidney-shaped swimming pool and, off to one side, a spa and a set of six tennis courts. There was a forty-seat cinema, a squash court, a bowling alley and a paddock filled with race horses. There was a gym, a fourteen-car garage containing fourteen cars, a merry-go-round, a zoo and a dolphinarium, with six dolphins who all leapt into the air in formation as we passed.

There was a cable car and a jet in its own warehouse and a landing strip and a ski-jump, and up on the roof of the building were 'his and hers' helicopter pads – with 'his and hers' helicopters astride them, mine in baby blue, Penny's in coral pink, with our names written on the doors.

'Do you like it, Mr Race?' said Tewfik.

'It's staggering, Tewfik,' I said. 'Just staggering.'

We drove back in stunned silence. That night at a sumptuous candlelit dinner in the Sheik's private residence, the Sheik and I talked football and I found him engaged, enthusiastic, deeply knowledgeable, magnetically ambitious but also realistic – pragmatic, even. His ambition was a strong Basran national side and then, beyond that, a World Cup in Basran, opening up the entire Middle East to the international football fraternity.

'But what about the climate?' I asked. 'Don't temperatures touch forty degrees here in the height of summer, when the World Cup is played?'

'Air-conditioned stadiums,' said the Sheik. 'The technology already exists.'

I must have looked doubtful.

'Mr Race,' said the Sheik. 'You might not approve of it, I might not approve of it, but neither of us can deny that it's a fact: with money, anything is possible. Now – more water?'

I returned to the hotel deep in thought and lay awake most of the night. The following day we had a few hours together as a family on the beach and then flew back on the private jet.

'It wouldn't be a big chunk out of our lives, Penny,' I said, as we sank back in the leather seats, stretching our toes in the complimentary in-flight slippers while the hostess served us smoked salmon blinis. 'Three years – two years, even . . . we'd be made for life.'

'I know, Roy,' said Penny, with a sigh. 'And that bedroom . . .'

'That bedroom!' I said, sighing too. I reached for Penny's hand and clutched it tight.

When I got back to the house, I found a gold-plated Rolls-Royce waiting for me on the drive, with silver ribbons wrapped around it and tied in a giant bow. 'For the future national coach of Basran,' said the hand-written gift-tag attached to the hood ornament.

I spent the next two days in a state of agonised indecision. All those exquisite wonders on offer to us – and yet only at the cost of abandoning what we had here, in Melchester.

It was time for another trip up Melbury Tor – my trusty thinking spot, the reliable bringer of clarity.

Once again, I sat on the bench and looked out across the city – my birthplace, the only place I had ever called home. And once again, as if on cue, the sun broke through the clouds and shafts of golden light illuminated the huddled rooftops and the chimneys of the pickled onion factory and the floodlight pylons of Mel Park beyond. And I realised, as I looked out and drank in this vista, that I had something that no amount of money and performing dolphins and swan-shaped taps and cinemas and luxury spa treatments, and the ability to travel almost anywhere in the world at the click of a finger, and delicious food prepared by cooks, and a complete absence of worry about the financial future, either for me or my children or even my children's children, and comprehensive medical cover, and balconies overlooking the winking blue sea could ever replace: I had my roots.

Back at the house, I made a call to Basran to decline the million-pound-a-year-plus-perks offer. Afterwards, as I sat at my desk, breathing deeply, Penny came and cupped my face in her hands. 'I'm very proud of you,' she said. 'I didn't really see myself in a coral pink helicopter, to be honest.'

I thought her lower lip trembled slightly as she said this, but I could have been wrong.

The Sheik did not give up easily. Over the following fortnight, two more Rolls-Royces and a speedboat turned up. I realised that the only real way to close this matter down was to find Basran another coach in my place. Conveniently, Lofty Peak was at the end of his contract with the Rovers. He had been a wonderful servant to the club but, as is often the way of things, over the course of the past season he had not been quite as wonderful a servant as he had been before, and I had not been looking forward to having to tell him that we would not be renewing his deal. This was the perfect solution. Lofty flew out for an interview, the Sheik loved him and everything was settled amicably, with me promising that the Rovers would undertake a summer tour of Basran at some point in the next few years.

Did my decision to refuse the Basran millions prey on my mind afterwards? I would say that it didn't, although the press at the time seemed to be suggesting differently. I'll confess that, every now and again, I would get a postcard from Lofty Peak, where he might casually mention that he was in the spa having his daily pedicure after morning training, or where he might say that he and his wife Delia were about to jet off to Rome for the weekend, or where he might complain that one of the dolphins was playing up, and I would reflect momentarily on what might have been. But the idea that this affected my concentration on important matters at the Rovers was nonsense put about by mischievous reporters with nothing better to write.

What's certainly the case is that, Basran offer or no Basran offer, we endured a torrid season in 1980–81 – as torrid as any I had experienced in my career, and certainly my most torrid ever as a manager.

It was relegation form all the way, with defeat after defeat and sloppily dropped points everywhere, and I was seemingly powerless to arrest our decline. Everything I tried – dropping Blackie into a holding role in front of the back four, utilising Vic 'Superbrat' Guthrie as a deep-lying left back with a brief to bomb on when necessary – failed. There were rumours of dissatisfaction from the board, and the fans, hitherto so supportive, were clearly restless. We went into the last day of the season needing to defeat Stambridge City by five clear goals to stay up. I was still backing us. Stambridge were already relegated and I knew the high stakes would inspire rather than intimidate my players, given the amount of character that there was in the side that I had assembled, which now included Nat 'Grandad' Gosden ('the comb-over king', who still had plenty to offer at fifty-seven, in my opinion, though many begged to differ) and Paco Diaz, signed from Zaragosa of Spain after absolutely pulling us to bits in a UEFA Cup quarter-final meeting. My confidence seemed to have been justified when we scored twice in the second half (both goals by me) and then twice more (me again) to make it 4–0 with ten minutes to go. Attack after attack then came and went, without that vital breakthrough. Merv Wallace scraped the crossbar, Blackie hit the post, I hit the bar, the post, the goalkeeper and the referee, whose positioning for that particular corner was questionable, not that I questioned it. But still that crucial fifth goal would not come.

Then, with just seconds remaining, I latched on to the ball just inside the opposition's half and looked up to see Noel Baxter moving into a dangerous position on the right flank. Using the outside of my left foot, I sent the ball bending up, over and behind the defensive line and, as Noel continued his run . . . heard the referee signal for full time.

The relegation trapdoor had opened up and swallowed us. Rovers were demoted to the Second Division – ejected from the top flight for the first time since 1929.

However, back in the dressing room, I urged the lads to look on the positive side. 'The lessons we learn about ourselves in defeat are as important as the lessons we learn about ourselves in success,' I pointed out, 'and possibly even more so. It's not losing – it's how you bounce back from losing. It's not going under, it's how you surface. Next season, we come back and we go again. And next season, we surface.'

'Inspiring words, Racey,' said Grandad Gosden.

'I'm feeling better about the prospect of a season spent facing the likes of lowly Railsborough and Northfield already,' said Vic 'The Superbrat' Guthrie.

'Iz not sech a kick in the pisser after all!' said Paco Diaz, whose grasp of idiomatic English had always impressed us.

Accordingly, it was an optimistic and forward-looking Rovers who departed almost immediately on the traditional summer tour, where we were kidnapped on the beautiful and remote Caribbean island of St Nita. (Forces Loyal To The Deposed Government of Prime Minister Denzil Johnson 6, Melchester Rovers 0.)

And, similarly, it was an optimistic and forward-looking Rovers who commenced the 1981–2 season in Division Two. We had held onto our top players, with the exception of Geoff Giles, and I was proud that everyone had bought into the project of rolling up their sleeves, getting their heads down and returning Rovers to the place where they belonged. That went for the fans too, who continued to fill Mel Park to capacity, regardless of the club's newly humbled status. We came out of the blocks fast with a 6–0 home victory over Dundermore Albion and tore off on a winning streak that lasted right through the autumn. All the indications were that we would absolutely romp back into the upper echelons.

All in all, in the circumstances, and given the upward direction in which things were finally heading, I think it's easy to see that an attempt on my life by a crazed gunman was the last thing I needed.

19

Gunned Down

'ROY RACE SHOT!'

The 48-point headline on the front of the *Melchester Evening Chronicle* on 21 December 1981 couldn't have put it more clearly. I had been shot.

Not that I was in a position to know much about it at the time. The full extent of my memories of this extraordinary moment, which was to send shockwaves round the world of football that can still be felt today, are as follows: that I returned to my office at the training ground late one Tuesday evening to collect some papers; that I became aware of someone in the doorway; that I raised my head from my desk and had enough time to catch a glimpse of the raised silver barrel of a revolver; and that when I came to, it was the end of February.

People often ask me, 'Roy, what's it like to be in a coma?' I wish I knew! It's like they always say: if you can remember being in a coma, you probably weren't in one!

Mostly, I have the memory only of blankness – a little, so I'm told, like the sensation when you come around after a general anaesthetic: one moment, the anaesthetist is counting down from ten and the next, almost at the click of a finger, the patient is waking up and it's all over, except for the pain and the stitches, etc. (I wouldn't know: I've never had an operation.) Except, in my case, I did have at least some vague sense of a period of lost time. Did I have an out-of-body experience, see myself from above, receive some intimation of the fate that awaits us all beyond our final breath? Sorry to disappoint you. I did, subsequently, pick up the strands of a few dreams that I must have had, lying there in the hospital. But they were mostly dreams in which I appeared to be living some kind of luxury life in a glorious mansion with an amazing bedroom and a balcony looking across to the sun-stippled sea – nonsensical, floaty, fantasy stuff. I don't think there is any point trying to interpret them in order to come up with any deep meaning there.

I got lucky: the shot turned out merely to have grazed my temple, minimising my rehabilitation period. A fraction of an inch to the right, and, without question, it would have killed me. But, of course, two inches to the left and it would have missed me altogether. These are the margins. You have to choose which ones you want to dwell on.

I just lay there, in Melchester General, amid the quietly bleeping monitors, entirely oblivious to the concern I was causing: the concern of Penny, ever watchful at my bedside when she could get away from the kids; the concern of the fans, staging candlelit vigils outside the hospital and at the ground; and the concern, touchingly, of the wider nation who sought news of my condition hourly on the bulletins – if bulletins isn't a slightly unfortunate word in this context.

Why shoot the player-manager of a leading English football

club? It was a question that inevitably preoccupied me after I woke up, brought back to consciousness that Saturday afternoon by the combined effects of Penny's sweet voice and the radio commentary from Melchester Rovers v Haddaway Town, where Rovers had just bagged a fourth, Paco Diaz latching on to a perfectly weighted through-ball from Vernon Eliot. And, on the surface, the shooting was indeed a mystery. But you have to remember the climate of the times. This was the beginning of the 1980s when an unprecedented economic boom, particularly in the banking sector, was under way, when synth-pop was on the rise, and when assassination, successful or otherwise, was enjoying a bit of a vogue. Popes, American presidents, rock stars, characters in long-running TV soaps . . . the person who hadn't had a potshot taken at him by a disenchanted loner was increasingly rare. Assassination seemed to be happening to everyone.

At the same time, I didn't think of myself as someone who had enemies. I had rivals, yes. And occasionally I had run-ins with people, which was only inevitable, given that I was in a position of responsibility, professionally speaking, and required to uphold certain standards in the workplace, as I saw fit. Of course, you never entirely know what people are saying behind your back, but my impression was that, on the whole (and without wishing to speak out of turn), I managed to dispense my duties as a leader without inspiring people to attempt to kill me. And I don't think you can ask for more than that, as a leader.

Nonetheless, when I thought about it, there had been a moment, back at the beginning of December, a couple of weeks before the shooting, when someone had tried to run me over on a motorbike. It was in the club car park, and the bike, with its headlights full on, had driven directly at me and kept on coming, forcing me to dive to one side into some waste bins. I had dismissed this incident at the time as just another one of Noel Baxter's pranks. I didn't even bother to tell anybody about it. However, in the wake of this altogether clearer attempt on my life, that close shave in the car park seemed to take on a less innocent and more troubling light.

I sat in my office and drew up a list of the people I considered to be suspects. Essentially, this involved thinking of the people I knew who might have a reason to want to try and kill me, twice. I wasn't expecting the list to be particularly long. I was certainly hoping it wouldn't be.

The first name I wrote down was Vic 'The Superbrat' Guthrie. This was more a procedural formality than anything else. Yes, Vic wasn't the easiest player to manage. Just recently he had decked Barnbury City's Brian Norton in an off-the-ball incident behind the ref's back, and I had immediately reported Vic to the ref (Mr K.T. Davies of Billbury) and got him sent off. This didn't make me popular with Vic, but, as I had to point out to him, the rules on violent conduct are the rules on violent conduct and they apply to everyone. I had also been forced to upbraid Vic on his discipline on a number of occasions, not least when I found him urinating into the petrol tank of an Austin 1100 belonging to Mr G.D. Malone of Ettringham Bay. Nevertheless, Vic was, underneath it all, a professional, and there was nothing in his prior conduct to indicate that he was the kind of player who would attempt to run his manager over using a motorbike and, having failed in that, shoot him. Vic was on my list simply because he was the person who discovered my body, lying bleeding on the floor of the office, and used the phone on my desk to alert the police and ambulance services, and, as with Blackie and the Great Mel Park Fire of 1959, he would necessarily need to be eliminated from the enquiries.

The second name I wrote down was Arthur Logan. Arthur was the father of Kenny Logan, a young Scots talent I had been trying to bring to the Rovers on a permanent deal. Arthur, however, wanted his son to stay in Scotland and help him run the family estate agency business, for which he was predicting great things over the next decade. He and I had had a number of phone conversations in which he had accused me, in so many words, of leading his son astray, despite the fact that Kenny, at eighteen, was, to my mind, capable of making his own decision and clearly preferred the idea of playing professional football for a living than the prospect of showing young marrieds round a three-bedroom semi in East Kilkirk offering excellent access to local amenities and priced for a quick sale, not that there's anything wrong with that. Was Arthur Logan a potential manager-killer? Unlikely, on the surface. At the same time, if growing up with my father had taught me one thing it was never to underestimate the anger of an aggrieved parent.

The third and final name I wrote down was Elton Blake, the actor and soap star. Now, this really was a long shot. A few months prior to the assassination attempt, a television production company had approached Melchester Rovers with a lucrative proposal to develop a bi-weekly drama series based on life at the club. I had argued forcefully against it, believing it would be a major and unhelpful distraction to our business on the pitch, but the money men had prevailed and the project had been given the green light. (It wouldn't have happened in John Mason's day, I feel fairly confident in saying. But Mason had retired and had been replaced by Sam Barlow, the millionaire owner of Brazzia, the women's lingerie chain, and the culture of the club had tilted slightly.) Elton Blake had been selected to play the part of me in this drama and had spent some time at the training ground, researching the role. Penny didn't think Blake was right for the part at all – and said so, within earshot of the producer. Blake was subsequently stood down just before filming was due to start and left the set cursing me for conspiring against him. That put Blake among the small number of people I could think of with a grudge against me. But did that make him a plausible suspect? I entirely doubted it. I was sure he was capable of riding a motor-bike. I was sure he was capable of handling firearms. But, at the same time, we know about actors: they are all talk. Anyway, in the absence of alternatives, his name was down.

I toyed with adding Buzzer Hawkins, the club commissionaire, to the list. After all, he had been rude to me on an almost daily basis for more than twenty-seven years at this stage. On the other hand, he was a lifelong servant to the club, much loved by everyone who worked with him, and, at the same time, I was almost certain, unable to ride a motorbike.

So that was it: three names. It wasn't an especially convincing piece of paper, with those six words on it, but it was all I had and I duly took it to the police.

Detective Inspector Plews from Melchester CID was extremely grateful for my research – apparently having no better suggestions of his own, or, indeed, any suggestions at all – and proposed that we summon all three of the suspects for interview at the station at the same time, and just as soon as it was possible to do so.

'You mean, like in the television dramas, where the detective calls all the suspects together in the sitting room and eventually reveals the murderer?' I said.

'Exactly like that,' said Detective Inspector Plews. 'There's a reason they put that scene in the dramas, you know.'

Three days after this, Guthrie, Arthur and Blake were ordered to report to the interrogation room at Melchester Yard. I sat secretly in the adjacent room, with a police annotator, watching events through a window fitted with one-way glass. It was extremely interesting to see how the three of them responded to their predicament. Vic was uncomfortable and sullenly uncooperative and lightly flushed with sweat. He almost seemed to incriminate himself just by the way he twisted in his chair and refused to meet anybody's eyes. Arthur Logan was boilingly angry and immediately aggressive under questioning – to the point where you were convinced very quickly that he had something to hide and was concealing it behind a wall of hostility. Elton Blake, meanwhile, sat calmly to one side, one eyebrow arched, clearly feeling that he had nothing to fear from the proceedings whatsoever and that his very presence at this meeting of oddballs was merely an amusing curiosity which could potentially furnish a decent anecdote in the very near future.

Detective Inspector Plews had been joined in the interrogation room by his colleague, Detective Sergeant Partridge, and the two of them had obviously made a prior arrangement to tackle the suspects using the classic good cop/bad cop approach.

'You shot him, didn't you Vic?' bawled DI Plews.

'No, I did not!' shouted Vic.

'Can I get you a cup of tea, Vic?' said DS Partridge.

'No thanks, I'm all right,' said Vic.

'You pointed the gun in the direction of that father of three's head and in cold blood, you pulled the trigger with the intention of ending his life, didn't you, Vic?' bawled DI Plews.

'No!' screamed Vic. 'I'm telling you the truth. I did not shoot Roy Race!'

'What about a coffee, Vic? Can I get you one of those?' asked DS Partridge.

'No, I'm all right,' said Vic. 'Thanks anyway.'

'Because you're a murderer and you're a liar, isn't that right, Vic? And you tried to kill a man and now you need to go to jail and pay for it,' bawled DI Plews.

'I did not shoot the gaffer!' howled Vic.

'How about a mint, Vic?' said DS Partridge.

'Are they Polos?' asked Vic.

And on it went, with Vic close to cracking under the strain and right on the verge of bursting into tears at several points, but at the same time eventually saying yes to a sandwich and a hot chocolate.

When Vic didn't confess, the detectives started in on Arthur Logan.

'You're an angry man, aren't you, Arthur?' said DI Plews.

'Too right I'm f***ing angry,' said Arthur Logan. 'I've come all the way from Scotland for this.'

'They do a very nice chicken wrap in the canteen, Arthur,' said DS Partridge. 'Any interest?'

And, again, on it went, with no ultimate capitulation on the part of the suspect. Then it was Elton Blake's turn.

'This is quite preposterous,' said Blake. 'Are you saying that I, Elton Blake, a renowned and popular star of the small screen, is the kind of person to go vulgarly running people over on a motorbike and firing a gun at their heads? Please, darlings.'

I shot bolt upright in my chair at this. The police officer who was alongside me, taking notes, said, 'Something awry, Roy?'

'Can I go in there?' I said.

'Well, it's not standard procedure . . .' began the police officer, but I was already leaving the room and bursting in next door.

'Gaffer!' said Vic, caught by surprise.

'That's the culprit, if you f***ing ask me,' said Arthur Logan, pointing at me.

'Shut it, Kenny,' screamed DI Plews.

'Piece of Battenberg, Roy?' asked DS Partridge.

'Officers?' I said. 'Arrest this man.'

My finger was pointing at Elton Blake.

'Oh, for goodness' sake, ducks,' said Elton Blake. 'The man's gone to fairy land.'

'What are you saying, Roy?' screamed DI Plews.

'The tape of this interview will, when rewound, demonstrate that Elton Blake makes reference, at the nineteen minutes and thirty-four seconds mark, to the act of running someone over with a motorbike,' I said.

'And what if I did?' said Elton Blake.

'How can you have known?' I said. 'I told nobody about the aforementioned incident involving said motorbike, including my wife Penny and the police officers here gathered. You, Elton Blake, have therefore incriminated yourself and it follows, as the night the day, that you are also guilty of the attempt upon my life with the revolver, in an act of stark vengeance, having wrongly attributed to me your loss of the role as the fictional Roy Race in a proposed drama upon the subject of Melchester Rovers FC. I hereby rest my case,' I said, unable to resist a small bow.

'Excellent work, Roy,' bawled DI Plews, 'although we may have to tighten it up a bit, legals-wise.'

'Would anybody like a nice refreshing cup of tea after all that?' asked DS Partridge.

And so it was that Elton Blake was sentenced to fourteen years in prison for two independent attempts upon my life, making me the first footballer in English league history to be almost killed by a soap star on two separate occasions – or certainly in the professional era. Not that this is a record that I'm particularly proud of. It was a sorry and sordid episode which did not reveal human nature in its best light. It also threatened to interrupt Rovers' league season, although, as it happened, we were on fire that year and beyond interruption. I returned to work at the end of March, the victories kept on coming and we romped to the Second Division Championship and automatic promotion.

Rovers were back where we belonged: in League Division One.

And I was no longer shot.

20

Doing the Unthinkable

We returned to the top flight rejuvenated and confident, although, sadly, without Vernon Eliot. Vernon suffered a career-ending leg injury over the summer of 1983 when he was trampled in a pitch invasion just before the tea interval in a charity cricket match. However, he wasn't completely lost to football: as soon as he was out of traction, he accepted a role at Carford City as Assistant Under-Eight Development Officer (eastern region).

Vernon's mishap only served to underscore the extent to which the unruliness of crowds was a pressing issue in these years. The blight of hooliganism had been upon the game for some time, but the early 1980s were unquestionably the high watermark for football thuggery, with pitched battles between rival fans frequently breaking out in and around grounds, as well as in trains and train stations, on planes and cross-channel ferries, in town centres, bus parks and municipal gardens and once, most shamefully of all, following a cup tie with arch rivals Walford

Rovers, in the grounds of the Quiet Rivers old people's home in Holbrook.

We had four games postponed as a result of pitch invasions during the first fortnight of the 1984-5 season alone. Rovers fans, let me make clear, were no worse than any others – and, in fact, better than most, I would argue. But when police made 34,569 arrests after a hotly contested league match against Westbury Town, it was clear that the old line about this being a tiny, lawless minority spoiling it for the rest was no longer holding as much water as it once had.

The way I understood it, hooliganism was a social problem as much as a football problem, but I didn't think that meant that football could absolve itself of its responsibility to tackle the issue. My approach, which I actioned via the board and following meetings with supporters' representatives, was to instigate fan-based initiatives, including meet'n'greets and entertainments (races, dancing, penalty shoot-outs and so forth) before the game and at half-time to attempt to make the match-day experience more family-friendly and generally involving. 'We want to create an environment in which violence can't take root,' I argued. And when that didn't work, we identified the ringleader (Trevor Brinsden of 24 Hall Dene Way, Melchester) and banned him from the ground.

But it was a time of unrest more generally. The running fights and the dart-flinging served to provide a somehow poignantly appropriate backdrop for the deterioration of my relationship with Sam Barlow, the Melchester Rovers chairman. We had fallen out badly when he had installed an electric fence around the perimeter of Mel Park for the purposes of crowd control. ('That'll teach those f***ers,' he had said.) I was also distressed when I heard him ask his secretary to find out the price of a water cannon and to see whether it was possible to get one in club colours. More pressingly, his visits to the dressing room after games were becoming more frequent and more irksome. I had barely had time to talk to the players sometimes before Barlow would come marching in with his always apologetic-looking vice chairman, Doug Clitheroe, and demand to know why I had made this change, and why hadn't I made that substitution and so on. In front of the players, I found this undermining, to say the least. John Mason had always trusted the manager to get on with managing. Barlow was different. He was an interferer – and I was beginning to resent the interference.

So, when a call came through, one wet Tuesday afternoon in 1982, from Harvey Rawson, the fertiliser mogul and chairman of Walford Rovers, I found myself more inclined to listen than I might otherwise have been.

'How would you fancy becoming player-manager of Walford Rovers?' I heard Rawson say. 'I can offer you three thousand per week.'

Those were the days when £3000 a week was a lot of money. But that wasn't what attracted me. What got my attention was the offer of five million pounds to spend on new players.

'Five million!' I gasped.

'Five million,' repeated Harvey Rawson.

Because those were the days when five million was a lot of money to spend on players.

'Let me discuss it at home,' I said.

'You can't be serious,' said Penny that night.

'I've come to feel hemmed in and untrusted, Penny,' I said. 'This would be fresh – a new challenge, with people who believe in me and what I can do.'

'Roy,' said Penny, 'we turned down the opportunity to go and live in luxury in Basran for two or three years – and now you're asking me to go and live in Walford, potentially indefinitely? Walford doesn't even have a decent café.'

'I think it could be the change of scene that my career needs, Penny.'

Penny looked at me in amazement.

'I'm sorry, Roy. You go if you want, but I'm not doing it. I'm not uprooting our children for the sake of a move to Walford. I mean, why would you even . . .'

She shook her head in despair.

'But Rawson's offering five million to spend on new players,' I said. 'It's an opportunity to build something really special.'

Penny's eyes now flashed with fire.

'Well, you go and build your "something special", Roy, and I'll stay here and get on with building our family.'

The kitchen door slammed.

And so began two of the most confused and miserable months of my life – my lost weekends, if you will. I packed a bag of clothes and moved into the Walford Premierlodge, returning on Sundays to see the kids when I could, but otherwise training and working in the day and retreating alone at night to a dull corporate hotel bedroom, feeling desolate inside.

My move had, of course, sent the world of football into a flat spin. The papers seemed to contain little else but stories and comment about my 'desertion'. 'All Over For Rovers' was one of the better headlines, above a piece by the always perceptive and stylistically intriguing Bob Dickens, who argued that Sam Barlow's failure to hold on to me bespoke a chairmanship in terminal decline. It was a point of view, and one of the more positive things I read about myself that week, when I became, for the first time in my life, the recipient of hate mail. There were letters and cards scrawled with crayon and lipstick and other fluids and bearing such messages as 'TRATER' and 'YOUR DOG FOOD RACE!' I guess you could tell how much it meant to people. There was a packet which I didn't open, knowing all too well from the smell what it contained. None of this in any way improved my spirits.

Running out for my first game in the blue of Walford, after all those years in the red and yellow of Melchester, was a deeply dislocating experience, to put it mildly. Harvey Rawson was on the pitch to welcome me, milking his moment in the spotlight as the man who had lured Roy Race away from Melchester Rovers – and fair enough, although something about the scene, and my part in it, as Rawson clasped my hand and, grinning, raised it aloft to the crowd, turned my stomach.

Obviously, once the whistle blew, I became a professional footballer, shut everything else out and locked into the game. A football match is a football match, after all, and your duty is to perform to the limits of your ability, no matter whose shirt you are wearing. I scored four goals that afternoon, the fourth of them an absolute peach of a left-foot shot into the bottom corner after a long diagonal run from one penalty area to the other, beating nine along the way. But of course, my only concern as soon as I got back to the dressing room was to find out how the Rovers had got on. (Answer: they drew 1–1 away at Honiton, a late equaliser from Jimmy Slade securing a vital point.)

That night in the Premierlodge, I called Blackie for a chat.

'Christ, Roy,' he said, his voice immediately descending to a whisper. 'Are we still allowed to talk? Is this a secure line?'

'I've only joined another football club, Blackie,' I said. 'I haven't defected to the Soviet Union.'

'Well, it feels a bit like it,' Blackie said.

'I guess so,' I replied. 'How are things, anyway?'

'Oh, not so bad,' said Blackie. 'Looks like we're signing Rob Richards.'

'Yeah, I heard,' I said. 'He's good.'

'I know,' said Blackie. 'Gets a lot of goals. By the way – they've made me caretaker manager.'

'You?' I asked, perhaps a little too quickly and in a voice that was possibly a little too highly pitched.

'What do you mean by that?' said Blackie and I heard him slam down the receiver.

Penny, my children, my club, and now Blackie: I seemed to be losing everything I cared about at an alarming rate. I was at my lowest ebb.

And what did the fixture list have to go and throw up, shortly thereafter? A visit to Mel Park.

You could have cut the atmosphere on that match day with a knife – a knife more than likely belonging to a member of one of the gangs of Melchester Rovers supporters who had gathered long before kick-off to jeer the Walford coach as it arrived. A couple of bottles bounced off the windows as the bus nudged its way through the baying mob. Two lines of policemen formed a corridor so that I could get from the coach to the visitors' door without getting molested – and even then, as I passed through, one of the policemen had a little dig with his elbow, which I didn't think was particularly professional.

As for the crowd in the stadium, I guess you would say I got a mixed reception. There were those who welcomed me back on the basis of what I had achieved at the club over my long years of service; and there were those who booed me onto the pitch on account of my perceived treachery. And, because this was the early 1980s, a fight broke out between the two factions and the game was delayed for forty minutes while the police went in on horseback, which did nothing to defuse the general atmosphere. I also noticed a lot of 'Sam Barlow Out!' banners, so clearly the chairman was experiencing some disaffection, too. At least there was that.

And again, it felt all wrong: the wrong shirt, the wrong team, the wrong opponent. But again, once the game got going I managed to shut all that out, along with the crowd, turning in a Man of the Match performance and contributing three goals and two assists in a 5–1 victory for the visitors which took us up to sixth place in the table.

Getting back onto the coach, two policemen had a go with their elbows and one had a kick at my shins.

That night, back in Walford, as depressed as I had ever been, I rang Harvey Rawson and asked him if I could see him at home the following day.

'Come for Sunday lunch,' he said gently.

'I'm not sure you'll want me to stay that long, Mr Rawson, given the state I'm in,' I replied.

'Come for Sunday lunch,' he repeated.

The next day I drove out to Rawson's mansion in Chesterly Edge and was shown through to the oak-lined library.

'Sam Barlow's gone, did you see?' said Rawson, waving a newspaper. 'Walked out as chairman of Melchester Rovers last night, citing public pressure. Doug Clitheroe's now in charge.'

I hadn't seen. I didn't know whether it made me feel better or worse.

Harvey Rawson dropped the newspaper onto a side table. I was about to start speaking, but he beat me to it.

'Listen, Roy,' said Harvey. 'I can tell when a man's not happy, and right now I'm looking at an unhappy man. And if you're not happy, then I'm not happy. So why don't you and I agree that this was simply one of those things that didn't work out – and then you can go home to your wife and children, and to your club, assuming they'll take you back, which I think these latest developments very strongly indicate that they will.'

'Are you serious, Mr Rawson?' I asked.

'More serious than I have ever been about anything, Roy. Hey – I'll still be the man who lured Roy Race away from Melchester Rovers. Just not for very long!'

'I'm extremely grateful to you, Mr Rawson,' I said.

'Good!' said Rawson. 'Now, let's have some lunch.'

When we had eaten, I went back to my room at the Premierlodge and phoned Doug Clitheroe.

'Have you back?' said Clitheroe. 'Are you kidding? Of course we'll have you back. But you owe us two points from yesterday! Actually, make that three points, because since 1981 it's been three points for a win, not two.'

'I'll be sure to make them up to you, Mr Clitheroe,' I said.

Then I phoned Blackie and apologised to him for having intimated by my careless tone of voice the previous evening that he wasn't management material. 'Of course you're going to be a great manager, Blackie,' I said, 'albeit not right now, because guess what: I'm coming back.'

'That's fantastic news,' said Blackie. 'Melchester Rovers is where you belong, Roy. I'll be proud to step aside and await my chance at a later date.'

Then I hung up, packed, settled my bill and drove home.

'Penny,' I said, standing in the kitchen doorway. 'I made a mistake. But now I've unmade it. And I intend to continue unmaking it for the rest of my life.'

'Welcome home, Roy Race,' said Penny, smiling and softly enclosing me in her arms.

The next morning I was back at my desk at the training ground, feeling thoroughly relieved and beginning to plan for the future, when the phone rang and a woman's voice said, 'Hello – Roy Race? I'm calling from Harbins, the salted snack company? Regarding our new Porky Pig Scratchings? We sent you a sample of our product a few weeks ago – just wondering if you'd had the chance to try it and whether you had been able to have a think about possibly coming on board as an ambassador for the brand.'

My mind spun back. This definitely rang a bell. That packet at Walford that I didn't open . . .

'Oh, my word!' I said. 'I thought it was hate mail!'

Not long after this, I signed a long and extremely lucrative deal to become the face of Harbins Porky Pig Scratchings – though, as I am always very careful to tell the kids, you should eat other things too.

21

Atrocity

What can I write about Basran in 1986 that hasn't already been written? What can I say that hasn't been said? What can I think that hasn't been thought? The simple, bare, inescapably tragic fact of the matter is this: eight men went to play football in an unstable Middle Eastern state in the middle of a military coup, and didn't come home. Were those of us who did make it back ever the same afterwards? No, we were not.

The summer tour of Basran – as faithfully promised to Sheik Ibn Hassan six years previously – had appeared to be proceeding entirely along the normal lines. Basran was now a more unsettled place than it had been when Penny and I had flown out for my interview for the coaching job with the national side – indeed, most of the reports I read before we departed described the country as being in political foment after an armed takeover of government buildings in Basran City by forces loyal to the former President Al Suki Kadiz, three days before we touched down.

It wasn't altogether surprising to any of us, accordingly, when our team bus was pulled over by armed rebels on a dirt road twenty-four miles south of the southern city of Gy Tabat. None of us were remotely surprised, either, when we were subsequently marched at gunpoint into a nearby encampment and forced to sit down in a rudimentary pen, under guard.

Eventually, causing exactly no one to raise a quizzical eyebrow, a rebel with a rifle approached us.

'You, Captain – come!' he barked, predictably enough.

'Where are you taking me?' I asked, already knowing the answer.

'To the Colonel,' he said, not disappointing me.

So once again I was taken to a large tent in the shade of a tree in the centre of the encampment and pushed through the flap where my eyes gradually grew accustomed enough to the darkness to make out a swarthy figure at a desk who first wanted to have a chat about some esoteric detail relating to the English domestic game and who then offered me the usual 'play to go free' deal.

When I reported back to the pen, the lads were already getting changed.

The final score was Loyalist Paramilitaries 1, Melchester Rovers 6 with goals by me (four), Blackie and – poignantly, as it would turn out – Vic 'The Superbrat' Guthrie, who was not to know that he had just got on a score sheet for the last time in his life.

Only when we were back on board the bus and heading south again did the trip finally summon the new, the shockingly new, the genuinely unforeseen, in the form of the squeal of brakes and the lurch of the coach and the sickening crunch of metal as the bomb-packed car – bound elsewhere, bound not for us – embedded itself suicidally, and worse, in the radiator grille and became only noise and light and heat. Followed after that by scenes and sounds, also novel, that I am not prepared to revisit – not here in this book, not anywhere else but in the private vigils held nigh on daily since then in my own mind.

Let me simply say that when the smoke cleared, the following players had lost their lives: Noel Baxter, Trevor Cassidy, Vic Guthrie, Carl Hunt, Neville Jones, Kenny Logan, Steve Naylor and Jimmy Slade.

Let me add that the following twenty-four hours were a living nightmare of grim accountings and consular administration and phone calls that you never want to have to make and the direly solemn business of the shipping home of bodies.

Those of us who lived flew back. The rest of the week was funerals and flowers.

There was talk of suspending the entire English league campaign, but I argued vociferously that none of the Basran Eight would have wanted that. They would have wanted football to continue as usual. So football did continue.

However, the first weekend of the new season was set aside for commemoration and, as a mark of respect, all league games kicked off at 5.33 a.m. (The bomb-laden car had struck at 8.33 in the morning, and Basran was three hours ahead of Greenwich Mean Time.) That was a wonderful show of solidarity from the wider football community, and everyone at the Rovers was touched by it. At the same time, I thought it would be appropriate for us to do something extra.

We were scheduled to be at home to Shermall United that day in a game where, as ever, the stakes would be high. Someone had raised the possibility of leaving eight seats empty on the Rovers bench, as a tribute to our absent friends. I thought that was a touching idea but I had a much grander and, to my mind, far more fitting suggestion.

I came up with the notion of fielding a team with eight players missing. I couldn't think of a more appropriate or a more evocative tribute to the Basran car-bomb victims than an actual gap on the field where they would have been standing, had they lived (assuming selection).

Realising that I would have to go down the proper channels, I had a meeting with Bert Weatherseed at the Football Association, seeking formal ratification for the plan. At first, I met with some resistance. Bert said, 'Roy, we understand where you're coming from on this, but at the same time we have to respect the integrity of the game, and also the integrity of the league. No disrespect to the players you end up picking, but to the rest of the world this could look awfully like fielding a weakened side.'

I tried to keep my calm and speak in a measured way, but I think the emotion betrayed itself in my voice.

'Bert,' I said. 'My club is hurting.'

Bert sighed and looked out of the window in silence for a few moments. Then he turned back to me.

'Leave it with me, Roy.'

Inevitably, I had mixed feelings in the build-up to the day. Part of me was reluctant to revisit those memories so publicly and anxious about the feelings that would be stirred. At the same time, I was also excited at the prospect of our club being involved in a show of respect like no other. It was a big ask, obviously, of the lads I selected – Olly Olsen, Duncan McKay and Charlie 'The Cat' Carter in goal; I would have selected myself but I was still nursing a shoulder injury following the coach crash – and I could tell they were a bit nervous at the thought of facing the might of Shermall, a side who were always imposing going forward, while being so undermanned. But in the dressing room beforehand, I urged the three of them to draw inspiration from the memory of the Basran Eight.

'You knew those guys, as I did,' I said, 'and you know what they meant to this club, and you know what their legacy stands for at Melchester Rovers: for the spirit that never gives up. So go out there and use it; draw on its energy, let it drive you on.'

I also mentioned that we were clearly the underdogs, so all the pressure was on Shermall to perform. And then, in a quieter voice, I added, 'You don't need to make me proud. I'm already proud of you. You don't need to make our fans proud, either. They're already proud of you. The only people you need to make proud are yourselves. Now, let's go.'

'Yes, boss!' came the resounding cry and off down the tunnel the three of them went. I had a quiet moment alone in the dressing room, in which I closed my eyes and thought, one by one, of those young lives so brutally cut short in the Middle East. And then I went to the dugout.

The ground was packed, and the atmosphere was uniquely charged, especially given that it was so early in the morning. There was a minute's silence before the match, impeccably observed. It's always an incredible and unearthly moment when a stadium falls still and the air seems to hang heavily, and the only movement is the wind gently ruffling the corner flags. It's all spoiled today, of course, with the fad for 'a minute of appreciation', with rounds of applause and even singing. Have we lost the capacity, as people, to be still? Have we outlived the value of silence? We hadn't done so then and I think the occasion was richer for it.

However, it was after that, when the players lined up for the kick-off, that the emotion really hit me hard. When you saw how empty our half of the field looked, with only three players in it . . . well, it brought it all home in the most devastating way, and even now, writing this, the memory of that unoccupied grass, impossibly bright in the early light, brings a lump to my throat.

Our tactic, obviously enough, was to try to sit deep and soak up the pressure, for at least the first twenty minutes, and then take anything that we were offered on the break. For a while this worked well, with Olly Olsen not pressing the ball and refusing to be drawn too high up the field, and with Big Dunc doing his best to track the runners in behind. Frustratingly, in the seventy-second minute, I noticed that Shermall's left back, Dave Tolworth, was beginning to flag, which might have created an exploitable opportunity had I been able to send on a quick, probing winger, such as Chico Alonso. But unfortunately, I had used up all my subs. Also, by that point, Shermall's extremely efficient use of the 'Christmas tree' formation and their superior manpower had already told, and the visitors ended up running out 36–0 winners.

The lads, and the fans, were very subdued at the end of the game but I think their reaction was understandable. It was a difficult day for all of us, marking the most terrible event in the history of the Rovers, the scars from which will never heal. But to the extent that we had made a statement and shown our solidarity with the past, and our determination to carry our memories forward, it was a day that I know we would always be glad to have been a part of. And it marked the beginning of the healing process.

22

Haunted by the Past

One morning in early 1989, I was at home on my own, cleaning my golf clubs, when the doorbell rang. I opened the door and found myself face to face with a woman in her late teens, who was wearing a blue puffa jacket and black track pants, and was trembling slightly and clearly extremely anxious.

'Can I help you?' I said.

She said, 'My name is Claire, and I think I'm your daughter.'

My mind reeled and I almost dropped the lofted wedge I was holding. I couldn't believe what I was hearing and was momentarily lost for words. I think my mouth may even have fallen wide open, like in some kind of cartoon.

I looked carefully at the figure in front of me: blonde hair, pulled back tightly into a ponytail; strong jawline; piercingly blue eyes, as blue as Diana's, my third-born's . . .

I said quietly, 'I think you'd better come in.'

I took Claire into the kitchen, sat her down at the table and made us both a cup of coffee, biding my time, trying to settle on a course of action, not knowing quite how to handle this. Eventually, I set the mug in front of her and suggested that, in view of the inherently awkward and unnatural nature of our meeting, maybe it would be best if I simply listened for a while and she told me what she knew.

Claire sipped at the coffee, breathed deeply and, with her eyes concentrated firmly on the table, began.

She said she had been given up for adoption at birth. She had been raised, comfortably enough, in Pondworth, a pretty village three miles south of Melchester. Her adoptive parents were a couple called Carol and David Spendlove – he, a quantity surveyor, she, a school secretary. Claire said Carol and David had been nothing but loving and generous in their support for her – had doted on her, indeed – all her life long, and had done everything they could to make her happy, but that she had always wondered about her true parentage and that, as she came of age, that wondering had grown to become an obsession.

Accordingly, she had begun to conduct some research into her past, as best she could – at first secretly, and then openly – and her enquiries, after many setbacks and false trails and much dashed hope, had in due course led her to a Saturday night, some nineteen years ago, in April 1970.

Claire paused to breathe deeply again, and then carried on.

On that occasion, she explained, several members of the Melchester Rovers team, me among them, had attended the seven-thirty performance of a show by Bobby Dazzle's Travelling Circus which had pitched its tent on Melchester Common for the Easter holiday period. For the players concerned, this was a celebratory outing in the wake of a 4–0 trouncing that afternoon of Everpool in which I had netted a hat-trick, the third a sweetly struck volley from a Duncan McElway cross which would go on to win *The Big Match of the Week*'s Goal of the Month competition for April.

Among Dazzle's featured entertainers that night, Claire continued, was a Polish-born trapeze artist called Magda Putzov. The players, who had been received as special guests, were invited backstage to the dressing rooms where, Claire indicated, I and the aforementioned Ms Putzov, who was still in her silver leotard, spangly tights and full circus make-up, struck up an immediate allegiance, and where other players struck up other allegiances, variously, with other performers including a couple of jugglers and a seal-handler. (Claire went into no further details on this.)

Apparently, the evening duly wore on and Claire's further allegation was that, buoyed up by the recklessness and general euphoria that is likely to be engendered by a comprehensive home victory over a title rival followed directly by a trip to the circus, I had consummated my rapidly kindled and well-received passion for Magda Putzov behind the elephant wagon. And there, to the clatter of the petrol-driven electric generator, and with the heady smells of popcorn, straw and surprisingly well-trained animals mingling in the warm spring air, Claire had been conceived.

'And now here I am, aged eighteen,' Claire concluded, 'and just wanting to say . . . well . . . hello, Dad, I guess.'

Claire sat back and drew a deep breath of relief, and the kitchen fell silent.

There was a lot to take in, and I needed a few moments to gather myself. I got up and made another cup of coffee, using the period while the kettle boiled to stare out across the garden, think back through Claire's story and start to compose my thoughts.

When I was ready, I turned to face Claire and began my response, in the most measured way that the emotions which were, for obvious reasons, coursing through me at that moment allowed me to muster.

First of all, I picked her up, as patiently as I could, on an error of fact: the goal of mine against Everpool which had won *The Big Match of the Week*'s Goal of the Month for April 1970 had not been the third I scored on that occasion, but the second. The third was a scruffy prod-in after a melee on the goal line following a viciously in-swinging corner – not the kind of strike that was ever going to win an award for prettiness, though, obviously, as I said to Claire, they all count.

My second point also related to a factual error in her telling of the tale – but perhaps a more damaging one, from the point of view of the tale's overall coherence. I informed Claire that at no point in my life had I gone to watch Bobby Dazzle's Travelling Circus – neither on that April night in 1970 nor on any other night. All circuses, I explained, and not just Bobby Dazzle's, were a no-go area for me on account of the fact that I was mildly allergic to horses. Also to clowns, but more specifically to horses. Moreover, even if the rest of the team had decided upon Dunkling's Big Top as a venue in which to relax and celebrate the afternoon's achievements, I would not have joined them, preferring to spend the evenings after matches at home, reviewing my own performance and the team's, and identifying strengths and weaknesses before drawing up a list of things to work on and then going to bed.

With those things established, I then moved on to address what I felt (and I made this clear) was the real, hurtful and preposterous core of Claire's allegation – namely, that I had been unfaithful to my wife Penny. Penny! My darling and only Penny, to whom, on our wedding day, I had sworn an oath of absolute fidelity, and she to me. This, above all else, was utterly unthinkable and rendered Claire's story not only ridiculous but deeply offensive. Even though

Penny and I were not yet married at the time of Bobby Dazzle's visit to Melchester, in my mind Penny was already, with no shadow of doubt, my future wife. Fidelity within marriage was an absolute point of principle with me, I explained, and I repeated to Claire those beautiful words from the ceremony:

'Will you love her, comfort and keep her, and, *forsaking all other*, remain true to her, so long as you both shall live?' (My italics.)

This was not – I bade Claire know – a vow that I would take lightly or idly. Once I had met Penny, there was no question of copping off with the first trapeze artist whose tights I happened to look up at. On the contrary, the certainty and the mutual honour that flowed between two people as a result of that unbreachable contract was, in my firm belief, the very heart of a marriage and, moreover, worth all of the lying awake at night, staring at the ceiling while the thought of lips unkissed and hands unheld churned over and over in your mind and crushed your chest like a bag of cement.

'So therefore, Claire, I am obliged to inform you in no uncertain terms that I have never had adulterous sex with a Polish circus performer, or any other kind of Polish woman, and that, consequently, whomsoever your real father may be, that man is, categorically and beyond any shadow of a doubt, not I – or not me, or whichsoever is the correct personal pronoun to be using at the end of this grammatically ornate and rather too lengthy sentence.'

Claire had looked gradually more wilted during all this but, credit to her, she found some defiance from somewhere and came back off the ropes.

'Well, maybe you were drunk at the time and don't remember anything about it.'

At this point, I reminded Claire that I was a lifelong teetotaller and that alcohol had never so much as touched my lips, except possibly on that one occasion when I was about eight and Dad came home in a rage about a disallowed goal in extra time during a home game against Goredean United, and, down on his knees in the grate, furiously and repeatedly beat a brandy bottle against the coal scuttle, causing the liquid to fly across the room and spatter, not only my lips, but also the lips, hair and trousers of Mr Sexton from next door, who happened to be visiting at the time.

I also pointed out that even an alcoholic stupor wouldn't have annulled the effects of the handicap I had already mentioned, viz my horse allergy, which would, likely as not, in the confines of a Big Top, have rapidly seen me debilitated by streaming eyes and extremely itchy hives, complicating simple conversation with my neighbour, let alone successful congress with a trapeze artist.

'Well, perhaps you were drugged and forced into the boot of someone's car and taken to the circus and . . . and . . .'

But, alas, it was clear even to Claire by this time that the plausibility of her story had collapsed like a soufflé in a high gale. And Claire herself now collapsed similarly, her head dropping to the table, her shoulders heaving.

I waited until the worst of the crying was over.

'Claire, dry your eyes,' I said, gently, handing her a piece of kitchen towel. 'Why don't you and I have a conversation and see where we can go from here?'

And that was the beginning of Claire's Foundation – a charitable organisation overseen by Claire, aimed at people who have reached a point in their lives where they are tempted to try and pass themselves off as the offspring of a famous person, either for the purposes of extortion or simply (and this is more common than you might think) for self-validation – because they have issues with esteem, or are struggling to find their place in the world, or because their real parents have come, with over-familiarity, to seem routine and boring. The Foundation offers such people access to counselling and guidance, and an opportunity to reappraise their own life journeys and arrive at a place where they can see the value in them.

It took a while to develop, of course, but the ground was broken that afternoon, right there in my kitchen, in the aftermath of Claire's failed sting.

'Claire,' I said at one point, as we talked some more, 'I'm interested to know: why me?'

Claire said that, in order for her story to be plausible, she had first to identify a celebrity whom she physically resembled. 'It was between you and Brian Thurman, the bassist with Seventies glam pop sensations, the Spangles.'

'Hold up!' I said. 'Isn't he the one who wore eye make-up and women's trouser suits?'

'Yes!' giggled Claire.

'Well, thanks a bunch!' I laughed. 'Not that there's anything wrong with that,' I added.

Claire had clearly also gone to a lot of trouble to make sure all the dates in her concocted narrative tied up, working back carefully, nine months from her birthday.

'Discovering that Bobby Dazzle's Circus was in Melchester on the night of that victory over Everpool was a real eureka moment for my plan,' Claire explained. 'Most footballers, I imagine, don't remember very much about the evening after a four–nil home victory in which they scored a hat-trick – so it was almost like I had a blank canvas. And the circus just walked right into the middle of it and plonked itself down! But I picked the wrong footballer.'

'There's probably more of us like that than you imagine, Claire,' I said.

That slip aside, I think her thoroughness was what impressed me most about Claire – her attention to detail and her willingness not to be daunted by the scale of a task, or the remote likelihood of its success, but to take it on in any case. To that extent, although she might not have been my daughter, and although what she had been attempting to do was borderline criminal, or even worse than that, I recognised myself in her. There were qualities in Claire which spoke loudly to me – and so much potential which simply needed to be channelled in the right direction. Sure enough, in the intervening years, since the Foundation got under way, Claire has shown herself to be a highly capable administrator and also an extremely effective motivational speaker. She is also someone who is completely dedicated to the Foundation's fundamental principle, which she herself put into words and which I wholly endorse: that 'everyone is special, but some people just haven't realised it yet'. The Foundation has opened drop-in centres across Britain and, at the time of writing, is hoping to expand into America. I'm very proud to be involved with it.

There's an interesting coda to this story. A number of years later, as a result of a couple of leads arising quite incidentally from some research the Foundation had done for an entirely unconnected client, Claire discovered that her father was, in fact, Brian Thurman from the Spangles. After some concerted work by intermediaries, the two of them were positively reunited, I'm pleased to say, and much of the money that Thurman subsequently agreed in court to pay out to Claire by way of compensation for his gross neglect down the years funded further important work for the Foundation. All in all, it couldn't have worked out more satisfyingly.

23

The Final Whistle

You go again. That's what you do. You pick yourself up and refocus and graft and graft until the trophies start to come – league titles, an FA Cup, a UEFA Cup, a European Cup.

And then you crash your helicopter.

So many ifs. If I hadn't decided at the last minute to go on a solo scouting mission to Shermall United, following up on a tip-off I had received from Vernon Eliot about a promising young sweeper. If I had chosen to go by car. If the mist hadn't closed in that night in 1993.

The investigation concluded that I had clipped a power line, though I knew little of it – just the loss of control and the sudden, dizzying plummet and then the blackout. And then waking up with a strange illusory sense of numbness where my left foot used to be.

If you had asked me before the crash, I'd have said I had a good few seasons left in me – maybe ten, maybe more. I wouldn't have been prepared to put a number on it. I felt good. I had been in the professional game for thirty-eight years, and I didn't seem to have aged. People always said that: 'Roy, you don't look any older now than you did when you were twenty-five!' Shame, then, to lose those years. Still, you could hardly say it was a career cut short.

Blackie came to see me in Melchester General, bringing a bag of grapes. He was, for him, unusually subdued.

'I'm sorry about your foot, Roy,' he said.

'Thanks, Blackie,' I said. 'It could have been a lot worse, though.'

'It was a very good foot,' said Blackie.

'It was, wasn't it?' I said. 'And I got a lot of good use out of it.'

'You certainly did, Roy,' said Blackie. 'We all did.'

After I had recuperated and had talked to a number of leading psychiatrists, Penny and I decided to go and live in southern Italy, where I had been offered the job as manager of AC Monza, who were then in Serie A. The warm climate felt like a good idea, the kids were grown up – it was the right time. We had a lovely shuttered house in the hills with a verandah and an orange grove, and Penny had a little convertible Fiat Barchetta that she used to nip in and out of the town, and we were finally spending time together in the way that we hadn't spent time together before, as if we had been granted a second chance.

And fortunately the gods only had one more cosmic joke to crack at my expense, albeit that this was their best one – their absolute masterpiece.

Did I know? Of course I didn't know. How can you know? And yet why did I feel the urge that sunny morning, seeing Penny start the car before she headed down to the town, to lean in over the side window and say, 'I've never been happier than I am right now'?

Perhaps because it was true.

Penny smiled and said, 'Me too.' Then she put her sunglasses on and waved and was gone.

I had always urged her to be careful, driving down that mountain road, and she always was except for then.

I went back to Melchester. In the circumstances, it was the obvious thing for me to do. In Melchester I didn't feel like I was alone.

We hadn't sold the house, so I moved back in. I passed some time, thinking things through, adjusting. Roy Jr, Melinda and Diana were often around and a comfort, though I was also frequently in the dark and very still. Eventually I was ready to be busy again, or so I felt. I managed the Rovers, just for a short while. Roy Jr was in the side by that time, really hitting form in my old number nine shirt. I was proud to manage him – even prouder to watch him. What a player he was, and still is, and probably still will be for another two or three decades, if he looks after himself. It's up to him. Together we put a couple more trophies in the cabinet – a league title, an FA Cup . . .

But something had changed. Something had faded. Something wasn't there.

I went home after training one day and stood in the hall, where there is a large mirror. I remembered what Penny used to say to me when I came in at the end of a particularly stressful day, feeling wired up and at the same time worn down.

'Roy,' she would say, taking my face between her hands, 'you look drawn, sweetheart.'

That's what I realised now, staring at the face in the mirror. I looked drawn.

It was time to stop.

24

Time Added On

People often ask me, 'What's the secret, Roy? How did you manage to sustain a thirty-eight-year playing career at the very top level of the game, when so many other players consider themselves fortunate if they manage twelve or fifteen?'

And obviously it's got a lot to do with how you take care of yourself – the way you train, what you eat. A few self-sacrifices along the way can really pay dividends. Early nights, too, are to be recommended.

But it's also in the genes. I look at my mum, for example, who is ninety-eight now, and sharp as a tack. Busy as ever in the kitchen too. Indeed, these days, on account of the programmes that she watches on the television, there's a growing continental flavour to her dishes. Last Sunday, for example, I went over there for lunch, as I usually do, and she produced spaghetti con vongole with all the trimmings – roast potatoes, carrots, swede and bread sauce. Mr Sexton and I were a long time sitting down that afternoon!

Mum keeps herself active, which is also part of it. She and Mr Sexton go on a lot of cruises. They must have been on about fifteen in the last three years alone – to Balakiri, Dessekhan, Maskevitch, through the Oslip Straits . . . all over the place. No kidnappings yet! Actually – one kidnapping, in Bhalti Old Town, during an organised visit to a souk when . . . But that's a story for Mum's book when she gets round to writing it!

I'm seventy-six now, and I make sure to keep busy too. I play a lot of golf and work out for two and a half hours in the gym every day. I've also recently been looking into the possibility of doing the annual Melchester Iron Man Triathlon, where you do six laps of the city centre on a monocycle, swim for nine miles up the River Mel, and then run up Melbury Tor with a bag of lit coal on your back. It sounds like my kind of thing.

I'm aware, of course, as all retired footballers are, of the intense need in myself to occupy the space once filled by football. And I'm aware too that this is, by its very nature, a battle I cannot win. When football filled up so much space in your life, there is necessarily a void when football is gone.

Now I must be content to watch, and sometimes that's hard. Nevertheless, as an honorary vice president of Melchester Rovers, I have my own seat in the directors' box, with a bronze plaque with my name engraved on it, and I never miss a game at Mel Park, crossing the concourse, shaking a few hands, made very welcome, and trying not to look too hard at the bronze statue of myself that now touchingly stands by the main entrance, arms aloft and beaming – myself as once I was.

And do I wish I was out there playing in today's game? Of course I do. To have the chance to engage with the talents that are currently in the domestic league, on the billiard-smooth pitches that football now takes for granted – I would leap at it. Football, it seems to me, gets better. I really mean that. The money certainly gets better! But do I regret that my career ended just before the cash for television rights flushed through the game and entirely transformed the prospects of those who play it? Not for a moment. It was never about the money for me. I would have played for nothing. I still would. And do you know what? Today's big-earning multi-millionaire stars would say the same if you could get close enough to ask them.

In any case, there are wonders available in football way beyond the merely material – and if this book could ever be boiled down to one message (pulped, as it were, into a single, take-away thought) then I would hope it was that.

'Roy of the Rovers stuff.' I still hear people use the expression – even now, some twenty-two years after I last kicked a ball in public.

When a team completes an unlikely turnaround with a last-gasp winner: 'Roy of the Rovers stuff.'

When the captain who was written off turns to the crowd and lifts the trophy: 'Roy of the Rovers stuff'.

When the ball explodes off a player's boot on the edge of the penalty area and rockets into the back of the net past the goalkeeper's despairing dive, and the referee doesn't even have time to restart the match: 'Roy of the Rovers stuff.'

When a boy from a humble home in a humble street gets to know a life of glory and love that he would never have imagined for himself: 'Roy of the Rovers stuff.'

I hear the phrase used and, I don't mind admitting to you, something inside me glows. To have a whole kind of stuff named after you, to become a brand of stuff, to be permanently associated in the popular imagination with amazing stuff . . .

. . . to be, in short, a synonym for wonder . . .

With all due humility, when I am finally obliged to be still, I'll settle for that.

INDEX